WHAT KATY READ

What Katy Read

Feminist Re-Readings
of 'Classic' Stories for Girls

Shirley Foster

and

Judy Simons

University of Iowa Press, Iowa City

Copyright © 1995 by Shirley Foster and Judy Simons
All rights reserved
University of Iowa Press, Iowa City 52242
International Standard Book Number 0–87745–493–0
Library of Congress Catalog Card Number 94–61440
01 00 99 98 97 96 95 C 5 4 3 2 1

Printed in Hong Kong

Contents

Acknowledgements

We should like to thank Gillian Avery, Julia Briggs and Kimberley Reynolds for so generously giving up their time to discuss this work and for sharing their ideas and their store of knowledge with us. Thanks too go to Dennis Butts for his advice and support, and to Bryan Burns and Barbara Dennis for reading parts of the manuscript in draft and commenting so constructively. Meg Moore and Marie Mulvey Roberts loaned out-of-print volumes from their personal collections of school stories. The National Children's Literature Research Association, the Modern Studies Seminar of the University of Sheffield and the School of English Research Seminar at the Queen's University, Belfast, all allowed a forum for dissemination and discussion of work in progress. We are also grateful to Judy Bottrill and Nicola Shultz whose typing skills ensured that the delivery of the final manuscript was delayed no longer.

Shirley Foster
Judy Simons

Sheffield, 1994

Preface

This work arose out of a conversation about favourite childhood reading, powerful memories of which had remained with us. In recalling how we had both longed to be Jo March, had sympathized with Katy on her broken swing, and had wept over *The Secret Garden*, we discovered that not only had we, two women who come from very different backgrounds, shared reading experiences in the past, but that our views on thinking about those works from a more mature perspective had in some cases radically altered their meanings. As girls we had bitterly resented the cruelty of Aunt Fortune to Ellen Montgomery in *The Wide, Wide World*, although a rereading of the novel finds her to be a model of a strong, independent woman with far more dynamism than her weepy niece. Similarly at the age of nine we were prepared to accept without question Jo March's meek adoption of the role of a 'little woman' at the end of *Little Women* even though it was her very challenge to conventional femininity with which we had passionately identified. Worst of all perhaps, we had completely failed to register Mary Lennox's exclusion from the inheritance of Misselthwaite Manor in *The Secret Garden*, so caught up were we in the sense of power and enabling fantasy that the central action of the story generated.

Spreading the net of our enquiry further we realized that we were not alone in our experience. Women both of our own generation and outside it, whether older or younger than ourselves, admitted to a surprisingly common store of juvenile literary experience. More interestingly, this collective cultural inheritance that had figured as an important ingredient in our formative literary education was one in which men had generally not participated. It was difficult to find either boys or adult males who knew exactly what it was that Katy did or why the garden had to be kept secret. To them the Railway Children were nothing more than vague names, characters in a book that their sisters had read but that was not considered worth their attention. We discovered moreover that not only was this gendered division of readership in existence in children's literature today but that it still applied to many of the same texts that we had enjoyed as girls. Despite the fact that they were written for a different generation – often of a century earlier

– books such as _Little Women_, _What Katy Did_ and _The Secret Garden_ still retain their place as standard items on the classics list of late twentieth-century publishing houses, and sales figures confirm their continuing popularity with girl readers. At the same time, as schoolteachers and librarians attest, they are treated with contempt by many boys, who cannot imagine that they could find in them any scope for personal imaginative identification.

What had started then as casual reminiscence became complicated with critical questions that in turn stimulated our thinking about the status of literature for girls and its identity as a discrete literary genre. What exactly _is_ girls' fiction? What makes it distinctive? Do 'classic' books for girls promote significant aspects of women's culture in an attempt to bridge the divide between patriarchal realities and the appeal to female individualism? How do they modify or continue the familiar narrative motifs and patterns of their age in the address to a juvenile audience, and why should such motifs continue to exert an attraction for girls who are products of a very different cultural climate and consciousness? To what extent can questioning of the age's gender ideologies operate in such literature and would a contemporary juvenile readership have picked this up? What problems do they raise for the twentieth-century critic intent on recognizing the influential part played by such works in providing models of behaviour and value systems for impressionable readers attracted by the thought of, in Elaine Showalter's phrase, 'a literature of their own'?[1]

In seeking to establish the parameters of the genre, the modern critic has to take into account not only assumptions of the time about what constitutes literature for the young but also the current reader response and literary conventions. Writing for children is not a completely separate form of creative production but a branch of literary practice which is informed by the same political and cultural movements as is serious adult fiction. Any discussion of juvenile fiction must be located therefore within the critical and ideological frameworks that operate in the analysis of both canonically received and popular adult literature. As literature for girls has been the virtually exclusive preserve of women writers, it is also important to see these works as part of women's overall contribution to the literary marketplace during the period 1850–1920, and to take into account issues relating to the marginalization and devaluation of women's writing generally. Similar sorts of tensions exist within girls' fiction as have been identified in other texts by women authors of the late nineteenth century and early twentieth century, a period which produced many of what are now perceived as the central classics of the juvenile female literary canon. Yet the positioning of that canon as essentially peripheral to the acknowledged literary establishment creates its own difficulties for the woman critic.

Modern critical theory has come relatively late to children's literature, in particular that written for girls. Indeed, until recently, little scholarly attention has been paid to it at all. A 1980s study of school stories for instance, devotes only one chapter to female practitioners of the genre,[2] and the establishment of the Henty Society, with its own newsletter, has not been complemented by one dedicated to, say, Angela Brazil. More work is now beginning to be undertaken in this area, especially in North America, but much of it hardly moves away from the mainly historical or biographical approach of pioneering studies such as those by F.J. Harvey Darton, Roger Green, John Rowe Townsend and Gillian Avery.[3] Yet the genre is eminently accessible to various strands of current critical theory, not only as material for cultural analysis but also for the textual and psycho-linguistic perspectives it discloses. Feminist criticism, incorporating as it does many of the debates about textual status, the positioning of the reader, and the coexistence of alternative readings and coded 'messages', offers a particularly rewarding mode of analysis for juvenile literature. In drawing on the diversity of current feminist critical practice, the analysis of texts in this study will reveal the ways in which these works both spoke to their age and speak to today's, and should go some way in helping to retrieve them from their neglected and marginalized position.

What Sara Mills has proposed as the 'key issues' of feminist critical practice – 'language, the constitution of the subject, the social construction of gender, author intentionality and the position of the author'[4] – all have obvious relevance to girls' literature. The merging of the essentially cultural- and text-based Anglo-American feminist criticism with the more psychoanalytic and linguistically oriented approach of French feminist theorists offers a range of analytical possibilities within what is arguably the widest and most flexible of current critical methodologies. The implementation of the openness that characterizes contemporary feminism must of course not carry any suggestion of theoretical evasiveness. The very flexibility of feminist literary critical practice, in its ability to accommodate

a diversity of approaches, recreates the text as a rich site of interpretative possibility. Moreover, as Mills has signalled, it assumes
and confirms its political base.

It is also important to retain a historicist grasp on the implementation of late twentieth-century theory in reading a literature of the
past. Analysis must not lose sight of historical contextualization,
with reference either to value-judgements or to interpretations of
ideological positioning. As Gillian Beer has observed, 'we are not at
work on a supine or docile text which we colonize with our meaning or meanings.'[5] There are dangers in separating texts from their
contemporaneity or in failing to take account of the periodicity of
their reception. Textual elements which today may appear to indicate a particular reaction to contemporary ideologies will have had
different meanings for the audience of the time: even 'coded' messages are inseparable from the context which produces them. For
example, what now may seem to invite a deconstructive reading
of gendered behavioural patterns may have been ignored or unde-
tected by contemporary readers. Moreover, women writing for
children are not in precisely the same category as women writing
for women, if only because the former are constructing a voice
which is self-consciously regressive and which assumes an audience
which is inevitably 'other', whereas the latter could be said to implement a shared author/audience discourse. Critical discussion of
juvenile texts in the light of current feminist thinking has therefore
to address questions of narrational stance and the vexed question
of intentionality from a somewhat different angle. Nevertheless,
as this study will show, feminist critical practice can as fruitfully reveal the complexities and richness of nineteenth and early twentieth-
century girls' fiction as it has those of the adult novels of the same
period.

The texts chosen for close analysis in the following discussion
conform to certain common criteria, although there are significant
differences between them. All are directed towards a predominantly
female readership and all engage directly with the conceptualization
of girlhood and the development of a gendered identity. Each marks
a milestone in the history of girls' literature, although some of the
works were of course better known in their own time than they are
today. *The Daisy Chain* and *The Wide, Wide World,* hugely popular
novels at the time of their original publication and for a number of
years subsequently, are virtually unknown to the modern reader.
Their influence, however, on the contemporary juvenile market was

considerable, and a number of the novels which followed them make explicit or oblique reference to these seminal texts. Similarly, *The Madcap of the School*, while currently out of print, provides an archetypal model of the sub-genre that is arguably the most compulsive of all, the girls' school story. Other works examined here, such as *Little Women*, have retained their appeal and are now considered to be almost required reading for young girls, not for the moral directives they contain but for their established place as part of a special female literary heritage.

In 1885 the novelist and critic George Moore dismissed girls' fiction as having no conceivable literary value. 'Let us renounce the effort to reconcile these two irreconcilable things – art and young girls,'[6] he wrote despairingly, rejecting as futile any serious critical consideration of such material. It is in an attempt to explode the fallacy of Moore's pronouncement that this book is written.

Notes

1. Elaine Showalter, *A Literature of Their Own: Women Writers from Brontë: to Lessing* (Princeton: Princeton University Press, 1977).
2. Isobel Quigly, *The Heirs of Tom Brown: The English School Story* (London: Chatto & Windus, 1982).
3. F.J. Harvey Darton, *Children's Books in England: Five Centuries of Social Life*, rev. edn (Cambridge, Cambridge University Press, 1982); John Rowe Townsend, *Written for Children: An Outline of English Language Children's Literature*, rev. edn (Harmondsworth: Penguin, 1987); Gillian Avery, *Childhood's Pattern: A Study of the Heroes and Heroines of Children's Fiction, 1770–1950* (London: Hodder & Stoughton, 1975).
4. Sara Mills, Lynne Pearce, Sue Spaull, Elaine Millard, *Feminist Readings/Feminists Reading* (Hemel Hempstead: Harvester Wheatsheaf, 1989), p.10.
5. Gillian Beer, 'Representing Women: Re-Presenting the Past', in Catherine Belsey and Jane Moore (eds), *The Feminist Reader: Essays in Gender and the Politics of Literary Criticism* (London: Macmillan, 1989), p.69.
6. George Moore, *Literature at Nurse, or Circulating Morals* (1885), quoted in Felicity Hughes, 'Children's Literature: Theory and Practice', *English Literary History* 45 (Johns Hopkins University Press, 1978), p.547.

1

Introduction

In 1886, Edward J. Salmon, discussing the wide range of books currently being written specifically for a young female audience, commented:

> Girls' literature performs one very useful function. It enables girls to read something above mere baby tales, and yet keeps them from the influence of novels of a sort which should be read only by persons capable of forming a discreet judgement.[1]

Although in this article as a whole he is dismissive of many aspects of this writing, in focusing upon girls' literature as a well-established genre, Salmon both acknowledges it as worthy of critical consideration and highlights its somewhat precarious status, poised between nursery or schoolroom tales and adult fiction. He also makes clear his anxiety about the potentially damaging effect of novels on susceptible young female readers. One of the major difficulties encountered in this study of girls' fiction during the period 1850–1920 is precisely that which Salmon articulates of its problematic critical status and the consequent positioning of its readers. In a period characterized by crucial changes in attitudes to women and in opportunities granted them for self-expression, literature for girls proves a productive site for ascertaining attitudes towards girlhood and for revealing the prevailing uncertainties regarding gender. Before embarking on the detailed discussion of the works themselves, the main task of this study, it is important to contextualize some of the issues relating to categorization and generic distinctiveness so as to establish an appropriate critical structure within which the specific texts can be located.

THE HISTORICAL BACKGROUND

Although it is generally noted by critics that from its beginnings – usually taken to be in the mid-eighteenth century – the majority of

authors in the field of children's literature were women, there is
less agreement about the development of a literature specifically
directed towards girls. In a recent study, Kimberley Reynolds,
arguing that juvenile books as a class did not really emerge until
the 1880s with the growth of commercial publishing for the young
and the general rise in literacy, claims that the marked subdivision
between girls' and boys' fiction did not appear until that time. Her
assertion that 'sexually differentiated popular juvenile fiction . . .
originated in the closing decades of the last century',[2] however, is
countered by other critics who discover this division much earlier
in the century. In her study of the nineteenth-century fictional portrayal of children, for example, Gillian Avery, while not directly
proposing a separate genre, highlights the importance of the female
reader with reference to pre-1860 children's writers such as Mary
Howitt, Margaret Gatty, Catherine Sinclair and Charlotte Yonge.[3]
These writers, foregrounding the heroines and matters of adolescent female concern in their stories, indicate the existence of a
gendered youthful audience in the early Victorian period. Julia
Briggs, in her discussion of women writers for children from Sarah
Fielding to E. Nesbit, shows the extent to which many of the novels
produced by women concentrate on young female protagonists and
characteristically feminine patterns of behaviour. More specifically,
she argues that:

> during the early nineteenth century . . . stories for boys and girls
> now began to be sharply differentiated: boys' stories often involved
> travel to far-flung places and advocated the less reflective virtues
> – courage, endurance, loyalty and patriotism. Stories for girls
> were typically set in the home and exemplified charity, kindness,
> patience and self-discipline, virtues which most girls had ample
> opportunity to practise.[4]

Significantly, Briggs bases her distinction on the gendered bias of
the didacticism in children's literature. As she suggests, girls' fiction
prioritizes feminine experience and consequently (whether implicitly or explicitly) explores the possibilities of female self-expression
and fulfilment in a male-dominated world. This prioritization of
heroic femininity and the ideologies of girlhood that children's
literature encodes (in a period undergoing dramatic shifts in the
conceptualization of gender relations) will form the central focus of
this study.

Mid-Victorian authors themselves certainly recognized the existence of a distinct category of literature for girls. In an article in *Macmillan's* in 1869, Charlotte Yonge, herself a writer of 'transitional' novels for adolescent girls, attributes the inception of this literary type to Harriet Mozley, Cardinal Newman's sister, whose *The Fairy Bower* (1841) and its sequel, *The Lost Brooch* (1841), Yonge claims, were pioneering publications:

> [A] work done by them was the creation of the class of literature now termed "books for the young", standing between the child's story and the full-grown novel. We do not mean that there were no such books before, but as a school they seemed to rise up either in imitation of, or almost in rivalry to, *The Fairy Bower* and *The Lost Brooch*.[5]

Furthermore, as well as noting that 'though boys seldom are influenced by story-books ... girls are,'[6] Yonge develops the important point (confirmed by primary schoolteachers today) that whereas boys will not read books which seem to be directed at girls, 'schoolboy' literature tends to be read as much, if not more, by a female audience than by the boys themselves.[7] In Yonge's view, the 'wider' literary field of tales for girls is a far more 'convenient' (and rewarding?) area of investigation 'inasmuch as those for whom they [the books] are written really do read them, and like them.'[8] Her distinctions are based partly on contemporary notions of gender roles: 'There are so many hours of a girl's life when she must sit still, that a book is her natural resource, and reading becomes to her like breathing.'[9]

The sex of the contemporary readership cannot necessarily be taken as conclusive evidence of generic distinctiveness, since in the nineteenth century many men enjoyed ostensibly female-oriented literature. Lewis Carroll, Tennyson, and Edward Burne Jones were enthusiastic readers of Yonge's fiction, and the works of Susan Warner and Louisa May Alcott had many male admirers. But contemporary role patterns were certainly influential on reader orientation. As Kimberley Reynolds has noted,[10] Ruskinian assumptions about the 'separate spheres' not only tended to dictate the content of boys' and girls' literatures but also generally directed readership along distinctively gendered lines. So boys were encouraged to read books which would reinforce contemporary ideologies of masculinity, while girls were led to works which would reassure them of the value and necessity of the feminine ideals inherent in their culture.[11] Recent theories of gendered responses to language and their centrality to children's psychological development have highlighted the crucial relationship between reading and the awareness of sexual difference. The texts chosen for discussion in this study formulate certain distinctive patterns of particular relevance to girls. It is this more than anything that defines their orientation as gender-specific, as they both reflect and help to shape the consciousness of their female consumers.

The question of genre boundaries cannot be separated from historical context, and any examination of these works must take into account their place in the social and literary ideologies of the age. As Jane Tompkins has argued in her study of American fiction from 1790 to 1860, fictional texts can be seen as powerful examples of the way a culture thinks about itself: such works, engaging with the religious, social and cultural questions of the day, provide a means of ordering the world for their readers. Tompkins argues that 'popular' novels, especially those by women, are as influential in revealing the age's self-images as the so-called 'serious' or canonical literary texts.[12] Though she concentrates on *The Wide, Wide World* as her prime subject of analysis, her thesis is equally applicable to the whole *oeuvre* of juvenile literature, which presents examples of youthful behaviour set against the standards of the adult world. The historical dimensions of the novels addressed in this study are important in other ways, too. All of them function in relation to earlier texts, adapting and repositioning the characteristics which they have inherited from a well-established tradition of juvenile as well as adult literature. Indeed, as is the case with Edith Nesbit's writing, challenges to contemporary ideologies are often effected through deconstructive or parodic imitation of previous literary models, a technique which enables a subversive voice to speak from within the text itself.

In the mid-nineteenth century, girls' fiction on both sides of the Atlantic takes domestic realism as its generic model, and all the works dealt with here owe their organizing principle to the realistic tradition as it was established in both England and North America, centred on a localized or domestic environment. Other literary types, such as romance or fairy tale, may feature subtextually, but the main engagement is always with the development and interplay of characters in a family'or neighbourhood setting, geographically specific and usually contemporaneous. This fictional type draws on two important literary influences, the Evangelical tract and the sentimental/domestic novel. The first emanates from the religious revival at the end of the eighteenth century, which emphasized moral earnestness in a context of soul-searching and individual righteousness. The didactic tales which were produced, particularly for the young, applied religious and ethical principles to everyday life and concentrated on sinfulness, guilt and punishment, before showing how eventual salvation could be achieved; stories by writers such as Mrs Sherwood, Mrs Cameron and Mrs Hofland depict naughty children brought to redemption by recognition of and expiation for their wrongdoing, the stern commands of God transmitted through parental or priestly authority. There is a particular emphasis on the suffering attendant on wrongdoing, which is shown as both the consequence of flouting moral strictures and the signs of God's beneficient chastisement. In Sherwood's tales, divinely-authorized parents exact punishments which can be as psychologically as they are physically horrendous. (In one story, quarrelling siblings are taken by their father to see a rotting corpse on a gibbet, the visible manifestation of brotherly hatred which culminated in murder; deeply shocked, the children vow never to fight with each other again).[13]

The second literary type is of especial significance for women, in that such fiction emphasized feeling and emotional or psychological development in the private sphere of home and family, and portrayed the heroine's growth to ideal womanhood. As Tompkins has noted, there is an important relationship between the two types; sentimental fiction can be categorized as a form of revivalist expression, its definition of true power being essentially spiritual, not material. Evangelical Protestantism elevated the sacred role of women in the domestic sphere, and this too is replicated in these novels.[14] Popular fiction such as *The Wide, Wide World*, *The Lamplighter*, and *Little Women* similarly provide a typological source of female characteristics with particular stress on the sacrosanct family ideal.[15]

As many social historians of the period have indicated, these ideals of womanhood were an inherent part of contemporary society's self-definition, not merely ideological constructions invented by the novelists themselves. Conduct manuals and advice books of the time promoted the centrality of motherhood in the prevailing social order and the necessity for female self-sacrifice, service, and domestic responsibility, and these lessons were echoed in current literature for the young. Recent studies comparing nineteenth-century American children's fiction with autobiographies of the same period confirm the suggestion that the creative works not only seek to shape ideology but also to reinforce it through replication. So what one critic has called the 'cult of domesticity', promulgated by advisory works and enacted by women themselves, reappears in the imaginative publications.[16]

In their reflection of a historical reality, the novels chosen for analysis in this study also show how ideas about women and female roles in general altered during the period under discussion. The relationship is not a simple one; often a dialectic is set up between prevailing ideology and alternative possibilities. But certain shifts can be detected, approximating to changes in contemporary opinions and circumstances. The first of these is connected with the gradual liberalization of attitudes towards women which occurred from the 1870s onwards. The growth of girls' schools, the entry of women to higher education, and the admission – albeit reluctant – by a male-dominated society that women needed more satisfying occupations than wifehood and motherhood all contributed to a questioning of female roles and challenges to the conventionally gendered hegemony. Although, in her discussion of late Victorian and Edwardian children's fiction, a recent critic states that the '"New Woman" and her young counterpart, "the girl of the period", with their short hair, loose habits and challenging behaviour, do not intrude into the golden afternoons of these stories,'[17] other critics have suggested that such literature at least tried to engage with the dilemmas and tensions produced by this sexual restiveness, even if it was unable or unwilling to resolve them.[18] The appearance of the 'madcap' in the girls' story, for example, is an indication of this, and it is certainly notable that in the later texts a more anarchic stance towards female independence is taken. Although in most cases the familiar behavioural codes of feminine self-effacement and domesticity are in the end reinforced, there are more suggestive 'gaps' in the discourse in many of these texts which allow at least glimpses of alternative possibilities.

Another observable change is the secularization of the later texts. While moral lessons of duty and obedience continue to be taught, the specifically religious or doctrinal nature of these disappears. Here, too, the woman's influence is important; it is often the female figures who, while articulating ethical priorities, challenge the dogmatic intervention of patriarchal and institutional authority in women's spiritual lives. In relation to this, too, is the gradual disappearance of fathers or father-figures from the novels, perhaps reflecting the increasingly divergent spheres of family life, as outlined by Ruskin in 'Of Queens' Gardens' in his *Sesame and Lilies* (1871). Many of the young heroines are fatherless or orphans; at the same time, there is increased emphasis on mothers or mother-figures, who have significant power, at least within the domestic environment.

The other important source of thematic and tonal shifts in the fiction emanates from changes in attitudes towards children and adolescents. Arguing from an American historical perspective, a recent article discusses the ideological shifts which occurred between 1820 and 1920: stemming partly from the influence of Rousseau and Locke, and partly from the Evangelical revival, the child came to be seen not as a depraved being deformed by original sin, but as an individual capable of being moulded and improved; with the advent of Romantic and post-Enlightenment thinking, this idea was in turn replaced by the notion of the naturally innocent child, worthy in its own right and, like the cherished mother, capable of teaching messages of love and charitableness to a corrupted (often male) adulthood.[19] These developments have a dual and somewhat contradictory effect on girls' literature. On the one hand, the iconography of the ideal child, foregrounded in some of the earlier texts, gives way to the more vigorous and naughtier heroine who, despite her innate goodness of heart, has to learn control and the right exercise of individuality. On the other hand, as is suggested in the compared openings of selected works below, there is a move towards a greater identification with the child reader and a more uncritical engagement with the characters. The image of childhood becomes sentimentalized and adulthood becomes less a state to be aspired to and more a sphere only reluctantly entered. Writers such as Lucy Maud Montgomery and Kate Douglas Wiggin in North America, and Frances Hodgson Burnett in England, could be seen as idealizing – even idolizing – girlhood in their works. Anne Scott McLeod, commenting on the nostalgia for an unfettered childhood which characterizes many mid-nineteenth-century American women's autobiographies, observes that the treatment of the adolescent heroine in female-authored girls' stories of the same period frequently reveals a similar sentimentalized regret for this transient phase in life. While Montgomery's Anne and Wiggin's Rebecca embody an idea of childhood which celebrates the child as child (and as McLeod notes both writers are clearly entranced by their heroines[20]), such indulgence towards pre-adult girls is certainly not a feature of Yonge's or Warner's work.

One final shift is evidenced by the less stringent moral emphasis in the novels as the century progresses. Distinctions between 'right' and 'wrong' behaviour are still the central concern in most of the narratives, but less insistently articulated. The texts also have some degree of greater freedom and openness. In connection with this, the emphasis on physical and emotional suffering, so prevalent in the earlier, evangelical-influenced fictions, diminishes. As Susan Coolidge, herself the author of stories which contain a good deal of fun as well as painfully-learned lessons, amusedly remarks in 1875:

> Perhaps we may live to see the day when wise mammas, going through the list of nursery diseases which their children have had, will wind up with, "Mumps, measles, chicken-pox – and they are all over with 'Amy Herbert', 'The Heir of Redclyffe', and the notion that they are going to be miserable for the rest of their lives!"[21]

Youthful experience is less traumatic and more frequently enjoyable in the later texts – compare Ellen Montgomery's constant distress over her own and others' behaviour with the Railway Children's carefree adventures, for instance – and even where some kind of moral is implicit it may well be, as Elizabeth Sewell remarked in the late 1890s, that young readers paid little attention to it:

> I have come to the conclusion that the young people of the present day leave out the reflections and advice in a tale, just as I used to leave out the texts and prayers in Mrs Sherwood's stories. It is decided that medicine must be medicine, and jam, jam; so that a choice may be made between them.[22]

THE JUVENILE AUDIENCE

In the nineteenth century there was a far less rigid division between adult and youthful readerships than is accepted today. Referring to juvenile-directed works by writers such as Charlotte Yonge, Elizabeth Sewell, and Harriet Martineau, Kathleen Tillotson comments that 'the line between tales for the young and novels is a wavering one; it was indeed felt to be specially so in the forties.'[23] The line continued to waver in the following decades. Yonge's *The Heir of*

Redclyffe (1853), for instance, was wept over by officers in the Crimea as much as by sentimental teenagers, and many of the authors under discussion drew – and expected to draw – an audience from a wide age range. Contemporary reviews of Alcott's *Little Women* (1868) illustrate this: the *Nation* saw it as 'not only very well adapted to the readers for whom it is especially intended, but [it] may also be read with pleasure by older people', while *Harper's* considered it . . . 'a rather mature book for the little women, but a capital one for their elders.'[24] Similar responses to other works ostensibly written for young people at this time confirm their contemporary width of appeal. Christabel Coleridge, Charlotte Yonge's biographer, records a mid-century family discussion about Elizabeth Sewell's avowedly child-oriented *Amy Herbert* (1844), with which the head of the household, Judge Coleridge, was closely familiar. She comments: 'It appears . . . that brilliant young men and learned judges were more ready to discuss with interest stories for little girls than would seem likely at the present day [1901].'[25]

The fact that Lewis Carroll's *Alice* books immediately became best-sellers and that Anna Sewell's *Black Beauty* (1877) had sold 180 000 copies by the second decade of its publication[26] is further indication that such works appealed not only to children but to the older generation. They were also considered worthy of public critical attention, as the comments on *Little Women* cited above demonstrate. Again, Tillotson points out that tales which 'would now be classed as "juvenile" . . . were read by adults in their own time, and were surveyed in serious reviews.'[27] In his early criticism, even that most highbrow of literary commentators, Henry James, not only discussed many contemporary 'juvenile' novels but judged several of them to be of considerable merit.[28]

Despite this evidence of generic indeterminacy, some features of the text themselves do indicate a specific readership. It may be possible to argue that the main tendency of children's writing is to accommodate the youthful reader to the cultural and social hegemony of the age and, at the same time, to define desirable value systems; whereas adult narratives may be assumed to initiate a process of recognition, juvenile fiction presupposes if not a wholly blank-paged receptor at least one more vulnerable to ideological manipulation. This distinction is evident in the period immediately preceding the one under discussion.

In early nineteenth century tales for children, such as those by Mrs Sherwood and Maria Edgeworth, the formulaic nature of the

plot and the direct intervention of a moralistic authorial voice clearly
establish the lesson being taught. In Mrs Sherwood's well-known
The Fairchild Family (1818–47), for instance, certain childish acts lead
to inevitable consequences, whose significance is underlined by a
sternly admonitory commentator. The section in Part I entitled 'The
All-Seeing God' deals with a young girl's greed. First alerting the
reader to the nature of the ensuing discourse – 'I must now tell you
of a sad temptation into which Emily fell about this time'[29] – the
narration goes on to describe how Emily, having stained her dress
with the juice from the bottled damsons which she has stolen out
of the store-cupboard, tries to wash out the evidence of her crime,
develops a high fever from the chill which results, and nearly dies.
On her sick-bed, she is consumed with guilt for 'knowing . . . as she
did, how she had offended God, by continuing so many days in
sin; and particularly in committing the sin again, after having been
warned of the greatness of it in the sermon which her papa had
read in the morning.'[30] Though on recovering, Emily confesses her
sinfulness and acknowledges God's benevolence in having so
chastised her, the narrator reiterates the story's moral meaning by
adding a fearful prayer about sin and punishment at the conclusion. Maria Edgeworth's more sophisticated *Moral Tales* (1801)
parade their moral teaching less insistently, but still overtly point
the youthful reader to a recognition of stupid or wrong behaviour
via an authoritative voice. 'Angelina; or, L'Aime Inconnue', a story
about vanity and self-importance, for example, concludes with a
reminder 'that it is possible for a young lady of sixteen to cure
herself of the affectation of sensibility and the folly of romance.'[31]

In the mid and late-century works with which this study deals,
there is a less clear-cut relationship between narration and discern-
ible 'message' although the text is still built on a substructure of
evaluation and recommendation. What makes these works more
complex is the subtler formulation of textual strategies: patterns of
behaviour enacted by female characters even within a seemingly
'free' or 'open' narrative can constitute an indication to adolescent
girls of the values considered intrinsic to the maintenance of social
harmony – that is, women's essentialist and subordinate role in the
patriarchal order. Although there may be no obvious moral directives
about female behaviour, thus allowing various kinds of possible
self-expression to be explored, the narrative closure usually indicates the prevailing ideologies endorsed by the text. So Jo March in
Little Women may write books in her attic but is finally confirmed

first as dutiful daughter and later in a domestic wifely role, and Ethel May in *The Daisy Chain* has to subordinate her intellectual aspirations to a recognition of her true worth as the support of her father and brothers; in each case, the narration finally validates acceptance of a dominant moral or social order, even though it may at the same time express coded alternative meanings.

If many of these texts, then, can be viewed as 'hybrids', appealing to both young and adult readers and consequently inviting complex critical readings, it is nevertheless also the case that as the century proceeded changes took place which re-established distinctiveness, though not of the earlier kind. In this later period the most marked evidence of child-directedness is in language register rather than moral foregrounding. So while mid-century texts, though clearly 'juvenile' in that they focus on a young heroine and her world, implement an essentially adult discourse, later texts represent the youthful female experience either in the voice of the protagonist herself or via an adult voice which has deliberately accommodated itself to childish articulation. This can be seen by comparing passages from the openings of Susan Warner's *The Wide, Wide World* (1850) and Susan Coolidge's *What Katy Did* (1872), or, in England, Charlotte Yonge's *The Daisy Chain* (1856) and Frances Hodgson Burnett's *The Secret Garden* (1911):

There was no one else in the room. Driven thus to her own resources, Ellen betook herself to the window and sought amusement there. The prospect without gave little promise of it . . . Daylight gradually faded away, and the street wore a more and more gloomy aspect . . . Yet Ellen still sat with her face glued to the window as if spell-bound, gazing out at every dusky form that passed, as though it had some strange interest for her.[32]

Katy's name was Katy Carr. She lived in the town of Burnet, which wasn't a very big town, but growing as fast as it knew how. The house she lived in stood on the edge of the town . . . Behind was a kitchen-garden sloping to the south; and behind that a pasture with a brook in it, and butternut trees, and four cows – two red ones, a yellow one with sharp horns tipped with tin, and a dear little white one named Daisy.[33]

"Good morning, Miss Winter," said a thin, lank, angular, sallow girl, just fifteen, trembling from head to foot with restrained eagerness, as she tried to curb her tone into the requisite civility.

"Good morning, Ethel, good morning, Flora," said the prim, middle-aged, daily governess, taking off her bonnet, and arranging the still little rolls of curl at the long, narrow looking-glass, the border of which distorted her countenance.[34]

When Mary Lennox was sent to Misselthwaite Manor to live with her uncle everybody said she was the most disagreeable-looking child ever seen. It was true, too. She had a little thin face and a little thin body, thin light hair and a sour expression. Her hair was yellow, and her face was yellow because she had been born in India and had always been ill in one way or another.[35]

In each case, the first of the two passages establishes the heroine and the world in which she is to operate, but makes no concession to a juvenile audience. Not only is the linguistic register essentially adult, using relatively sophisticated vocabulary, but the narrational positioning is that of a distanced, interpreting observer who aligns the (adult) reader's viewpoint with her own rather than with the characters'. In the second passage, from the later works (though it is worth noting that *What Katy Did* is considerably earlier than *The Secret Garden*), the discourse immediately sets up an intimate relationship between narrator and child. The syntax and vocabulary are simpler, and far less depends on implied knowledge of social mores. Though there is no attempt to replicate actual juvenile speech patterns (this is not a regular feature of children's literature until well into the twentieth-century, *Huckleberry Finn* [1884] excepted) and the speaking voice is obviously adult, the engagement is with an implied young reader who is invited to adopt a position of close identification with that of the protagonist. This carries important implications for thinking about the process of gender construction in this period. As a recent critic of children's literature has remarked:

The most important concept for children to grasp about literary fictions is always that of narrative point of view, since this has the function of constructing subject positions and inscribing ideological assumptions.[36]

The shift in narrative perspective can then be deceptively seductive. For with the later texts in this study, although there is apparently less ambiguity of focus, the themes and issues treated – the progress from childhood towards adulthood, the significance of gender roles, the dilemmas facing young girls – remain basically similar, and continue to make their impact within an ostensibly less insistent but still determined ideological framework.

NATIONAL DISTINCTIVENESS

If political relationships between Britain and America during the nineteenth century underwent periods of strain, literary ones flourished and each nation's books were eagerly received by the other. Even when merciless satirists such as Fanny Trollope and Charles Dickens caused a furore with their acerbic commentaries on the United States, curiosity outweighed animosity and each country's successful authors continued to attract a transatlantic as well as a home audience. Children's literature was no exception to this. Amy Cruse talks of an 'invasion' of England by American children's stories in the 1850s and 1860s.[37] *The Wide, Wide World*, for example, was one of the most popular books of its time in England, while *Little Women* and the *Katy* books immediately became best-sellers on both sides of the Atlantic. Similarly, the frequent references to Charlotte Yonge's works – albeit not always flatteringly – in contemporary American texts suggests widespread familiarity with her fiction.

It is probably true to say, however, that North American[38] girls' books were more popular in England than vice versa. In her study of patterns of childhood in nineteenth-century juvenile fiction, Gillian Avery suggests that there was no English equivalent of *Little Women* or *What Katy Did* in terms of their accessibility to the ordinary young reader. In her view, not even Yonge or Mrs Ewing were able to achieve contact with their readers in the same way as these American children's writers.[39] Publication details of representative texts from both sides of the Atlantic give evidence of this. New editions or re-issues of *Little Women* appeared simultaneously in both countries, often annually, until well into the twentieth century. All the *Katy* books continued to be produced in England at regular intervals for at least forty years after their initial publication and have of course, like Alcott's and Montgomery's novels, been revived in recent paperback editions. In contrast, Nesbit's *The Railway Children* seems to have gone into only two American editions up to the First World War, with no constant re-issues like the American texts in Britain. Even Yonge's fiction, although enjoying considerable popularity in

the States, could not compete with the transatlantic market for
Little Women or *What Katy Did*: nearly thirty years after publication,
The Daisy Chain, for example, had reached only three American
editions, and the phenomenal success of *The Heir of Redclyffe* in England, which had reached its seventeenth edition by 1868, was not
matched by American figures, although it appeared in America at
least seven times in the period up to 1888.[40] This imbalance may be
due to certain textual differences, reflecting each nation's respective
ideologies and patterns of conduct. In whatever way these differences were perceived, however, for the female reader, beginning to
learn to reconcile her own sense of selfhood with the requirements
of society at large and in the process questioning some of the latter's
demands, exposure to another country's treatment of similar concerns must have been illuminating, even challenging.

One of the major differences between English and American
juvenile texts relates to the framing of their didactic message. As
has already been suggested, the Evangelical revival had a profound
effect on juvenile literature in the United States, but this was rarely
attached to any specific sectarian doctrine beyond the intrinsic
tenets of Christianity. So whereas the plot of *The Daisy Chain* hinges
on matters such as a child's worthiness for Confirmation and the
imperatives of sacramental observance, novels such as *Little Women*
or *What Katy Did* promote the ideals of goodness and righteousness
within a general framework of Christian principles but without reference to any specific dogma. Even the intensely-focused religiosity
of *The Wide, Wide World* centres on realizing an individual's direct
relationship with God, via the Bible, and not on institutionalized
piety.

American children's novels also seemed more attractive to contemporary English readers because they presented a more romantic
world, encouraging wish-fulfilment of a highly emotional kind;
orphaned heroines gain parents or even lovers, passions are allowed
vent, and the harshnesses of life are transformed by the intervention of Fortune. This fantasy element, building on the notion of a
non-determined world of endless opportunity, has of course a
particularly American resonance. The spirit of optimism and belief
in progress which nineteenth-century British visitors to the New
World constantly remarked permeates the literature too. From the
self-confident pragmatism of Franklin's *Autobiography* (1818), reiterated later in the century in the popular Horatio Alger stories
rehearsing the 'rags to riches' myth of success, to the Emersonian

and Whitmanesque creeds of self-reliance and inner autonomy, the nation's creative works articulate that most peculiarly American combination of spirituality and self-interest. What is loosely termed 'the American Dream' influences juvenile as well as adult American texts, in their emphasis on literal rewards as well as on a pioneering impulse towards exploration and self-determination: Warner's Ellen Montgomery and Cummins's Gerty in *The Lamplighter* are not only spiritually purified by the end of their respective stories but have also gained material and emotional satisfaction; and the March family are sustained with gifts and luxuries from their wealthy benefactor in the figure of Laurie's grandfather, old Mr Laurence.

In this context, it is particularly interesting to recognize the merged national sources of Burnett's novels. Effectively of dual nationality (born in England, she moved to the United States in her teens and married an American, but returned to her homeland later in life), Burnett was responsive to twin cultural influences, and her work achieved popularity on both sides of the Atlantic. Her fiction persistently draws on an archetypal fairy-tale plot which depicts the transformation from deprivation to some kind of enrichment, her own version of the American dream of success. Yet her most enduring novels, *Little Lord Fauntleroy* (1886), *A Little Princess* (1888) and *The Secret Garden* (1911), locate their narratives almost entirely within a British setting and a fully realized domestic and class structure. The shifts between the modes of realism and romance in *The Secret Garden* also reflect to some extent the double literary influences on the text, and although Mary Lennox's triumphs are finally subsumed by the restoration of the masculine order, Colin's confidence in a future of endless possibilities for himself voices an American rather than a British self-confidence.

The notion of a secret place of autonomy and freedom from adult control, which *The Secret Garden* celebrates and which is a central feature of Nesbit's and Brazil's fiction, can perhaps be traced back to the joyfully anarchic juvenile world of that most American of childhood narratives, *Huckleberry Finn* (1884). Huck's delight in the refuge of the uncivilized, bounded by the limits of adult respectability, recurs with Nesbit's and Brazil's heroines and their discovery of natural sanctuaries. Both *The Railway Children* and *The Madcap of the School* show the appeal of these Edenic worlds of innocence and licence which exist in the wild surroundings beyond the confines of house and school. It is the North American texts, however, which are characterized most forcefully by a context of geographical

expansion, and this in turn links with their representation of girlhood. The extension of the physical environment beyond the domestic interior is accompanied by a related movement beyond the
spiritual 'closet' for the women and girls who figure in them. The
outdoor activities in which Ellen, Jo, Katy and Anne luxuriate reflect
moreover the impact of the pioneering society on American models
of girlhood, a society in which 'woman' was less easily definable in
terms of the 'angel of the hearth' ideology. Even at the turn of the
century, British texts such as *The Secret Garden*, *The Railway Children*
and *The Madcap of the School*, while acknowledging the attractions
of the outdoor environment – the garden, the moors, the woods –
are more tentative about their beneficial effects, and ultimately return
their heroines from the potentially liberating derestricted territory
they find so exhilarating to the safe enclosure of solid buildings
with their associated clear moral and social objectives.

The fictional model of freedom and fulfilment which characterized American texts in the latter part of the nineteenth century also
offered the young English readers a more liberated vision of girlhood, in contrast to that experienced in duty-ridden, restrictive
British society. Not only are American heroines allowed more physical freedom than their British counterparts, but they seem less
hemmed in by proprieties. This to a considerable extent reflects the
historical situation of the time. Anne Scott McLeod's analysis of
the autobiographies of women who grew up in America before the
late 1870s includes a quotation from Lucy Larcom's *A New England
Girlhood* (1889) which effectively shows the contrast between the
picture of English childhood generated by English books and the
reality of the American experience:

> We did not think those children had so good a time as we did;
> they had to be so prim and methodical. It seemed to us that the
> little folks across the water never were allowed to romp and run
> wild; . . . [we had] a vague idea that this freedom of ours was the
> natural inheritance of republican children only.[41]

As McLeod indicates, the licence allowed to young girls changed
with the onset of puberty, as the adolescent entered the more
restricted sphere of young womanhood. Certainly American writers
incorporate this closure into their narratives, particularly in mid-
century when both Coolidge and Alcott, despite their ambivalent
celebration of female unruliness, finally prioritize conventional

concepts of womanly virtues and show their heroines moving into the discrete operational arena of the feminine. As McLeod points out, however, attitudes shift in the latter part of the century and writers such as Wiggin and Montgomery portray their heroines' passage to womanhood as more gradual and freer of conflict, in line with contemporary altered perceptions of gender development. And even the earlier heroines Jo March and Katy Carr, as well as Anne Shirley and Rebecca Randall (in Wiggin's *Rebecca of Sunnybrook Farm*) – find opportunities for self-expansion through the expression of physical energy in a way denied their English counterparts. They are encouraged to be hardy and their defiance of traditional gender roles in childhood and early adolescence remains a fundamental feature of their appeal.

The nationally distinctive features of American and British texts relate too to the significance allocated to the concept of family. Despite the fact that Alcott is credited with initiating a new genre of American family novels, the prevailing pattern in American texts for girls in this period is one that focuses on individuals or small groups rather than on the tightly-knit interlocking relationships of family life which constitute the narrative not only of mid-Victorian British tales but also of Nesbit's fiction at the turn of the century. This diminished emphasis on family could be attributed, as Gillian Avery suggests, to differences in English and American family ideals in the nineteenth century. English children's books reflect a society that was morally self-conscious, class-ridden and institutionalized, moulding its young according to principles of restraint, obedience, and reference to authority; in contrast, American texts portray an essentially classless society, in which children are encouraged in self-reliance and independence as well as in a more pragmatic and domestic virtue (Avery notes that it would be hard to imagine a young English Victorian heroine relishing the delicious food which she herself had prepared in the kitchen).[42] Even the weepiest and apparently most conformist heroine, such as Ellen Montgomery, possesses a spirit of resistance and an inner resourcefulness that would be regarded as both undesirable and dangerous in an English novel for girls of the same period.

The notion of female power with which to some extent all the texts in this study engage, is thus more firmly implanted in the American novels, which do not merely rely on the suggestion of woman as God's agent with her own spiritual autonomy in a world of patriarchal authority, but depict strong women whose vigour has influence beyond as well as within the immediate family. Even the archetypal family novel, *Little Women*, contains mother and daughters who have employment in the outside world, while Anne grows up in a world where women such as Marilla occupy a position in a community structure not bound by an overriding concept of domestic duty. In contrast Ethel's involvement in parish affairs is subject to establishment mores which maintain a traditional view of gendered hierarchies and Roberta in *The Railway Children* fifty years later is similarly restricted. It is only with the introduction of the school story in the form pioneered by Brazil that family is replaced in English fiction for girls by the notion of an independent female community within which female adolescence can find scope for redefinition.

Instead of being located within a familial context, American girls are encouraged to define their selfhood through a strong sense of patriotism and national identity. American national characteristics, including a more developed spirit of independence, are seen to affect models of girlhood that challenge the more rigid standards of conduct prevailing for their English counterparts. This is most strikingly apparent in a revealing episode in Alcott's *Little Women* which depicts the March girls on a picnic with a group of English visitors. The scene is defiantly pro-American, pointing to fundamental differences between the two cultures and the concepts of female identity they promote. The English girl, Miss Kate, has a 'stand-off-don't-touch-me air, which contrasted strongly with the free and easy demeanour of the other girls,'[43] and although elegant and accomplished, her reading of Schiller's verse is cold and unemotional. Her English reserve emanates from a mistrust of the new, and her hidebound English standards, which prevent genuine self-development, are affronted by the democratized ethos of the New Englanders, where Laurie and the March girls are on equal terms, despite the disparity in their respective incomes. Kate, as an inheritor of old world values, patronizes Meg for her position as governess and John Brooke's spirited defence of American girlhood – 'Young ladies in America love independence as much as their ancestors did, and are admired and respected for supporting themselves'[44] – contextualizes Meg's personal situation within a determinedly nationalistic framework of Emersonian self-reliance and independence, according her a representative cultural status.

Although much of the following study is devoted to recognizing the many similarities which exist between English and American texts in their re-enactment of contemporary debates about girlhood, it is important not to discount the impact of national and cultural differences which colour, while not subsuming, their gender orientation. American ideals of freedom and independence, the greater ambivalence regarding a clear-cut gendered identity, and the consequent emergence of the tomboy figure all have an impact upon English fiction for girls which often contains explicit acknowledgement of transatlantic influence. Similarly the English literary tradition is clearly inspirational for many American writers and the intertextual dimension of a number of the works under consideration testifies to the interactive relationship between the two cultures, which could almost be considered a dialogue on the nature of girlhood in this period and its appropriate fictional representation.

THE DEVALUED GENRE

The issue of cultural status and artistic excellence of 'non-canonical' literature continues to pose a vexed question for feminist literary critics. It remains an important task for twentieth-century commentators to rescue devalued texts from conventional critical hierarchies so that questions of literary exclusion and determinants of taste can be addressed with some understanding of their sources. As Jane Tompkins has commented with regard to the establishment of the American literary canon, criteria of aesthetic value emerge in response to a complicated system of cultural, commercial and evaluative codes that are by no means reliant on literary considerations alone.[45] The double marginalization of children's literature and of women writers in the critical establishment can be traced to sources that relate more to commercial conditions than to artistic merit. Gaye Tuchman, in a study of nineteenth-century publication policies in England, has shown how manuscripts submitted to publishing houses were placed in a rank order by editors according to gender specialism, with categories designated as 'high prestige', 'men's specialities', 'mixed specialities' and 'women's specialities.'[46] Writing for children was inevitably allocated to the last category, and it is this critical inheritance, based initially on market considerations, that has contributed fundamentally to the devaluation of popular women's writing and children's literature within that gradation system.

The low esteem in which nineteenth-century women writers were

(with a few exceptions) held by a male-dominated critical establishment has been well documented elsewhere. Women writers of juvenile fiction in the period under discussion constituted a specially
marginalized group writing for an equally disregarded audience.
Although, as Tuchman has so ably demonstrated, market forces
and the attitudes of editors combined to relegate their work to the
bottom of the literary hierarchy, contemporary cultural attitudes
to women also contributed to these authors' self-deprecating views
of their own achievement. As Julia Briggs points out, women were
assigned to domestic and maternal roles and shared with children
'subordinate positions in society, both groups being regarded as
weaker, less capable, and less responsible than men.'[47] It is significant that many of the authors under consideration in this study
felt highly equivocal about their achievement as children's writers,
uncomfortable with their participation in a genre which, as they
were well aware, was generally considered inferior. The hybrid
nature of some of their books, which as has already been noted are
directed towards the young yet contextualize the narrative within
an adult-centred world, may well be an indication of their nervous-
ness in this respect.

Almost all the writers under discussion here aspired to writing
adult novels, regarding these works as more serious and worth-
while than the juvenile works which brought them essential financial
rewards. Indeed, once they had achieved unanticipated fame with
a best-selling juvenile text, it was often mainly the prospect of future
economic security which kept them writing in an area which they
had entered only reluctantly. Alcott's personal diary, for example,
after the phenomenal success of *Little Women*, contains frequent
references to the drudgery of maintaining the level of production
necessary for the family's support. 'Feel quite used up', runs a typical
entry in April 1869. 'The family seem so panic-stricken and helpless when I break down, that I try to keep the mill going.' And in
a letter to her publishers that same Christmas she notes how her
financial situation has been finally alleviated by her entry into the
market of girls' fiction, 'after toiling so many years along the uphill
road, – always a hard one to women writers.'[48] Financial pressures
kept Susan Warner tied to the writing of juvenile literature, too. As
her sister notes in her biography, the economic insecurity caused
by their father's ill-advised speculations and commitments could
be ameliorated only by Warner's constant production of books for
young people. Extracts from her journal quoted in the biography,

increasingly refer to the burden of having to keep the family afloat in this way.[49]

Even within the lowly category of children's writing there were further divisions which militated against women who wrote specifically for girls. As Jacqueline Rose has observed, in the first issue of *The Girls' Own Paper*, which was published in 1880 as a complement to the already highly successful *Boys' Own Paper*, there was a marked absence of contributions from well-known writers or those established in other fields. In addition, whereas books for boys followed a consistent practice in marking out distinctive literary sub-genres with clear masculine prototypes and recognized narrative rituals – the adventure story and the public school story for instance – girls' literature frequently seemed to be little more than an arbitrary collection of material thought appropriate for untrained female minds. The critical implications of this division on the reception of writing for girls are severe. As Rose comments:

> In the distinction between the two, literature for boys appears as a marked term of the opposition which stakes out its territory against the rest . . . The sexual differentiation of children's literature was, therefore, not so much an equal division as a breaking away of one form into a more 'adult' space. In this sense, girls' literature is best described as what got left behind (an old story).[50]

It is precisely this miscellaneous, hotch-potch nature of typical girls' fiction that E. Nesbit satirizes in *The Story of the Treasure Seekers* (1899) and *The Wouldbegoods* (1901), texts which function as a sustained critique of contemporary children's writing and its gendered bias. In *The Story of the Treasure Seekers*, the Bastable family's efforts to produce a children's magazine, *The Lewisham Recorder*, result in a sophisticated pastiche of the type of children's journal to which Nesbit had herself been an active contributor and which significantly reflects on her own complicity in contemporary practice. The children's version of a juvenile text incorporates irrelevant advice columns, sentimental cliché, travesties of juvenile fiction and trite precepts for children which conflate to the point of absurdity the domestic, the moral and the instructive. The distinctive contributions made by boys and girls to the newspaper draw heavily on their own supposed reading experiences, with the girls rewriting romantic narratives which feature trapped and endangered heroines.

The satire is further developed in *The Wouldbegoods* with the

creation of Daisy, a meek, gentle and obedient child who has absorbed the full impact of conventional girls' literature, or as Albert's
uncle describes it, 'reading the wrong sort of books.'[51] Until Oswald
Bastable introduces her to the right sort of books, Daisy's literary
diet has consisted of Mrs Charlesworth's *Ministering Children* (a work
which has itself been taken as the model for the parodic *The
Wouldbegoods*),[52] *Anna Ross or The Orphan of Waterloo*, *Ready Work for
Willing Hands*, and *Elsie, or Like a Little Candle*, typical Victorian
educative and sentimental texts for girls. The effect of such works
has been to stifle Daisy's imagination and her individualism, and
she has to learn from the untamed Bastable children how to play,
a lesson which involves abandoning the feminine decorousness
she has had instilled into her by her previous assiduous reading.
The distinction between boys' and girls' fiction is pointed up most
scathingly when Oswald changes his narrative style in order to write
'in a different way, like the books they give you for a prize at a
girls' school.'[53] In an exaggerated parody of sentimental formulae
and the exploitation of stylistic banalities, Nesbit openly satirizes the
literary conventions which underlie much girls' fiction of the late
nineteenth century and the quality of the hack writing it contains.

The division that existed between work written for boys and for
girls and that forms the focus of her attack was thus the product of
a combination of forces that led in turn to the consistent downgrad-
ing of girls' literature as a genre. Kimberley Reynolds' study of the
development of fiction for girls at the turn of the century confirms
this assessment and its consequences:

> Because it failed to meet the usual requirements for acceptance as
> high-status juvenile literature, was written by women and read
> by girls, the new girls' fiction was assumed to lack literary merit.
> Its offerings were set aside as an uninteresting but useful mass of
> pulp. This became the starting point from which books for girls
> came to be seen as a sub-genre within the already devalued areas
> of juvenile publishing.[54]

At the same time it can be argued that writing for children was
a means of validating the profession of letters for nineteenth-century
women. Indeed, especially later in the period, it frequently enabled
them to adopt a subversive position through articulating the child's
viewpoint. Nesbit's work in particular can be taken as a supreme
illustration of the irreverence with which establishment views could

be handled within the licence of a juvenile perspective. Both *The Story of the Treasure Seekers* and *The Wouldbegoods* contain a number of comments on the state of the literary market place and the position of women within it, from the references to Mrs Leslie who 'wrote better poetry than any other lady alive now'[55] to the comments on the role of the male editors and the power they wield.

It has become almost axiomatic for critics of nineteenth-century literature by women to reveal the coded messages such texts contain, with their emphasis on entrapment and enclosure, and the strategies for subversion that women writers adopt so as to speak from the margins to a knowing if equally repressed audience. Children's books expose similar motifs and subversive impulses. Lissa Paul, one of the few critics to apply feminist theory to a reading of children's literature, has remarked on the similarity between the two and the ways in which 'both women's literature and children's literature are devalued and regarded as marginal or peripheral by the literary and educational communities.'[56] Paul goes on to argue:

> as long as the signs and language of women's literature and children's literature are foreign, other, to male-order critics, it is almost impossible to play with meaning. So one of the primary problems feminist critics and children's literature critics have is how to recognize, define, and accord value to otherness.[57]

It is with this enterprise that this study crucially engages, and, as the subsequent section makes clear, the critical perspectives afforded by feminism disclose the texts' interplay with meaning that in the current critical climate has most frequently become associated with literary value.

FEMINIST CRITICAL PRACTICE AND GIRLS' FICTION

Because they are written by women for a primarily female public, novels for girls invite treatment according to the second of Elaine Showalter's two varieties of feminist criticism – that which concerns itself 'with *woman as writer* – with woman as the producer of textual meaning, with the history, themes, genres and structures of literature by women'[58] and which she termed *gynocritics*. For the same reason, they can be seen as part of what she has controversially defined as 'the female literary tradition' with its emphasis on female experience and aspirations, and on the construction and analysis of gender roles in a male-dominated society. Although not without its own critical difficulties in its exclusions and assumptions, Showalter's argument relies on certain fundamental principles that can be usefully applied to girls' fiction, in identifying a distinctively female literary heritage composed of writers who, consciously or not, as marginalized producers in a male profession are bonded together by gender affiliation. Other feminist literary historians, such as Ellen Moers and Nina Baym, have given weight to this view of women's writing by indicating recurrent plot patterns and themes of which such a tradition is constituted. Certainly the juvenile texts which form the subject of analysis in the succeeding discussion not only exhibit pervasive motifs in their narrative and representational patterns, but contain a marked degree of self-referentiality in locating themselves within a line of women's writing for children. Charlotte Yonge acknowledges Harriet Mozley and Elizabeth Sewell as her predecessors in the field. Alcott's heroine, Jo March, weeps over Yonge's *Heir of Redclyffe*. In *What Katy Did*, the children read Mrs Sherwood and Sewell's *Amy Herbert*. Books by well-known juvenile writers are also given as presents: Aunt Helen gives Cecy Yonge's *A Book of Golden Deeds*, and Katy receives *The Wide, Wide World* for Christmas. *The Railway Children* makes oblique reference to *The Daisy Chain* and *What Katy Did*, and Brazil's schoolgirls devour the work of the American writer Gene Stratton Porter, whose heroines open up for them exciting vistas of female possibility.

Although, as has already been suggested, it is not always easy to designate texts of the mid-nineteenth century as being written specifically for girls or young women, subject matter alone would indicate their essentially female orientation. In all the narratives discussed here, the central part is played by a heroine or heroines, and questions of feminine behaviour and values as defined by the prevailing (masculine) hegemony are prioritized. With varying degrees of didactic insistence, the works teach lessons of specific relevance to girls and young women, and offer models of desirable womanhood. Discussing early and mid-nineteenth century women's fiction, Nina Baym has characterized the genre as exemplifying a young girl's negotiation from childhood through the trials of adolescence to sound adulthood; the didacticism of such texts operates by encouraging the reader's identification with the heroine and foregrounds the lessons she learns.[59] As Judith Rowbotham has indicated, these features are also intrinsic to Victorian girls' fiction as a whole which aimed to explain and justify the female position in contemporary society, in both class and gender terms, and to convince readers to conform to conventional gender expectations.[60] Their recurrence in the texts examined in this study helps to locate these 'classic' works of literature within that same didactic tradition, and to explore women's negotiation between available narrative models and a personal voice.

For despite the fact that female children's writers may not appear to be directly political in the sense of engaging with what Chris Weedon has called the universal women's 'struggle to transform patriarchy,'[61] the issues and themes with which their works deal may well be iconoclastic in challenging existing gender hierarchies or behavioural patterns. The apparently 'innocent' and non-central arena within which they operate also empowers them to speak in disguise, as it were. Certainly, in their depictions of the move from an adolescent questioning of female sexual roles to an institution-alized womanhood, these texts can be seen to be at least disturbing the prevailing ideologies of their societies. Their 'protest' may be muted or indirect because children's literature, like women's, deals with a group which is subordinate and marginalized within the prevailing hegemonic structures, and which, at least until very recently, has not been allowed a voice. As already noted, Lissa Paul demonstrates the similarities between children's literature and women's literature, arguing that they share content and language and that this provides 'good reason for appropriating feminist theory to children's literature.'[62] Though this thesis evades the central difference between them – that whereas women's literature speaks from a position of subject-experience, children's literature is the product of one (adult) voice superimposing itself onto another (the child's) via regressive transference – it provides a helpful rationale for developing a feminist methodology in this context.

As Paul argues, both child and women fictional protagonists use deceit or guile as survival tactics in a world unaccommodating to their desires, and in each case the texts reveal a skewed relationship between plot and signified meaning. This position has obvious links with the theories of pioneering American feminist critics such as Auerbach, Showalter, and Gilbert and Gubar, whose claims of covert subversion and coded messages in female-authored texts have transformed critical readings of nineteenth-century women's writ-ing. The idea that literature for girls or young women articulates an

iconoclastic creed of protest or rebellion from within its conventional
generic boundaries has been powerfully argued by many of these
critics. Not all make such extreme claims as Helen Waite Papashilvy's
that nineteenth-century sentimental/domestic novels are handbooks
of feminine revolt 'so subtly vicious that by comparison the ladies
at Seneca appear angels of innocence . . . [they are] a witches' broth,
a lethal draught brewed by women and used by women to destroy
their common enemy, man.'[63] But some of her more persuasive
assertions – that the emphasis on the marked practical ability of
women, or on their effectiveness as moral and spiritual teachers,
empowers them in the novels, for example – can be convincingly
applied to several of the works considered in this study. Similarly,
in her much-quoted study of New England women in the early and
mid-nineteenth century, Nancy Cott focuses on the way in which
the growing importance of female domestic and religious authority
both allowed women to assert themselves and legitimized the
scrutiny of gender roles in the literature of the time;[64] and Baym also
argues that the 'cult of domesticity', with its religious contextualization, which mid-century women's fiction promotes is not wholly
conservative or passive but becomes a value scheme permeating
the whole of American life with women at its centre.[65] In greater
detail, Tompkins foregrounds the elements of covert rebellion
in sentimental texts such as *The Wide, Wide World*, arguing that
they are essentially preoccupied with the nature of power, and
that women's apparently helpless submission to Divine and human
patriarchal authority is in fact an assertion of autonomy according
them 'a place from which to launch a counter-strategy against their
worldly masters that would finally give them the upper hand.'[66]
Basing the notion of a gendered reader-response on the assumption
that a female audience, even a young one, could and did read in the
'gaps' or 'silences' set up within the narratives, this kind of feminist
revisionist reading offers a helpful approach to the texts in this
study. All the novels to a greater or lesser degree engage with the
scope for action available to girls and women, and, in their creation
of a female space through domestic or imaginative means, suggest
oppositional practices that can empower the protagonists and release their potential for self-realization.

Indeed, the exploration and construction of female subjectivity
is central to girls' fiction of this period, which experiments with a
variety of narrative models, in the process often drawing on experiences from the authors' own past in the attempt to redefine the

processes of female socialization and selfhood. Almost all the novels treated in this study reveal a dependence on autobiographical narrative sources and replicate to some extent the writers' own childhood and adolescent experiences, not only in terms of locale and temporality but also in the more intimate details of family and neighbourhood relationships. Viewed collectively they tell versions of a single female story and many of the heroines seem thinly disguised self-portraits of their author's struggles to come to terms with their own inner resistance to social or family pressures, or with fears of abandonment and loss of security. There is of course a danger in predicating the extent to which women in particular reproduce autobiographical narratives in their fictions, what Mary Jacobus terms the 'autobiographical "phallacy" – whereby male critics hold that women's writing is somehow closer to experience than men's, that the female text *is* the author, or at any rate a dramatic extension of her unconsciousness.'[67] At the same time, theorists of women's autobiography have been keen to emphasize 'the many distancing devices by which a woman writer weaves her strategy of self-representation'[68] into texts that appear on the surface to conform to regulated modes of female discourse. As Francoise Lionnet has remarked:

> Since it is notoriously difficult for women to recognize ourselves in the traditional images that literature and society (sometimes including our own mothers) project or uphold as models, it should not be surprising for an autobiographical narrative to proclaim itself as fiction: for the narrator's process of reflection, narration, and self-integration within language is bound to unveil patterns of self-definition (and self-dissimulation) which may seem new and strange and with which we are not always consciously familiar.[69]

Children's literature, as an approved outlet for women's publication, functions as a perfect vehicle for the 'alienated' woman writer to work through her own dilemmas and preoccupations via imaginative constructs within a conventional format. The texts' concern with female psychological and social development, and the experimentation with transgressive configurations of identity – Jo's crossdressing, Katy's daring, Mary Lennox's sullenness and temper – takes on a particularly personal resonance, indicating a closeness between the writer's life and her creative inspiration which can only find formulation in a fiction with an ostensible moral or educational bias. Theories of women's autobiography, in the exploration of the relation of the self to narrative and language, offer valuable insights into literature for girls. The positioning of the heroine as storyteller in a number of the works considered here, together with her ability to deploy narrative as a means to empowerment, indicates the complicated nature of the interrelation between autobiographical source material and its fictional transformation.

Feminist adaptations of Lacanian theory, making particular reference to the constitution of the subject in language help further to disclose the psychoanalytic dimensions of these works in their view of childhood and gendered subjectivities. Lacan's notion of the child's move from the Imaginary, a state of undifferentiatedness and oneness with the mother, to the Symbolic Order in which the individualized self is formulated is important here. Developed most influentially by French feminist critics such as Luce Irigaray and Julia Kristeva, his theories have radical implications for the rereading of juvenile literature. Building on Lacan's definition of the Symbolic as a state prioritizing the Law of the Father, embodied in language, in which elements of the Imaginary are repressed and thus silenced, these critics locate the feminine in the Imaginary (or what Kristeva calls the semiotic), arguing that women remain estranged within the Symbolic since it predicates the 'I' on a male-ordered articulation. Thus women, like children, operate at the level of the unconscious or pre-verbal, and cannot engage with the master discourse except as aliens borrowing a non-native language. The texts examined here, focusing on the problems of expressing meaning, the significance of naming as a means of establishing identities, and the separateness of juvenile and adult discourse, similarly suggest a link between the child and the feminine in a Kristevan configuration. In the same way, their portrayal of the young heroine's education into adulthood, during which she learns socialization as a process of adaptation to a patriarchal sign system, parallels feminist psychoanalytical concern with female subjectivity and self-identification in the work of critics such as Shoshana Felman and Nancy Chodorow.[70]

Although none of the texts scrutinized here attempts linguistically to articulate a female Imaginary in the self-conscious manner of some modernist works or the revolutionary mode of *écriture feminine* proposed by Hélène Cixous and other French feminists, they are in several ways concerned with establishing a discourse which disrupts the Symbolic. This is observable, for instance, in the nature of the metaphors and imagery which they employ. Moers and Gilbert and Gubar, among others, have shown how women writers tend to explore matters relevant to their sex through a particularly defined metaphoric language, and the repeated tropes embedded in these juvenile texts suggests the existence of a coherent feminized perceptual framework which stands in opposition to a dominant order. The importance of domestic interiors, suggesting both enclosure and security, the recurrent references to private or secret places, and the linkage between the heroine and the natural world, have been read by both cultural and psychoanalytic critics as having a specially feminine resonance, and carry significant implications in reading the narratives of escape (whether overt or covert) which are intrinsic to juvenile literature. Many of these novels depict the fantasy world which the heroine creates for herself and other children – Katy's imaginary queendoms, Anne Shirley's mysterious forest, Mary Lennox's secret garden. These are places of make-believe, autonomous and with their own sets of rules and talismans; they are also protected from intrusion by the dominant (adult) world.

The works also bear out Shirley and Edwin Ardeners' theory of 'muted' and 'dominant' language groups, as expanded by Showalter in her well-known essay 'Feminist Criticism in the Wilderness.'[71] Starting from the Ardeners' notion that in constituting the muted group women have to borrow the language of the dominant (male) group, which controls society's mode of communication, Showalter develops the concept of the 'wild zone' of woman's culture which exists outside the dominant boundaries of experience and language and in which female 'difference' is located. This has obvious application to children's literature, since children are also a muted group who speak and act in a 'wild zone'. In contrast the emphasis on the defining power of textuality itself – Ethel May's immersion in the romantic world of literary heroism, Jo March's Gothic tales of violence and desire, and Raymonde Armitage's rejection of school textbooks in favour of stories of adventure, together with her construction of a specialized schoolgirl slang – suggest the disruptive potential of an alternative female discourse fermenting beneath the weight of patriarchal language systems.

The novels also set up their own challenge to the Symbolic through a transgressive or subversive intertextuality. Many of them rewrite archetypal male myths, fairy tales, or formulaic literary types so as to prioritize the feminine. For instance, both *The Wide, Wide World*

and *The Secret Garden* are at one level fairy tales in which the prince
is transformed or controlled by the heroine/princess; many of the
plots, as that of *Anne of Green Gables,* can be seen as female versions
of the *Bildungsroman;* and the narrative formulations of works as
varied as *Little Women* and *The Madcap of the School* dramatize ways
in which girls and women are empowered in fictional worlds that,
temporarily at least, relate only tangentially to the external establishment structures. In connection with this, too, female authority is
foregrounded in the ability to name, considered a male prerogative
in patriarchal theories of language. Like women in the alternative
system proposed by feminist critics, the children in these stories
produce their own world of meaning by ordering and naming,
creating identities opposed to the pre-existing ones offered them in
the Symbolic order and in whose establishment they play no part.
Girls and women also adopt the roles of storyteller, replicating the
position of author as they use narrative as a means of empowerment.
Usurping the authority of linguistic definition, they give shape and
meaning to their personal visions, in the process gaining control
over their own psychological landscapes. Mary Lennox weaves her
magic narratives to hold Colin and Dickon spellbound in *The Secret
Garden;* Jo March and Katy Carr are authors in their own right, with
written texts to prove their effectiveness as producers of meaning;
Anne Shirley's fantasies recreate her self image in resistance to the
reality of her identity as unwanted orphan child; and Mother in *The
Railway Children* literally sustains her family through her imaginative
invention, her stories' success resulting in buns for tea.

The importance accorded in these novels to the exploration of
motherhood provides a further ingredient in the radical reconstruc-
tion of these texts in the light of current feminist critical practice.
Cathy N. Davidson has shown how the rhetoric of motherhood
which pervades much nineteenth-century women's fiction and which
is conjoined initially with a submerged language of feminism becomes transformed into a repressive ideology later in the century.[72]
Novels for girls, in their representation of motherhood as providing
a potential role-model for daughters, reflect the problematic nature
of this shift in the political textual agenda. Moreover, the position
of the daughter *vis-à-vis* the mother figure is inextricably associated
with her search for autonomous selfhood. Mothering, both in terms
of the representation of actual parents and as a metonymic signifier
of a core element in femininity, is central in virtually all the works
examined here. The analysis of gendered identity and female

autonomy with which the novels engage finds especial significance in the relationship between mothers and daughters in for example *Little Women* and *The Railway Children*. Conversely, the repeated motif of the dead or absent mother figure – as in *The Daisy Chain, The Wide, Wide World* and *The Secret Garden* – carries multiple inferences which are rarely as conventional in terms of the contemporary iconization of motherhood as an initial reading might allow.

The application of these multiform feminist critical principles to the texts chosen for discussion is not intended to be either exhaustive or limiting. As Annette Kolodny has argued, pluralism is essential to a genuinely feminist methodology in its uncovering of meanings and its refusal to strait-jacket the text in any over-prescriptive framework. Furthermore:

> If this kind of pluralism appears to threaten both the present coherence of and the inherited aesthetic criteria for a canon of "greats", then . . . it is precisely that threat which, alone, can free us from the prejudices, the strictures, and the blind spots of the past.[73]

The aim of this enterprise therefore is not to isolate texts from their contemporary meanings. Revisionist readings are set against contemporary reactions and ideologies in as far as these can be posited, suggesting both how fictional patterns in girls' literature may illuminate the text's contemporaneous culture and how a more radical critical positioning may offer new insights into the representation of gender roles and women's writing practices. Both surface and covert aspects of the narratives are thus explored, including elements of textual disruption or slippage – tensions between conflicting significations which Susan K. Harris has defined as a deliberate discontinuity between 'cover-plot' and 'underplot.'[74] In the context of the socio-historical changes which were taking place over the period under review, the rich possibilities of meaning embodied in a non-canonical but paradoxically less restricted genre can be revealed.

Notes

1. Edward J. Salmon, 'What Girls Read', *Nineteenth Century*, vol. XX, no. 116 (1886), p.522.

2.   Kimberley Reynolds, *Girls Only?: Gender and Popular Children's Fiction in Britain, 1880–1910* (Hemel Hempstead: Harvester, 1990), p.47.

3.   Gillian Avery, *Nineteenth Century Children* (London: Hodder & Stoughton, 1965).

4.   Julia Briggs, 'Women Writers and Writing for Children: From Sarah Fielding to E. Nesbit', in eds Gillian Avery and Julia Briggs, *Children and Their Books* (Oxford: Oxford University Press, 1990). p.238.

5.   Charlotte M. Yonge, 'Children's Literature of the Last Century', *Macmillan's Magazine*, vol. XX, nos. 117–19 (1869), p.449.

6.   Ibid., p.309.

7.   Ibid., p.453.

8.   Ibid., p.454.

9.   Ibid.

10. Reynolds, op.cit. Chapters 3 and 5.

11. Twentieth-century boys too have found girls' stories attractive, even if they have been ashamed of admitting it. Fred Inglis, Professor of Education at Nottingham University and a specialist on children's fiction, confesses to reading Alcott and Angela Brazil as a child, concealing the books' bindings behind brown paper covers on which he had written 'Billiards for Boys' so as to keep their true identity hidden from his schoolmates. Inglis's taste for works that were notably female in orientation and his furtiveness in reading them indicates the division that exists in assumptions about gendered reading. See Fred Inglis, *The Promise of Happiness: Value and Meaning in Children's Fiction* (Cambridge: Cambridge University Press, 1981), p.65.

12. Jane Tompkins, *Sensational Designs: the Cultural Work of American Fiction 1790–1860* (New York: Oxford University Press, 1985).

13. Martha Mary Sherwood, *The History of the Fairchild Family (1818–1847)*, Part I, 17th edn (London: J. Hatchard, 1848), p.112.

14. Tompkins, op.cit.

15. Nina Baym, 'Portrayal of Women in American Literature, 1790–1870', in ed. Marlene Springer, *What Manner of Woman: Essays on English and American Life and Literature* (Oxford: Basil Blackwell, 1977), pp.211–34.

16. The term 'cult of domesticity' is used by Nancy F. Cott in *The Bonds of Womanhood: 'Women's Sphere' in New England, 1780–1835* (New Haven: Yale, 1977). Other relevant studies of the relationship between women's lives and the fiction of the period, in England and America, are Carol Dyhouse, *Girls Growing Up in Late Victorian and Edwardian England* (London: Routledge & Kegan Paul, 1981), and Anne Scott McLeod, 'The *Caddie Woodlawn* Syndrome: American Girlhood in the Nineteenth Century', in Heininger et al., *A Century of Childhood 1820–1920* (Rochester, NY: Margaret Woodbury Strong Museum, 1984), pp.97–119.

17. Reynolds, op.cit., p.96.

18. See, for example, Gillian Avery, *Childhood's Pattern: a Study of the Heroes and Heroines of Children's Fiction, 1770–1950* (London: Hodder & Stoughton, 1975), and J.S. Bratton, *The Impact of Victorian Children's Fiction* (London: Croom Helm, 1981).

19. Mary Lynn Stevens Heininger, 'Children, Childhood and Change in America', in Heininger et al., op.cit.
20. Anne Scott McLeod, op.cit.
21. Susan Coolidge, *Nine Little Goslings*, 1875 (English edition, 1876), pp. 2–3.
22. Eleanor L. Sewell, ed., *The Autobiography of Elizabeth M. Sewell* (London: Longmans, Green, 1907), p.202.
23. Kathleen Tillotson, *Novels of the Eighteen-Forties* (Oxford: Oxford University Press, reprint 1962), p.5.
24. *Nation*, vol. 7 (22 October 1868), p.335; *Harper's*, vol. 39 (August 1868) pp.455–6. Quoted in Alma J. Payne, 'Louisa May Alcott', *American Literary Realism*, vol. 6, no. 1 (Winter 1973), p.29.
25. Christabel Coleridge, *Charlotte Mary Yonge: Her Life and Letters* (London: Macmillan, 1903), p.152.
26. Figures from Richard D. Altick, *The English Common Reader*, (Chicago: University of Chicago Press, 1957).
27. Tillotson, op.cit., p.136.
28. James reviewed Alcott's *Eight Cousins* in the *Nation*, October 1875 (reprinted in *Literary Reviews and Essays by Henry James*, ed. Albert Mordell [New York: Grove Press, 1957], pp.245–7). He praises Yonge's *The Heir of Redclyffe* and *The Daisy Chain*, and Warner's *The Wide, Wide World* as representatives of a 'school' which has achieved a compromise 'between the interest of youth and those of maturity . . . an attempt to provide a special literature for women and children', in '*The Schonberg-Cotta Family*', *Nation*, 14 September 1865 (reprinted in *Notes and Reviews by Henry James*, ed. Pierre de Chaignon la Rose [Freeport, New York: Dunster House, 1921], pp.77–81.
29. *The History of the Fairchild Family*, p.112.
30. Ibid., p.117.
31. Maria Edgeworth, *Tales and Novels*, vol.I *Moral Tales* (London: George Routledge, 1893), p.282
32. Susan B. Warner ['Elizabeth Wetherell'], *The Wide, Wide World* (New York: Feminist Press, 1987), pp.9–10.
33. Susan Coolidge [Sarah Chauncey Woolsey], *What Katy Did* (London and Melbourne: Ward, Lock, n.d.), p.1.
34. [Charlotte M. Yonge], *The Daisy Chain: or Aspirations* (London: Macmillan, 1870), p.1.
35. Frances Hodgson Burnett, *The Secret Garden* (Oxford: World's Classics, 1987), p.1.
36. John Stephens, *Language and Ideology in Children's Fiction* (London: Longman, 1992), p.56.
37. Amy Cruse, *The Victorians and Their Books* (London: George Allen & Unwin, 1935), p.25.
38. In this study, 'North American' refers to works by writers from Canada as well as the United States.
39. Gillian Avery, 'Home and Family: English and American Ideals in the Nineteenth Century', in ed. Dennis Butts, *Stories and Society: Children's Literature in its Social Context* (London: Macmillan, 1991), p.42.

40. Figures from US Library of Congress National Union Catalog, and British Library Catalogue.
41. Anne Scott McLeod, op.cit., p.104.
42. Avery, 'Home and Family', op.cit., p.46.
43. Alcott, *Little Women* (London: Puffin Books, 1953), p.171.
44. Ibid., p.183.
45. Tompkins, op.cit.
46. Gaye Tuchman, *Edging Women Out: Victorian Novelists, Publishers and Social Change* (London: Routledge, 1989), p.143.
47. Julia Briggs, op.cit., pp.223–4.
48. *Louisa May Alcott, her Life, Letters and Journals,* ed. Ednah D. Cheyney, (London: Sampson, Low and Marston; Searle and Rivington, 1889) pp.202–3.
49. See Anna B. Warner, *Susan Warner ('Elizabeth Wetherell')* (New York: G. P. Putnam's Sons, 1909).
50. Jacqueline Rose, *The Case of Peter Pan, or the Impossibility of Children's Fiction* (London: Macmillan, 1984), p.48.
51. E. Nesbit, *The Wouldbegoods* (London: Puffin Books, 1958), p.64.
52. See Juliet Dusinberre, *Alice to the Lighthouse: Children's Books and Radical Experiments in Art* (London: St. Martin's Press, 1987), p.44
53. *The Wouldbegoods*, p.128.
54. Reynolds op.cit., p.105.
55. E. Nesbit, *The Story of the Treasure Seekers* (London: Puffin Books, 1958) p.54.
56. Lissa Paul, 'Enigma Variations: What Feminist Theory Knows About Children's Literature', *Signal*, vol. 54 (September 1987), reprinted in Peter Hunt, *Children's Literature: the Development of Criticism* (London: Routledge, 1990), p.149.
57. Ibid., p.155.
58. Elaine Showalter 'Towards a Feminist Poetics', in ed. Mary Jacobus, *Women Writing and Writing About Women* (London: Croom Helm, 1979), p.25.
59. Nina Baym, *Women's Fiction: a Guide to Novels by and about Women in America 1820–1870* (Ithaca, NY: Cornell, 1978).
60. Judith Rowbotham, *Good Girls make Good Wives: Guidance for Girls in Victorian Fiction* (Oxford: Blackwell, 1989).
61. Chris Weedon, *Feminist Practice and Post-structuralist Theory* (Oxford: Blackwell, 1987), p.2.
62. Paul, op.cit., p.149.
63. Helen Waite Papashilvy, *All the Happy Endings: a study of the domestic novel in America, the women who wrote it, the women who read it, in the nineteenth century* (New York: Harper, 1956), p.xvii.
64. Nancy F. Cott, op.cit.
65. Nina Baym, *Woman's Fiction*, op.cit.
66. Jane Tompkins, op.cit., p.162.
67. Mary Jacobus, 'Review of The Madwoman in the Attic', *Signs* vol. 6 no. 3 (1981) quoted in ed. Marlene Kadar, *Essays on Life Writing: From Genre to Critical Practice* (Toronto: University of Toronto Press, 1992), p.165.

68. Vita Fortunati, Introduction to *Representations of the Self in Women's Autobiography*, ed. Vita Fortunati and Gabriella Morisco, (Bologna, University of Bologna Press, 1993), p.xv.

69. Francoise Lionnet, *Autobiographical Voices: Race, Gender, Self-Portraiture* (Ithaca and London: Cornell University Press, 1989), p.92

70. Shoshana Felman, 'Re-reading Femininity', *Yale French Studies*, 62, 1981, pp.19–44; *Writing and Madness* (Ithaca: Cornell University Press, 1985); Nancy Chodorow, *The Reproduction of Mothering: Psychoanalysis and the Sociology of Gender* (Berkeley: University of California Press, 1978).

71. Elaine Showalter, 'Feminist Criticism in the Wilderness', in ed. Elaine Showalter, *The New Feminist Criticism* (London: Virago Press, 1986), pp.243–70.

72. Cathy N. Davidson, 'Mothers and Daughters in the Fiction of the New Republic', in *The Lost Tradition: Mothers and Daughters in Literature*, ed. Cathy N. Davidson and E.M. Broner, (New York: Frederick Ungar, 1980).

73. Annette Kolodny 'Dancing through the Minefield: some observations on the theory, practice and politics of a feminist literary criticism', *Feminist Studies* 6 (1980), reprinted in ed. Elaine Showalter, op.cit., p.161.

74. Susan K. Harris, *19th-Century American Women's Novels: Interpretive Strategies* (Cambridge: Cambridge University Press, 1990).

2
Susan Warner:
The Wide, Wide World

In January 1853, looking back over the year's novels, the *North American Review* records the enthusiastic reception of 'a new venture in the new path [of American moral fiction] . . . *The Wide, Wide World* struck a chord that was still vibrating when *Queechy* came to prolong the thrill.'[1] The amazing success of Susan Warner's first novel, which appeared under the pseudonym of Elizabeth Wetherell[2] at the end of 1850, is attested by its sales figures on both sides of the Atlantic. It became a best-seller almost overnight: in the United States it went through fourteen editions in two years, its sales exceeded only by those of *Uncle Tom's Cabin*; and in England Routledge alone sold 80 000 in the first year of its publication.[3] Its readership ranged from highbrow critics like Henry James who compared its realism to Flaubert's[4], to ordinary families seeking domestic entertainment. As Warner's publisher informed her:

> I think I may say we have now got up a *Wide, Wide World* fever: I am told by a correspondent that the trade in Manchester and Liverpool is simply inundated with *Wide, Wide World*s. Ten thousand copies were sold at one English railway station.[5]

The novel's success depended to a large extent on its popularity with adult and youthful readers alike, for as has already been indicated, in this period there was a far less pronounced generic gap between children's and adult literature than there is today. The *North American Review* critic stresses the universal appeal of Warner's first novel: initially bought for 'nice little girls', it soon extended its readership:

> Elder sisters were . . . found poring over the volumes, and it was very natural that mothers next should try the spell . . . After this, papas were not very difficult to convert . . . [and] we are much mistaken if the *Wide, Wide World* and *Queechy*, have not been found under the pillows of sober bachelors.[6]

Warner's first biographer, her sister Anna, confirms this, claiming that all classes and ages read it, and illustrating the fact by reference to a family of avid enthusiasts ranging from a thirteen-year-old girl to a grave father of fifty-seven. Moreover, Warner's publisher, Putnam, seems to have considered it more of an adult's than a child's novel. After the appearance of *The Wide, Wide World* and *Queechy* (1852), he requested her to write a 'juvenile' work, a comment which suggests that he considered the two former books to be outside this category. Warner herself called a later fiction, *Daisy* (1868), 'a child's story'[7] apparently distinguishing it from her first two novels.

The Wide, Wide World spoke most specifically, however, to a contemporary female audience. It is one of the earliest and best examples of what was to become probably the most popular nineteenth-century fictional genre in America – the sentimental/domestic novel, written by women for women, and implementing an archetypal plot in which an unprotected heroine overcomes suffering and tribulations to achieve spiritual perfection and moral maturity. The genre both reinforced and was itself reinforced by current ideologies of feminine behaviour: female readers accepted the fiction as an accurate picture of their own lives in many respects, and also drew on it for social and spiritual guidance.[8] As Nancy Schnog has argued, as a quintessential instance of this type *The Wide, Wide World* represents and analyses emotional and psychological experiences familiar to many of its readers, reproducing

> an emotional and psychological terrain particular to the lives of many middle-class women in mid-nineteenth-century America . . . the intimate experiences of Warner's female heroines mirror and repeat some of the most important emotional events known to this class of women . . . [and] also tries to reduce their traumatic significance by showing women readers how to prepare for and manage them.[9]

It also needs to be stressed, though, that the novel has an especial appeal to a young female readership. Its heroine, Ellen Montgomery, is about ten when the story opens. An only child, living a secluded life in New York, she is suddenly confronted with the news that, having lost the lawsuit in which he had been involved, her father is about to leave for Europe, taking her mother with him but leaving his daughter behind in the care of an aunt who lives on a remote up-state farm. Ellen's intense distress at the separation and her subsequent loneliness and grief in the unfamiliar surroundings, where she is abused by her disagreeable aunt, speak particularly to girls, and to their fears of maternal deprivation and loss. Moreover, Ellen's endurance of harshness, humiliation and psychological bullying, and her feelings of being misunderstood and spiritually isolated, have a peculiarly feminine resonance, replicating the sense of helplessness and inequity in a male-privileged environment familiar to girls from an early age. The close tie, too, which Ellen establishes with Alice Humphreys, her aunt's neighbour – a tie which is broken after Alice's death and Ellen goes to live with her uncongenial Scottish relatives in Edinburgh – emphasizes the importance for girls of sisterly relationships which are both tutelary and affectionate.

The novel also combines didacticism and narrative realism in a way that has youthful appeal. While offering a behavioural model in the figure of Ellen, who triumphs over adversity and is rewarded materially as well as spiritually, its vivid details of life in an isolated rural community – the apple bee or the ham-smoking, for instance – have a similar kind of attractiveness to that of Twain's portrayal of regional life in *Huckleberry Finn*, another novel of child/adult appeal. Indeed, the back cover of the Feminist Press edition of *The Wide, Wide World* calls it 'a feminist *Huckleberry Finn*'. Ellen's delight in the far more opulent environment of the Marshmans' house at Ventnor, at which she spends Christmas, also creates the kind of nostalgic recall of childhood which Catherine Maria Sedgwick, herself an early American novelist for the young, experienced when reading the novel – 'Its simplicity and truth to nature are remarkable . . . [it makes] you turn back to your childhood when everyone was good or bad – when you loved or hated without analyzing character or dissecting nature.'[10] At the same time, as Nina Baym has indicated, by exemplifying 'the difficult but successful negotiation of the undifferentiated child through the trials of adolescence into the individuation of sound adulthood,'[11] the story reminds its young female readers that girlhood is merely a temporary state on the way to being a woman. Whereas in *Little Women* and *What Katy Did*, maturity is represented as a state of restraint and limitation in contrast to the utopian freedom of childhood, *The Wide, Wide World* does not romanticize its heroine's early years. For Ellen, her youthful experiences are merely stages – frequently disagreeable ones – in her undeviating progression to the full responsibilities, social and moral, of adulthood.

The popularity of *The Wide, Wide World* encouraged Warner to continue in the same vein. *Queechy*, her next novel, published in 1852, reproduces the same narrative pattern of girlhood refined and purified by suffering and submission to God's will, and it was equally successful. In the first couple of years after its appearance Routledge sold 62 000 copies in England, and Elizabeth Barrett Browning certainly thought it was as good as Mrs Stowe's work.[12] Like many other women writing in this genre, Warner realized that she had, in the words of the *North American Review*, 'struck a chord' that was to prove rewarding. The reward was much needed. Warner came from a prosperous middle-class family; her father, Henry Whiting Warner, was a successful New York state lawyer, and Susan and her younger sister, Anna, were brought up in relative luxury in New York City. But in 1837, Mr Warner lost most of his money and took his family to live on Constitution Island, near West Point, which he had previously bought as a paradisal retreat. The shock of the sudden move from financial ease to comparative poverty was considerable; and matters worsened when he lost his remaining assets in a legal battle over land improvement. Extra resources became essential for even the most basic necessities, and, as was the case with so many nineteenth-century women novelists, female creative talents had to be exploited for the purpose.

Anna, describing how their aunt (who had taken over the household after Mrs Warner's death in 1828) suggested that Susan write a story, remarks, 'Whether she added "that would sell," I am not sure; but of course that was what she meant.'[13] Money worries continued, as is indicated by the ever increasing references in Warner's journal to the burden of writing in order to keep the family going. But ironically enough, the very hardships and the ensuing self-sacrifices, bitter though they were, brought her popularity as well as some financial relief. The kind of domestic trials she suffered were familiar to many of her female contemporaries who recognized the survival strategies, social and spiritual, depicted in the novel. As Susan Williams argues, Warner's 'financial stability depended on her success as a sentimental novelist, a success due in turn to her responsiveness to the desires of her readers . . . she *chose* to write in the sentimental mode and to invest Ellen with the virtues of piety and self-discipline venerated within the domestic "woman's sphere." '[14]

The novel also owed its widespread appeal to the fact that it accurately reflected the spiritual preoccupations of the age. Like the tract literature of the early nineteenth-century Evangelical Revival, which in some ways it draws on, it joins a sentimental/domestic ideology with a pervasive evangelicalism. Right womanly behaviour is presented in the context of the individual's relation to God: Ellen's progression to an ideal Christian state via obedience to a heavenly authority, renunciation of personal desire, and endless conscience-searching and self-discipline embodies not a fictional ideal but historical reality, as the biographical and autobiographical writings of contemporary women reveal. Warner herself, in the possibly over-sanctified portrait of her offered by Anna, was a highly self-critical religious woman, preoccupied with her spiritual state. Soon after their move to Constitution Island, she underwent a religious conversion, becoming a full member of the Church and dedicating herself to Christ's service. Her diary entry for her twenty-second birthday, in 1841, for instance, stressing her need for constant self-examination and her intention of starting a new life with God, sounds remarkably like the kind of resolution which Mrs Montgomery and, later, Alice and John Humphreys exact from Ellen:

> Hoping as I do, that the future years of my life may bear very little resemblance to the preceding ones, it is fitting that on this day I should seriously consider the ground I stand upon; and considering the deceitfulness and evasiveness of the heart, it is as well perhaps that I should do it in writing.[15]

Such sentiments are echoed in Ellen's confession to Alice that all her determinations to be good have failed because she has allowed herself to feel resentment towards her aunt; to her remark that: " 'Isn't it strange, dear Alice, that I should do so when I have resolved so hard I wouldn't?" ', her friend replies, ' "Not very, my darling, as long as we have such evil hearts as ours are." '[16] Ellen's struggles to subdue wilfulness and resign herself to whatever God sees fit to send reflect not only her creator's obsessive self-searchings but also those of a whole female generation of which she was representative.

Critical reception of course shifts its emphases according to changes in moral and social ideologies. For contemporary readers, the ethical insistence of *The Wide, Wide World* was its chief – and by and large most attractive – feature. Contemporary reviewers praised its portrayal of 'individual loveliness and virtue', showing its heroine brought 'by careful gradations, to the state of self-governed and stable virtue which fits woman for her great office in the world' and offering 'some most salutary hints of united modesty and firmness;'[17] it was also felt that Warner 'has succeeded . . . better than any other writer in our language in making religious sentiment appear natural and attractive.'[18] Anna, too, notes 'How many of whom even I have heard, trace their heart conversion straight to that blessing [of the Lord] on the pages of the "Wide, Wide World." '[19] As these quotations make clear, most of Warner's early readers accepted her representation (and validation) of the age's conception of ideal womanhood; the North American Review's admiration for heroines who 'are conscious of having a power and place in the world, and . . . claim it without assumption or affectation, and fill it with a quiet self-respect, not inconsistent with modesty and due humility,'[20] for instance, voices approval for the essentialist and separatist view of female roles which the novel seems to endorse.

In the light of later twentieth-century attitudes towards women and gender roles, however, critical evaluations of The Wide, Wide World are markedly different. Recent feminist criticism has transformed readings of this sentimental/domestic genre, deconstructing its overt coding and suggesting that the authors are employing 'strategies of subversion'[21] in order to undercut their ostensible messages. Mary Hiatt, for example, argues not only that the novel contains 'an engrossing sub-text that is replete with conflicting desires, the disquieting possibility of independence, and the tumultuous but alluring toils of sexuality', but also that contemporary female readers themselves participated in these alternative readings – 'The tension between text and sub-text guaranteed the novel's wide appeal.'[22] The notion of collusion between text and audience has been posited by many feminist critics of the novel. Jane Tompkins claims that its subversive validation of female power enabled its readers to transcend their narrow culturally-assigned roles.[23] Similarly, Joanne Dobson, arguing that 'the ethos of female self-abnegation as it appeared in women's popular novels, although sincere, was often shot through with indications of dissatisfaction and dissent . . . [causing] a profoundly eloquent disruption between professed intention and realization,' finds in a work such as The Wide, Wide World an author/audience relationship which implicitly acknowledges this kind of textual dislocation.[24] According to such analyses, the story of a young girl's triumph over adversity covertly articulates more radical or iconoclastic possibilities of female autonomy and empowerment.

This kind of deconstructive reading of the novel depends on a reinterpretation of fictional iconographies whose nineteenth-century significance was undoubtedly different from today's. Women readers of the time may indeed have colluded with the author in her unease, but in suggesting a deliberate discrepancy between text and sub-text historicity and biographical evidence must not be ignored. Warner herself was undoubtedly only too familiar with the tensions and paradoxes inherent in the female condition of her time, but there is no evidence of her commitment to a clearly feminist position. She apparently accepted the feminine ideal of submission and inscribed it in her fiction. Nevertheless, this does not preclude the existence of 'powerful unspoken messages'[25] within it. There are certainly fascinating complexities and ambiguities in *The Wide, Wide World*, which allow for the possibility of a revisionary and more subversive interpretation. These are focalized in three interlocking narrative preoccupations – gender roles, power relations, and moral themes. The novel also effects a degree of iconoclasm in its rewriting of literary genres and in its nationalism.

In dealing with gender roles and characteristics, Warner both upholds and challenges the conventions of her age, suggesting her own ambiguity about them. Like many single women of her generation, she was at one and the same time dutiful daughter and family breadwinner, self-effacing spinster and participant in the public, male-dominated world of publishing. Devoted to her father and accustomed to deferring to him, she was nevertheless wearied by his continuing interference after she and Anna had taken over the family's business affairs. The unease which she must have felt in living out such apparently contradictory positions articulates itself in her portrayal of character and relationships between the sexes. The novel's prime concern is with what constitutes ideal womanhood. This ideal is explored through representative female figures who function as possible role models for the heroine, a narrative strategy employed by many of the writers in this study. The highest level of womanly perfection, incorporating virtues of submission, self-forgetfulness, loving-kindness and piety, is embodied in three separate characters: Mrs Montgomery, Alice Humphreys, and old Mrs Vawse.

Mrs Montgomery is a central icon in the narrative in several respects. Firstly, she is herself emblematic of womanly suffering, the victim of both ill-health and male tyranny. When the novel opens, she is already a fast-failing invalid, subject to her husband's wishes and unable to oppose his European travel plans: 'to the pressure of argument Captain Montgomery added the weight of authority, insisting on her compliance' (12). She is equally power-less to object to the suddenness with which he engineers Ellen's departure for Aunt Fortune's, with no advance warning. As well as the long-suffering, abused wife, Mrs Montgomery embodies another archetypal fictional figure – the saintly mother who functions as mentor and spiritual guide. The importance of motherhood in the women's texts of this period has already been indicated, but ma-ternity has an especial significance in *The Wide, Wide World*. Ellen's emotional and spiritual dependence on Mrs Montgomery is sugges-tive of the pre-Oedipal phase of identification with the mother. The two enjoy an extraordinary closeness as is demonstrated in the scene where in the sacred inner sanctum of their private parlour, the curtains drawn and the lamp lit, Ellen makes tea for her in a kind of ritualistic ceremony of mutual devotion:

> Ellen's whole soul was in her beloved duty . . . Mrs Montgomery arose with her usual kind smile, to show her gratitude by honoring as far as possible what Ellen had provided. (24)

For Ellen, maternal love is supreme even over God's – an order which Mrs Montgomery works to reverse – and her whole being is centred on her mother:

> "I always feel safe when you are near me, because I know you'll take care of me. And I am glad to think I belong to you, and you have the management of me entirely, and I needn't manage myself, because I know I can't; and if I could, I'd rather you would, Mama". (18)

> [Ellen] was thinking how very, very precious was the heart she could feel beating where her cheek lay – she thought it was greater happiness to lie there than anything else in life could be – she thought she would rather die so, on her mother's breast, than live long without her in the world. (38)

Mrs Montgomery's insistence on the supremacy of Divine love is reiterated by the old man on the boat who comforts Ellen on her way to her aunt's. He tells her that God ' "saw that his little child was in danger of forgetting him, and he loved you, Ellen; and so he has taken your dear mother, and sent you away where you will have no one to look to but him"' (70). But it is a long time before Ellen can school herself to learn this lesson, as is shown by her passionate grief and anger when her aunt retains her mother's letter, by her constant reliance on the memory of maternal support, and by her intense distress when she learns of Mrs Montgomery's death. Part of the novel's subversiveness, in fact, lies in this constant tension between ideology and desire. Spiritual perfection, as all Ellen's mentors teach her, depends on the rejection of earthly love in favour of God's: Ellen is reprobate in continuing to yearn for emotional fulfilment from a human source, and, like Jane Eyre, in insisting that 'I don't care a fig for anything people do for me without that [love]' (21). Yet all her needs are always focused on one individual – Mrs Montgomery, Alice, John – and, as will be shown, her final satisfaction is more secular than spiritual. Thus while the surface orthodoxy of the narrative validates one message, its subtextual acknowledgement of women's need for human affection and support undermines and changes the meaning of that message, particularly for female readers.

Alice Humphreys, the gentle and saintly young woman who befriends Ellen at Thirlwall, takes over from Mrs Montgomery as a mother substitute and central role model after the latter's death, continuing her lessons of self-control and submission to the Divine will. Alice herself is another archetypal angelic figure. At twenty-four already with the sinister signs of disease on her loveliness, she is linked with Mrs Montgomery in the text's iconography of blessed womanhood: it strikes Ellen 'that the bright spots of colour in Alice's face were just like what her mother's cheeks used to wear in her last illness' (427). Like Mrs Montgomery and like, too, that other emblem of female sanctity, little Eva in *Uncle Tom's Cabin*, she is carried away to a heavenly utopia after she has fulfilled her purpose in this world. Mrs Vawse also, though playing a more minor part in the story, represents female excellence and teaches Ellen the same lessons of humility and resignation to God's will.

Set against these embodiments of the female ideal are the women characterized by pride, lack of affection, selfishness, and bad temper. These include Mrs Dunscombe and Margaret, her daughter; Aunt Fortune; and Ellen's grandmother, Mrs Lindsay. Their deficiencies are evidenced not only by their neglect of spiritual duties – Aunt Fortune has no time for religious activities, and Mrs Lindsay tries to hinder Ellen's morning prayer and meditations – but also by their attitudes towards the young girl. Their cruel or thoughtless treatment of her, and the way in which they sneer at her piety become a measure of their lowliness in the text's hierarchy of moral goodness. Far from being role models, they themselves need to be redeemed by the kind of saintly influence enacted by Ellen, though the young girl, unlike the impossible child heroines of the novel's didactic precursors, does not effect any remarkable conversions.

The novel's female gender-stereotyping is not, however, as simple as this oppositional structuring would suggest. As various critics have noted, its potential subversiveness lies in its questioning or undermining of contemporary sexual ideologies. Thus this apparently straightforward positive/negative dualism is not stable and breaks down to show the relativity of commendable womanliness. Whereas forthrightness and self-assurance are clearly discreditable when manifested as cool arrogance, such as Mrs Dunscombe's, they are inherent elements in the strength of character exhibited by the old Swiss woman, Mrs Vawse. Mrs Vawse refuses to bow to convention: she lives alone in the mountains in independent isolation, and runs her own life in the way she wishes; she also acts in defiance of local custom, rejecting the architectural fashions of the region by having a high pointed roof put on her house ('she said her eyes were tired with the low roofs of this country' [187]). Her self-sufficiency, however, is commensurate with allegiance to God, and is not a rebellion against Divine authority. She represents an alternative version of femininity in which self-determination and saintliness coexist. Her granddaughter, Nancy, in contrast, is far from saintly, but even her wild, rough ways signify healthful feminine energy unrestrained by social regulation. Though she worries and upsets Ellen, leading her through the mud and water so that she ruins her shoes, and tormenting her when she is ill in bed, she is not wholly unkind. Moreover, Ellen needs some of her physical vigour and resilience in order to cope with life in the country: Nancy's early scorn at her companion's reluctance to cross the brook – 'Afraid of wetting your feet! . . . what a chickaninny you are!' (125) – is well deserved. Her basic good-nature, betokened by her kindness to Ellen at the bee-supper, and by her later rescue of all Mrs Montgomery's letters which Aunt Fortune has kept from her niece, responds gradually to Ellen's piety. As Ellen leaves for Edinburgh, she cries, and accepts Ellen's urgings that she look after her grand-mother and read her Bible. A contrasting example of girlhood, she can to some extent be seen as Ellen's alter ego. Interestingly in this respect, at the bee-supper, at which she is allowed to help but Ellen is not, she remarks pertly but relevantly, ' "I say, Ellen, anyone would think I was Miss Fortune's niece and you was somebody else, wouldn't they?" ' (249–50). Not only is the suggested identity by no means entirely to Ellen's disadvantage, but Nancy's spirited-ness introduces into the novel a potent challenge to ideologies of youthful passivity and conformity. More truly a female Huckleberry Finn than the self-doubting Ellen, she is the precursor of the tomboy figure who comes to feature so prominently in later juvenile texts. Though morally redeemed by the end of the novel, she is not written out of the narrative, and her very American independence remains as a frame of reference in the story's gender patterning.

Aunt Fortune is an even more equivocal figure. On the one hand, in terms of the paradigmatic fairy-tale structure of the novel, she is the wicked stepmother. Apparently incapable of affection and bearing deep grudges, she tyrannizes over Ellen: she cheats her of her mother's letters, she refuses to make it possible for her to attend the local school, and in order to vindicate herself in the eyes of Mr Van Brunt, her farm manager, she makes her niece confess to faults of which she is not guilty. She also uses Ellen as a servant, yet denies her participation in the bee-supper which the young girl has worked so hard to prepare. In gender terms, indeed, she seems not only more male than female, but embodies a domineering and aggressive masculinity. Yet this very aggression and assertiveness cast her as an image of female strength which has a particular national significance in this period: like so many pioneering Ameri-can women left on their own in isolated homesteads, she manages her own farm, and is ruthlessly efficient and economically successful. As has been pointed out elsewhere, her full name, Miss Fortune Emerson, carries resonances of frontier self-reliance and native entrepreneurial skills, qualities which were by this time already embedded in the American consciousness. When, unkindly but per-tinently, she tells Ellen that she has no time for effete Scotch women like the latter's mother – 'Give me Yankees!', she declares (158) – she is voicing a spirit of patriotic and democratic independence which would have been echoed by many contemporary readers. Importantly, too, she teaches Ellen some useful lessons. In the secular context of rural life, Ellen learns through her to share in the work of farm and household; she becomes healthier, is enabled to deal with physical hardship, and is introduced to the uncompromising realities of agricultural occupations such as pig-killing, activities which in a curious way she comes to value, if not to enjoy. Removed from the hot-house domestic enclosure of her New York existence, Ellen develops some of her aunt's physical vigour and well-being which come from open-air living.

The representation of Aunt Fortune is another instance of the tension between overt and coded messages in the narrative. Ellen's initial reactions to farm life are finicky and priggish: she does not like the rough sheets, demurs at having to wash at the spout, resents the everyday domestic tasks which to her are very different from making tea for her mother, and snobbishly objects to Mr Van Brunt's participation at meals. Thus contextualized, Aunt Fortune's exasperation at her querulous and uncooperative niece becomes comprehensible if not wholly excusable, enabling some sympathy for her position. Another victim of Mr Montgomery's cavalier treatment of women (he is her step-brother), Miss Fortune has to receive an uninvited, weepy, apparently ungrateful child into her home, a child furthermore who escapes from her whenever she can, sometimes without explanation, and who clearly prefers anyone's company rather than hers. Apart from her attempts to break Ellen's continuing preoccupation with her mother – a psychologically credible reaction to a jealous sense of exclusion – Aunt Fortune is rarely deliberately cruel to her niece: she looks after her carefully when she is sick, and allows her considerable freedom. She is also shown as capable of deep hurt when her attempts at tenderness are roughly repelled. She never becomes a wholly admirable figure in the novel, but her dominant and memorable positioning in the narrative structure disturbs the signification of conventional female excellence which the text prioritizes.

The novel's subtextual gender subversiveness also operates through its presentation of masculinity. Unlike *Little Women* or *What Katy Did*, *The Wide, Wide World* is not primarily female-centred in terms of social interaction, nor does it set up what Nina Auerbach has termed a 'community of women.'[26] There are many male figures in the narrative, some of whom serve as ostensible guides and models of goodness. The treatment of these male figures threatens the gender stereotyping rather differently from that of the women in the novel. Not only are positively evil male characteristics portrayed, but whereas seemingly 'unwomanly' qualities are accommodated within the novel's empowering ideology of female excellence, the equivocal elements in even apparently ideal masculinity are foregrounded so as to challenge the whole notion of patriarchal superiority.

Indeed, the text presents several examples of men in whom gendered attributes have become distorted or dangerous. Men like Mr Saunders (the clerk who bullies Ellen in the store and who later threatens her when she goes alone on her errand of mercy for Mr Van Brunt), Mr Montgomery, and Uncle Lindsay embody tyrannical authoritarianism, cruelty, vindictiveness and insensitivity, qualities which they activate to render women helpless. Especially in the case of Mr Saunders, sexual-sadistic overtones in their relationships with Ellen suggest the powerful male desire to master the 'otherness' of female individuation. In this context, the concept of paternalism comes under critical scrutiny, as it does in much other women's fiction of the period. Ellen's own father is an ogre, tyrannizing over his wife and daughter when he is present and leaving them without adequate financial resources when, as is so often the case, he is away from home. It is not insignificant that the cause of the traumatic disruption which motivates the ensuing narrative is Mr Montgomery's failed lawsuit; while recognizing the dangers of autobiographical interpretations, it is hard not to read this as expressing Warner's personal resentment at the disastrous consequences of paternal legal mismanagement. Ellen's substitute fathers are less evidently destructive, but Mr Humphreys is stern and remote, only latterly accepting Ellen as his daughter, and Uncle Lindsay conceals beneath his apparent concern for Ellen's welfare a self-aggrandizing possessiveness which will tolerate no resistance – he forces her to drink wine and will not return to her the book given her by John, compelling her obedience by telling her, ' "you are mine, you must understand" ' (553). Even the Heavenly Father, reference to whom constructs the narrative's overriding spiritual doctrine, embodies a patriarchal authority which in its uncompromising equation of love and suffering seems a questionable power.

The text also functions to deconstruct conventional notions of male virtue. The ideals of masculinity seem to be strength of character, moral rectitude, instructive paternalism, and justness. Representatives of these qualities include Mr Van Brunt, George Marshman (the old man on the boat who befriends Ellen), and John Humphreys. The story, however, quite clearly shows how ideologies of masculine perfection threaten women, as well as how certain aspects of femininity – such as extreme submissiveness – encourage and even collude with this tyranny. In this respect, one of the most interesting relationships in the book is that between Ellen and John Humphreys. Other aspects of this relationship will be discussed in more detail later, but it is worth noting here that John achieves his control over Ellen as much by authoritarianism as by kindness. His pleasant demeanour conceals an imperious and unyielding streak as is demonstrated in Alice's account of his horse-breaking:

> "It was a clear case of obstinacy. The horse was resolved to have his own way and not do what his rider required of him; it was necessary that either the horse or the man should give up; and as John has no fancy for giving up, he carried his point, – partly by management, partly, I confess, by a judicious use of the whip and spur." (377)

John effects his 'management' of Ellen through psychological rather than physical domination, but the result is the same. Ellen herself, on their first acquaintance, 'was quite sure from that one look into his eyes that he was a person to be feared' (275), and he commands her obedience by playing on her hyperactive sense of guilt. At the Christmas party at Ventnor, for example, after she has confessed to cheating in order to get the coveted piece of blue morocco, one look from John is enough to send her running out of the room in tearful distress. If he is a loving brother, he is also an oppressive moral tutor who wishes to control and dominate his pupil.

The subtextual radicalism of *The Wide, Wide World* is also focalized in the close link between gender roles and patterns of control and influence. As many recent feminist critics have noted, the novel is extensively concerned with questions of power and powerlessness. Joanne Dobson, for example, reads the story as an expression of Warner's anger at enforced female powerlessness and the trauma of abuse by male authority.[27] More revisionist critics argue that the narrative subtext actually endows the female characters with a subversive authority. So Mary Hiatt claims that Ellen's submissiveness and sweetness mask her assurance and arrogance in the spiritual sphere;[28] and Jane Tompkins sees female compliance here as an assertion of autonomy, a willed mastery of self bringing women access of divine power and bypassing earthly (male) authority – 'while it [submission] fulfilled the social demands placed upon them, [it] gave them a place from which to launch a counter strategy against their worldly masters that would finally give them the upper hand.'[29] It has also been suggested that even the novel's excessive sentimentality, in the shape of Ellen's endless fount of tears, represents freedom of expression, an acceptable response to the outrages of patriarchal domination where open rebellion would be impossible.

As has already been mentioned, iconoclastic readings are not always wholly suitable for such a text as this. The notion of a female power which is constituted through obedience to a patriarchal Divinity demanding self-abnegation hardly seems an assertion of independence, let alone compensation for earthly suffering. It is also the case that women in this novel are frequently presented as objects of male control. Wives are subject to husbands, and daughters to fathers; even Aunt Fortune has to submit to Mr Van Brunt's wishes concerning Ellen (and it seems likely, though amazing, that he will have the upper hand in their somewhat incredible marriage). Class and age hierarchies also operate against women. Ellen is vulnerable in the New York store not only because she is young but also because she is obviously poor; she is also sneered at on the boat by the Dunscombes because she is dressed so unfashionably. On the other hand, when she is with her wealthy relatives in Scotland, the material benefits with which they indulge her are a means of according her a status which will enhance their own sense of superiority.

Nevertheless, the emphasis on female influence which pervades the narrative certainly suggests a validation of womanly authority and self-determination, encouraging contemporary readers to exploit such influence in their own interests. Maternal authority is particularly significant in this respect. Nancy Schnog claims that through its linguistic strategies the book places maternity on a level with God, inculcating 'a theology of divine maternity . . . that works so ingeniously against the problematics of female dependency and loss.'[30] To illustrate this, she points to the ambiguity of Mrs Montgomery's inscription in the Bible she gives Ellen before her departure: 'I will be a God to thee, and to thy seed after thee' (42), an ambiguity also noted by Jane Tompkins. Though in their scriptural context, the words are spoken by God, in isolation the pronominal identification is unclear, thus the statement 'takes divinity into the hands of the mother and reshapes maternity as the divine.'[31] Tompkin's and Schnog's arguments are persuasive, especially since Mrs Montgomery's act of textual insertion here is accompanied by an oddly disturbing narrational comment – 'the . . . words were not for [Ellen]; what made her write them? . . . They were written almost unconsciously' (42) – suggesting an anarchically unwilled articulation of self-empowerment. But though it is true that Mrs Montgomery's influence has God-like attributes, rather than defining the text's subversiveness in terms of its sanctification of maternal power, it is perhaps more convincing to read it as effecting a secular transference of Divine authority, the supreme moral force residing instead in human female ascendancy. It is the memory of her mother, rather than reliance on God's law, which continues to direct Ellen long after the former has physically disappeared from the story. Alice, her successor (as sister/mother figure) also influences the friendless girl through her personal affection and example as much as through her orthodox teaching; her death, too, like Mrs Montgomery's, represents for Ellen a traumatic emotional loss for which religious consolation can compensate only with difficulty.

Ellen herself is empowered in the narrative through her role of spiritual teacher. Continuing the iconographic tradition of the girl child as a powerful agent of conversion, most compellingly presented in the figure of little Eva in *Uncle Tom's Cabin*, she 'converts' Mr Van Brunt, and triumphs finally in her ideological struggle with Uncle Lindsay, winning his respect for her religious principles and the concession that she may have her quiet hour every morning. She also, as has been seen, gains Nancy's somewhat grudging admiration for her piety and selflessness. Ellen is also accorded secular power at the end of the novel, in the final chapter which was omitted from the original edition and all subsequent editions, apparently because having initially failed to reach Putnam it did not seem to him worth including.[32] This chapter returns Ellen, now married to John (though curiously, this is nowhere directly stated), to America, where she takes her place in the Humphreys' parsonage as its mistress. Not only can she enjoy the many luxuries in what is designated as '*her room*' (574) – books, engravings, statues, easy chairs – but she is now the possessor of her own kingdom over which she has total control (John tells her she can lock the door whenever she chooses). She is also given charge of the domestic finances, becoming a 'steward in all that concerns the interior arrangements of the household' (582). Though she is diffident about her capabilities for this, and envisages having to rely on John for advice, the narrative closure clearly places her in a central and authoritative role, a role moreover which is operative in the secular, material sphere.

Perhaps the most fruitful area for deconstructive criticism of *The Wide, Wide World* is its moral and social patterning, through which the ideologies it represents are both formulated and challenged. The novel is framed on two linked literary genres – the sentimental/ religious novel and the *Bildungsroman*, both of which were seen as suitable for appropriation to the needs of girl readers. With each of these, an unwritten sub-plot permits a more subversive reading than the surface plot allows. As an example of nineteenth-century sentimental/religious fiction, the novel focuses on Ellen's progress towards an ideal Christian state. As has already been indicated, this involves negation of self-will and personal desire, and acceptance of tribulation as part of God's testing and strengthening of the soul. Ellen herself is a prototypical figure in this pattern; she has to undergo endless conscience-searching and reminders of her own unworthiness before she is deemed fully sanctified and can operate alone in the temptation-ridden secular world of her Scottish relatives. A leitmotiv of her spiritual development is her fascination with *The Pilgrim's Progress* – a seminal text in several such novels of the period, most notably *Little Women* – to which John introduces her and which becomes an emblem of her spiritual goals. When Uncle Lindsay punishes her for her insistent referral to the past by taking the book from her, her obedience to his will is an indication that she has indeed reached the Celestial City.

The idea of 'progress' is also central to the *Bildungsroman*, in which a young individual develops through a series of stages to maturity and self-knowledge. In this feminized version of the genre, Ellen not only learns to become a true Christian, but she also becomes more socially adept, well-read and discerning; she astonishes the guests at her uncle's with her knowledge of history and foreign languages, and she displays the accomplishments, though not the artificiality, of young ladyhood. Without abandoning the ethical lessons she has internalized, Ellen is now ready to enter the more complex and sophisticated world of adulthood.

These conventional narrative patternings are, however, variously changed or adapted. Warner refocuses some of the elements of the *Bildungsroman* so as to both radicalize and nationalize her text. It has already been suggested that Ellen's spiritual education is accompanied by a physical one which to some extent is antithetical to the sentimental/feminine; learning to be the embodiment of truly Christian womanhood is set against learning to be an American in a still evolving society. Aunt Fortune's harsh but not unwholesome domain is in many ways a sound environment for Ellen. In this environment, she is not subject to the restrictions of young ladyhood, with its emphasis on propriety and refinement: she is allowed to go off on her own, and getting dirty is a punishable offence not because it is unfeminine but because her aunt has to do the washing. The freedoms which Ellen enjoys, allowed to women in rural areas, are similar to those enjoyed by Coolidge's and Montgomery's young heroines who show a more marked American spirit of independence. Part of Ellen's educative experiences here, too, involve accepting the democratic mix of American society, although Warner seems somewhat equivocal on this point: cultivation and gentility are prioritized with Mrs Montgomery and the Humphreys, and though the latter are not antipathetic towards their neighbours they offer Ellen what is clearly to be regarded as more refined way of life. Significantly, their ancestry is English.

Set against the rough openness of the farm, the emotionally-charged atmosphere of the New York home and the Humphreys household (though Ellen does have some fun with John and Alice), with their insistence on moral distinctions and self-examination, seem somewhat cloying and enervating. Even hard domestic work, though wearisome, has a character-strengthening element as powerful as that of religious instruction. And although in Scotland some of the more republican qualities which Ellen has learnt while in Thirlwall seem to have disappeared, and she readily complies with the conventional social requirements of her class-conscious relatives, it is important that she refuses to forget her New World allegiances as they would like. In her discussion with her uncle as to the relative merits of the Scottish Bruce and the American Washington, she stoutly defends her preference for the latter ' "because he was an American" ' (515).

The ethical implications of Warner's generic manipulation are also significant. The novel's Evangelical lesson of submission to God's will has already shown to be morally ambiguous, because while negating it also empowers the individual self. More disruptively, the moral message is compromised by the nature of the causal relationship depicted in the novel between overt purpose and achievement. Ambiguity in this respect is characteristic of American Puritan narratives, from the earliest settlement literature in which worldly success is represented as the sign of God's favour to his worthy elect, to the secular materialism of the work ethic in Franklin's *Autobiography* and other later 'rags to riches' stories. *The Wide, Wide World* reveals something of this materialist slant, as Susan Williams has argued;[33] Ellen gains a horse and a wealthy family during her spiritual pilgrimage, and, as the omitted last chapter shows, she certainly takes pleasure in tasteful luxuries. But the text's most marked subversion of its prototypes occurs in the link it sets up between moral development and the fulfilment of desire. In a secularized reading of the novel, the religious fiction becomes a fairy tale, in which Cinderella's dutifulness is rewarded by her gaining her prince; the orphan finds not just a heavenly father but an earthly husband.

Particularly questionable here is the suggestion of female complicity, enhanced by the indistinctiveness of the childhood and adolescent states and the ensuing vagueness about female sexual awareness. The ambiguous nature of the relationship between John and Ellen was a feature of the novel which disturbed two of the best-known English Victorian writers for girls, Elizabeth Sewell and Charlotte Yonge. The former, deeply concerned about the possible danger to the young of reading unsuitable novels, cavils at the notion that genuine love stories are forbidden territory but that 'a book which treats of young people' is considered harmless:

> So . . . half the children in England would be permitted to read such books as "The Wide, Wide World", and "Queechy", in which fascinatingly simple little girls of ten or twelve are petted and caressed by respectable gentlemen of five-and-twenty or thirty, who afterwards take the form of lovers, and marry them. No one calls these books novels, and yet they are novels, just as strictly as the most exciting love story to be procured from a circulating library. And what is more, they are much more likely to do injury to a child's mind.[34]

Charlotte Yonge similarly emphasizes the potential danger to young female readers of books like *The Wide, Wide World* and *Queechy*, which

> have the very grave and really injurious effect of teaching little girls to expect a lover in any one who is good-natured to them. Nothing ought to be more rigidly avoided, for it fills the child with foolish expectations and dreams, which poison her simplicity of mind and her present enjoyment.[35]

Despite their somewhat strident moral tone, both writers perceptively foreground the moral subversiveness residing at the heart of the novel. There is an evasiveness about Ellen's sexual development, linked to doubts about her actual age – subjects of equally tantalizing indeterminacy in the case of the heroine of Henry James's *What Maisie Knew* (1896). What in fact does Ellen know? Is she quite innocent of her potential as an object of male gaze, or does she knowingly act out a role which will bring romantic as well as spiritual reward? At the beginning of the book Ellen is about ten; by the end she is fourteen, on the verge of adolescence, certainly in nineteenth-century terms. But there is much discussion of her age in connection with her appearance and behaviour. During her Christmas sojourn at Ventnor, the family debate how old she is: John calls her 'a simple intelligent child of twelve or thirteen', only to be instantly corrected by Sophia – 'Twelve or thirteen! . . . what are you thinking about? Alice says she is only ten or eleven' (295). The discrepancy between her physical smallness and her gravity of demeanour is frequently observed by other characters; indeed there is some surprise that she can in fact react like a child. The contradictory signals which Ellen puts out are also noted by her Edinburgh relatives: Lady Keith thinks she is too child-like and unsophisticated, with ' "that curious grave innocent look you see only in infants" ', whereas Mrs Lindsay asserts ' "*I* never saw one so much a woman" ' (521). Later, Ellen herself, having been called 'little daughter' by Uncle Lindsay, somewhat disingenuously meditates: 'I wonder . . . why every body calls me "little"; I don't think I am very little. Every body says "little" ' (535).

Within the narrative, Ellen plays roles pertaining to various ages: the orphaned child needing a parent; the carefree little girl opening her stocking at Christmas; the capable female domestic, making butter and doing the ironing; the wise interpreter of spiritual mysteries to those as yet uninitiated in them. The problematics of the multiplicity here both link to the novel's generic indeterminacy and to its ambiguous presentation of the pre-pubescent/adolescent period. Apparently mature in mind but young in body, Ellen is shown as negotiating the difficult transition between unconsciousness of self and self-awareness, with all its psychological complexities. The full implications of this transition, however, are not addressed openly in the text but reside in the tensions between the surface representation and the submerged undercurrents. This aspect of the novel provides a good illustration of Kristeva's thesis that a text's 'meanings', although inscribed within the symbolic, remain embedded in the semiotic, evident only in contradictions, gaps and absences. Her concept of a textual unconscious, working from within signification and indicating what is lacking in the codified discourse, can help in the analysis of the disruptive implications of this narrative.[36]

The disruption is most centrally focalized, as Sewell and Yonge note, in Ellen's relationship with John Humphreys. On one level, this is a conventional master/pupil relationship: John functions as God's representative on earth, teaching lessons of submission and obedience to Divine commands; like his inspirational source, he speaks the language of the Father, situated in the Symbolic. Ellen, on the other hand, her semiotic feminine repressed, is reduced to passivity and silence, speaking only with the words which the patriarchal authority has taught her and relying on his strength and counsel. John, it seems, has taken over her personality: Ellen is aware that ' "he always knows what I am thinking of just as well as if I told him" ' (414), and it is notable how many times she cannot say anything to him, able to express herself only through the pre-verbal mode of tears. But, as has been indicated, there are psycho-sexual undertones to their relationship, suggesting a more enabling feminine which actually constructs itself as the desired other and manipulates the male response.

Ellen's differing reactions to the men who seek to master or engage with her are sexually revealing. When she first meets Mr Van Brunt, good-humoured though he is, she resists his offer of lifting her into the cart with 'an evident shrinking from the proposal' (94), and later when in return for making her a swing he requests a kiss, she is appalled and enraged:

> when, with a good-natured smile upon his round face, he came near to claim the kiss he no doubt thought himself sure of, Ellen shot from him like an arrow from a bow. (116)

Her passion increases when her unsympathetic aunt merely laughs and ask her ' "Well, why didn't you let him kiss you?" ' (117). Ellen's indignation is partly based on snobbery, but it also articulates a fierce self-protectiveness against the threat of violation by male physical desire. A similar fear of violation, though far more well-founded, occurs in the scene where Ellen, having ridden alone to the neighbouring town to fetch a doctor for the injured Van Brunt, is (in a somewhat unlikely coincidence) accosted by Mr Saunders, the shop assistant who treated her so cavalierly in New York. Saunders begins to threaten her by tormenting Brownie, her pony; as with John, the male brutality towards a horse symbolizes the wish for sado-sexual domination of the female. His torture culminates in his threat to force her to dismount so that he can teach her a lesson by whipping Brownie, a horror from which she is rescued only by the timely appearance of John who hurls Saunders 'quite over into the gully at the side of the road, where he lay at full length without stirring' (401). Ellen's intensely emotional reaction to her escape (again, she has 'no words' and just shakes 'with convulsive sobs' [ibid.], contextualized by the sexual suggestiveness of the incident, hints at her dread of more than mere bullying.

From the first, however, she seems to welcome John's physical advances. When, at their initial meeting, he kisses her 'gravely on the lips' (274), she offers no resistance; the deliberate evasiveness of the accompanying narrational commentary implies that already Ellen finds the older man attractive:

> Probably Ellen thought there was a difference between John Humphreys and Mr Van Brunt, or the young gentlemen of the apple-paring; for though she coloured a good deal, she made no objection and showed no displeasure. (274)

After the incident with Saunders, when John leaves her without the kiss which by now she has come to take for granted, the description of her response implies a more than childish sense of disappointment:

> Something was the matter; for she stood with swimming eyes and a trembling lip . . . What *was* the matter? Only – that Mr John had forgotten the kiss that he always gave her on going or coming. (403)

The indirect discourse which moves between Ellen's consciousness (with its significant hesitancy) and external observation creates an underlay of textual meaning: what is suppressed here is that Ellen desires John's embraces, even if her sexual awareness is not yet fully awakened and though she persists in the myth that he is her adoptive brother. When, several years later, he comes to Edinburgh to claim her from the Lindsays, she welcomes him as a long-lost lover, throwing herself into his arms 'in an agony of joy' (559) and clasping his hand in a passion of emotional agitation. And in the omitted chapter in which Ellen is now John's wife, there is a coyly oblique exchange between them, suggestively referring to the physicality of their earlier relationship:

> "There is one comfort – you will not touch my lips if I say anything you do not like."

"Touch your lips?"

"No, no!" said Ellen, laughing and blushing – "You know what I mean." (572)

In the mid-nineteenth century the socially recognized parameters of gendered and sexual emotion were wider than they are today; love between siblings, for instance, expressed itself more vehemently than would currently be acceptable. But the subtextual implications of Ellen's feelings for John are certainly of sexual awareness and desire, however much concealed beneath the surface representation. Moreover, these implications are morally as well as psychologically subversive. On the one hand, they reveal that the desire for spiritual amendment may be inspired by earthly, not heavenly, influence. Ellen comes increasingly to obey John's commands not because they are righteous but because they emanate from him. This is made clear by her different responses to Alice and John: 'What [Alice] asked of her Ellen indeed *tried* to do; what John told her *was* done' (351). John himself becomes her God, and her life is devoid of meaning in his absence. When he comforts her after Alice's death, the language used to describe her feelings is charged with emotional intensity – 'to Ellen the arm that held her was more than all words; it was the dividing line between her and the world, – on this side everything, on that side nothing' (443). In Scotland, 'her love for her brother [*sic*] and longing remembrance of him' (538), together with her adherence to the godly lessons he has taught her, alone prevent her from rebelling against the Lindsays' authoritarian demands. Her religious awakening is thus at least partly dependent on her sexual awakening, the agent of both being one and the same.

The other subtextual 'meaning' of the linkage of religion and sexuality here is that spiritual rectitude and obedience to Divine commands will be rewarded with earthly, human satisfaction. While, as a recent critical study has indicated, the linkage itself is a traditional one and a prominent feature of much nineteenth-century American literature,[37] its particular signification in this text is disruptive of the overt didacticism. The novel's ostensible evangelicanism teaches that fulfilment will be attained only in the world of the spirit; Ellen's success story is a lesson in how a young, vulnerable female can achieve financial and emotional security through which she is accessed to power.

The Wide, Wide World is less overtly subversive than some of the later texts discussed in this study: it does not openly challenge the patriarchal and establishment value systems which it reproduces. From the beginning, it establishes its gender and moral ideology, and the narrative portrays the individual's process of alignment with this framework rather than any fantasy of escape from it. But from within these parameters, through subtextual dislocations and oppositional representation, it reinterprets some of the contemporary dicta about women and their roles. On its constant tendency to break out of the moulds according to which it is constructed it depends its fascination for readers today.

Notes

1. [C. Kirkland], 'Novels and Novelists: Queechy, and The Wide, Wide World', *North American Review*, vol. 76 (January 1853), p.112.
2. Warner and her sister, Anna, both wrote under pseudonyms which they took from their great-grandmothers. Though Warner retained hers for most of her literary career, in line with recent feminist criticism of her work her own name will be used throughout.
3. These details are taken from Richard Altick, *The English Common Reader: A Social History of the Magazine-reading Public, 1800–1900* (Chicago: University of Chicago Press, 1957), and Edward Halsey Foster, *Susan and Anna Warner* (Boston: Twayne Publishers, n.d.).
4. James makes this comparison in an article entitled 'The Schonberg-Cotta Family' in the *Nation*, 14 September, 1865.
5. Quoted in Amy Cruse, *The Victorians and Their Books* (London: George Allen & Unwin, 1935), pp.255–6.
6. 'Novels and Novelists', p.113.
7. Anna B. Warner, *Susan Warner ('Elizabeth Wetherell')* (New York: G.P. Putnam's Sons, 1909), p.420.
8. See Jane Tompkins, *Sensational Designs: The Cultural Work of American Fiction 1790–1860* (New York: Oxford University Press, 1985).
9. Nancy Schnog, 'Inside the Sentimental: The Psychological Work of *The Wide, Wide World*,' *Genders*, no. 4, Spring 1979, p.12.
10. Quoted in Mary Kelley, *Public Woman, Private Stage: Literary Domesticity in Nineteenth-Century America* (New York and Oxford: Oxford University Press, 1985), p.147.
11. Nina Baym, *Women's Fiction: A guide to novels by and about women in America 1820–1870* (Ithaca: Cornell University Press, 1980), p.12.
12. Quoted in Amy Cruse, op.cit. p.256.
13. Warner, op.cit., p.263.
14. Susan S. Williams, 'Widening the World: Susan Warner, her readers, and the assumption of authorship', *American Quarterly*, vol. 42, no. 4 (December 1990), pp.565–6.
15. Warner, op.cit., p.208.

60   *What Katy Read*

16. Susan B. Warner ('Elizabeth Wetherell'), *The Wide, Wide World* (New York: The Feminist Press, 1987), p.269. All subsequent references are to this edition and are included in the text.
17. 'Novels and Novelists', pp.114, 115, 118.
18. From an article in the *Christian Review*, quoted in Warner op.cit., p.344.
19. Warner, op.cit., p.264.
20. 'Novels and Novelists', p.115.
21. Joanne Dobson, 'The Hidden Hand: Subversion of cultural ideology in three mid-nineteenth-century American women's novels', *American Quarterly*, vol. 38, no. 2 (Summer 1986), p.224.
22. Mary Hiatt, 'Susan Warner's subtext: The other side of piety', *Journal of Evolutionary Psychology*, vol. 8, parts 3–4 (1987), pp.250, 252.
23. Tompkins, op.cit.
24. Dobson, op.cit., pp.226–8.
25. Ibid., p.227.
26. Nina Auerbach, *Communities of Women: An Idea in Fiction* (Cambridge, Mass: Harvard University Press, 1978). In this work, Auerbach discusses *Little Women* as an instance of the depiction of female bonding in nineteenth-century women's fiction.
27. Dobson, op.cit.
28. Hiatt, op.cit., p.252.
29. Tompkins, op.cit., p.162.
30. Schnog, op.cit., p.19.
31. Ibid., p.20.
32. This chapter was published for the first time in the Feminist Press edition used here. An introductory note explains the putative circumstances of this omission: when Putnam eventually received the final chapter, which had been mislaid, he apparently felt that it did not add anything significant to an already over–long manuscript.
33. Williams, op.cit., pp.577–9.
34. Elizabeth Sewell, *Principles of Education* (London: Longman, Green, Longman, Roberts & Green, 1865), II, pp.119–20.
35. Charlotte Yonge, 'Children's Literature of the Last Century', *Macmillan's*, vol. XX, no. 118 (1869), p.309.
36. The most useful overview of Kristeva's work with reference to this study is to be found in Toril Moi (ed.), *The Kristeva Reader* (Oxford: Basil Blackwell, 1986). There are also helpful discussions of her theories in Greene and Kahn (eds), *Making a Difference: Feminist Literary Criticism* (London: Methuen, 1985) and Sara Mills et al., *Feminist Readings/Feminists Reading* (Hemel Hempstead: Harvester, 1989).
37. See Ann-Janine Morey, *Religion and Sexuality in American Literature* (Cambridge: Cambridge University Press, 1992).

3

Charlotte Yonge:
The Daisy Chain

Although by no means obliterated from the classic canon of juvenile literature, *The Daisy Chain*, like *The Wide, Wide World*, has not undergone a major revival of interest today as have many of the other texts in this study. Its reprint in 1988 by Virago Press, instead of by a popular children's publisher such as Puffin, indicates a scholarly, feminist readership rather than a wide-ranging, youthful one, and its failure to be taken up by the media suggests that it lacks obvious twentieth-century appeal. Yet in its day it was one of the most extensively read of Charlotte Yonge's novels, reaching nine editions in twelve years and second only to *The Heir of Redclyffe* (1853) in popularity. Yonge herself did not anticipate such success for the book. In the Preface she dismisses it with characteristic female self-belittlement:

> No one can be more sensible than is the Author that the present is an overgrown book of a nondescript class, neither the "tale" for the young, nor the novel for their elders, but a mixture of both.[1]

Her apologia, however, points to the innovative nature of the work both in terms of genre and content, and her continuing comments in the Preface foreground this originality as she asks that it 'be considered merely as what it calls itself, a Family Chronicle – a domestic record of home events, large and small, during those years of early life when the character is chiefly formed' (v). Published in book form in 1856 (it was earlier serialized in a magazine for the young), *The Daisy Chain* cannot be said to have pioneered the family novel in England in the way that Alcott's work did in America, Yonge's most notable predecessor in this respect being Jane Austen. What is new in the novel, and what most clearly appealed to a contemporary audience, though, is its focus on the family as a unit of young people, interrelating with each other and maturing within this context. Though the story certainly deals with the outside world of school, parish affairs, and religious and political concerns of the day, its main themes and emphases centre on the May children in a domestic environment in which home values are paramount.

At the same time, because the narration is not oriented exclusively towards childhood but spirals actually and referentially outward to the adult world, the book constitutes – as Yonge herself recognized – a mixed genre. Like Harriet Mozley's fiction for the young just previous to it, whose innovativeness Yonge much admired,[2] it is neither purely a children's book nor a really 'grown up' novel. Yonge wrote many specifically children's tales, examples of which include *Henrietta's Wish* (1850), *The Little Duke* (1854) and *The Stokesley Secret* (1861), but she was more interested in experimenting with the mode which Mozley had initiated and which she turned into a much more complex and lively fictional form. Her first real success with this form was her immensely popular *The Heir of Redclyffe*, published three years before *The Daisy Chain*, and its extraordinarily wide-ranging contemporary audience attests to the appeal of this middle-ground orientation. Obviously popular with those readers to whom it was most directly addressed – middle-class girls of Anglican affiliation – it also drew a public from a multiplicity of sources. Its hero, Guy Morville, with his high aims and chivalric ideals, was taken as a behavioural model by William Rossetti and Dante Gabriel Rossetti; Julian Yonge, Yonge's brother, reported that nearly all the young men in his regiment in the Crimea had a copy; and Christabel Coleridge, Yonge's first biographer, notes that 'scholarly gentlemen wept over Guy's death.'[3]

The *Daisy Chain* has the same mixed generic and gendered appeal. The plot itself is somewhat rambling, consisting of a series of incidents loosely linked together, rather than a tightly organised structure; indeed Yonge herself commented on its lack of obvious coherence.[4] But there are several key incidents or issues around which the narrative is built: the carriage accident which causes the mother's death and the serious injury of the eldest daughter, Margaret, very early in the story; the negotiations for and establishment of a Sunday School and new church at the 'godless' nearby village of Cocksmoor; and the contrasting educational experiences of school and university. These are contextualized within the framing history of the May family, which traces the development of each member over a period of five years or so, from childhood through adolescence into early adulthood. Within this chronology, it deals with matters familiar to its intended public – the choice of careers for the boys, sibling rivalries and jealousy, early romance, academic misadventures or successes, and the traumas of illness or disappointment.

While this prime emphasis on life in the home and the tensions between public and private responsibility speaks especially to a female audience, it also addresses questions pertinent to male readers such as the nature of ambition and of courage. Likewise, though its lively and perceptive portrayal of family life would have been attractive to many of Yonge's younger contemporaries, both its language (as has already been shown, it makes no concessions to a juvenile readership in this respect[5]) and its thematic concerns point to an audience capable of making fine moral distinctions and of learning the lessons which these impart. Unlike Alcott's, Coolidge's or Nesbit's subsequent fiction, it contextualizes children's behaviour almost wholly with reference to an adult code of values, and the narrative positions itself from without, rather than from within, its youthful world, albeit sympathetically. This is partly a question of the novel's periodicity. Written at almost the same time as *The Wide, Wide World*, like that work it not only validates current social ideologies which seem particularly demanding on young women, but it also identifies children as potential adults. The rules of propriety, for instance, forbid the older May girls from walking out unescorted or in the company of unmarried men, and the ritualistic formalities surrounding death prevent Ethel and Flora from attending their baby sister's christening while they are still in mourning for their mother. Yonge does not romanticize childhood, and while permitting her young characters a degree of autonomy she does not allow them a make-believe world to which they can escape from the demands of adult society. Ethel's imagination, fired by the novels and poetry which she devours, must be kept constantly in check by recognition of the surrounding outer world of duty and responsibility and in this she is far more restricted than that later romantic dreamer, Anne Shirley, in L.M. Montgomery's *Anne of Green Gables*.

At the same time, Yonge by no means replicates the somewhat grim vision of childhood offered by earlier juvenile writers such as Mrs Sherwood and Mrs Cameron, who portray children either as innately corrupted or as impossibly good. Yonge herself deprecated such tract-like representations, and briskly dismisses those stories which deal in the young child who goes about asking people whether they are Christians, or else in the equally unnatural one who is always talking about its white robes. Both alike die young, and are equally unreal and unpractical.[6]

She also disliked those stories which 'represent aunts and uncles as uniformly unjust and cruel to orphan wards'[7] – perhaps a slyly oblique reference to Warner's *The Wide, Wide World* and *Queechy*.

Yonge's own fictional children are certainly not type-cast in this way. She both acknowledges and uncritically replicates many aspects of childish high-spiritedness, and the young Mays are shown engaging in the normal activities of their age group: the brothers tussling together, the 'spoof' archaeological picnic at which Norman plants fake Roman artefacts for his gullible siblings to discover, the uproar at the family dinner table. At least part of this verisimilitude derives from autobiographical sources. Early on, Yonge, an only child until she was six, metamorphosed her large troupe of dolls into children and sisters about whom she made up stories; she also created 'an imaginary family of ten boys and eleven girls who lived in an arbour' and who, according to her biographer, were the source of the large families in her novels, including the Mays.[8] The strong element of wish-fulfilment enacted by a solitary, imaginative child is obvious here. But there were also real-life prototypes for Yonge's juvenile characters. Every year until she was ten or eleven, and sporadically thereafter, the Yonges of Otterbourne (Yonge's father settled in this Hampshire village when he married) paid an extended visit to the main branch of the family, natives of south-east Devon. Of greatest joy to the young girl was the time they spent at Puslinch, a few miles outside Plymouth, where the large family of Alethea and John Yonge lived. Yonge was particularly happy here because she could enjoy 'all I longed for at home – the cousins who have been all my life more than cousins, almost brothers and sisters to me.'[9] Here, too, released from her more constricting home environment, she could express her innate high-spiritedness. That Yonge's observations and experiences here provided her with material for her fiction is attested by the fact that she transcribed many of the conversations between herself and her cousins, later adapting them for inclusion in her novels. She gained further personal acquaintance with large families via the ever-increasing progeny of the Moberleys, near neighbours of the Yonges, when the young Dr Moberley came to the area as headmaster of Winchester in 1835; they gave her another source for her fictional material.

In reproducing the lively interrelations of an average middle-class Victorian family – especially through dialogue which constitutes a large element of *The Daisy Chain* – Yonge makes a very different kind of appeal from that of Warner. Whereas *The Wide, Wide World* encourages the girl reader to identify with its heroine in a wholly imaginative way (most of Warner's young readers would have experienced neither orphanhood nor Ellen's translation to material and romantic fulfilment, the very point which made Yonge so critical of the novel's effect), Yonge's work aims to inspire its audience first to recognise themselves in its textual representations and then to follow the lessons which its characters learn. As Christabel Coleridge comments, 'trying to be very good was made interesting and romantic to thousands of good girls,'[10] and certainly Yonge's depiction of these efforts has more realistic application than Warner's creation of a world of rarefied emotion, compelling though this may be.

Set against later texts, of course, the freedom which the author allows her child characters appears fairly limited. Although she permits her children to be children, youthful exuberance can go only so far before it is checked by the adult-centred value systems which surround it. A good example of this occurs in the incident where the wildcap Harry dresses up as an old woman and pretends to pay a call on his invalid sister, Margaret; the latter is so frightened when she suspects a trick that her already precarious health is further undermined; and Harry is punished, as for a grave moral offence, by being told that he can no longer be considered worthy of Confirmation and must be excluded from the sacrament. The exaggerated moral treatment to which the incident is subjected, more reminiscent of juvenile tract literature, caused a later children's novelist, Edith Nesbit, to expose its absurdity in her own *The Wouldbegoods* (1901). In this novel, Daisy, whose name comes to acquire its full intertextual connotations through her identification with *The Daisy Chain*, gives an amusing and garbled plot reduction of the work which reduces it to a set of boring moral lessons, only to be interrupted by her brother who offers a much more attractive revised version:

> "*The Daisy Chain* is not a bit like that really. It's a ripping book. One of the boys dresses up like a lady and comes to call, and another tries to hit his little sister with a hoe. It's jolly fine, I tell you."[11]

Although Nesbit's mockery suggests more about the differences between girls' and boys' interpretations of the same text, than about Yonge's outmoded didacticism, ironically enough it testifies to the ongoing popularity of her novel with young readers into the twentieth century.

Another, earlier, intertextual reference also points up the high and demanding ethical ideals to which Yonge's child characters are subjected. In Margaret Oliphant's *Phoebe, Junior* (1876), one of the young heroines, Janet May, disclaims all similarities to Yonge's family of the same name: 'We are not a set of prigs like those people. We are not goody, whatever we are.'[12] Later, Phoebe herself, seeking to identify her friends in terms of Yonge's clergymen's families, comments to Janey's brother, 'I can recognise you quite well and your sister, but the younger ones puzzle me; they are not in Miss Yonge; they are too much like other children, too naughty.'[13] The objection to the kind of 'difference' which these fictional children voice with regard to Yonge's characters helps to validate Gillian Avery's claim that, in contrast to their American counterparts, Yonge's families were not generally accessible enough to the ordinary reader of the time.[14]

The particular characteristics and appeal of *The Daisy Chain* can also to some extent be defined in terms of nationality. Comparison has already been made with *The Wide, Wide World*, and although in some ways the two novels share a similar didactic orientation their differences highlight, among other things, their separate countries of origin. For all her subjection to an oppressive religious value system, Ellen Montgomery has greater physical freedom than her British counterparts. It is hard to imagine Ethel May, for example, being permitted to roam the countryside on her own without the company of her governess or one of her brothers, a regulation mindful of personal safety as well as of propriety. Yonge's world is strictly hierarchical, dependent on a rigidly class-structured society[15] whose closely observed behavioural significations are largely absent from the American text. The May children gladly give away some of their food from the picnic to the poor boy they encounter nearby, but he has to eat his feast away from the rest of the party; similarly Dr May is uneasy about the education his sons are getting at the local grammar school, because it is starting to fill up with lower-class boys who will be a bad influence. In contrast, Ellen's initial snobbish reaction to Mr Van Brunt's eating at the same table as herself and her aunt is shown as a failing which must be corrected. And later, now more attuned to the democratic tendencies of rural America, she feels uncomfortable in the class-conscious environment of her Scottish relatives. Yonge's work was very popular in the

States – in her biography, Coleridge includes tributes from Yonge's American admirers – but contemporary New World readers noted what to them was a different and less desirable cultural ethos. Jo March in *Little Women* (1868) cries over *The Heir of Redclyffe*, but Alcott's unflattering representation of English youth in her novel as arrogant and stand-offish (The English 'young lady', Kate, keeps herself apart from the crowd, treats Mr Brooke as an inferior because he is a tutor, and patronisingly commiserates with Meg for having to go out as a governess) suggests the questionings of a more democratic sensibility. Alcott made her first European trip in 1865, where she would have seen the English social system at first-hand, but she may have imbibed some of her notion of British class-consciousness and the restrictions imposed on young people from her reading of Yonge's fiction.

Alcott's unease would not have been shared by *The Daisy Chain*'s intended audience who were familiar with, and ready to accept, its social and moral configurations. As has already been suggested, the novel has a strong controlling moral impulse, but it makes its appeal by channelling this moral didacticism through the representation of recognisable human activity, measured but not overwhelmed by ethical considerations. Like many of the novels in this study, it is implicitly built on the pattern of *The Pilgrim's Progress*, a work which Yonge knew from an early age and which she recommended for Sunday School children – 'the dear old *Pilgrim's Progress*, where I am sure they could learn nothing but good.'[16] The parallel is suggested early on in the story when the May children read the unfinished letter which their dead mother has written to their aunt in New Zealand, describing them all and detailing their strengths and weaknesses. For each child, she gives a thumb-nail character sketch which indicates the areas in which improvement must be striven for. Of greatest interest here, is her analysis of Ethel, the figure with whom girl readers would most readily identify:

poor Ethel's old foibles, her harum-scarum nature, quick temper, uncouth manners, and heedlessness of all but one absorbing object, have kept her back, and caused her much discomfort; yet I sometimes think these manifest defects have occasioned a discipline that is the best thing for the character in the end. They are faults that show themselves, and which one can tell how to deal with, and I have full confidence that she has the principle within her that will conquer them. (49)

The tension between the foregrounding of moral progress, encap-
sulated in Mrs May's letter which posits codes of self-forgetfulness,
self-control, and gender-appropriate behaviour, and a less restrictive
portrayal of youthful experience is sharpest in the case of Ethel
herself, who, as the letter suggests, in many ways anticipates the
tomboy figure who features so prominently in several later juvenile
texts. She can certainly be seen as the predecessor to Jo March in
Little Women. At the beginning of the novel she is the antithesis of
conventional femininity – awkward, ungainly, untidy, impetuous,
and plain. She takes no thought for her appearance, rushing through
the house wild and dirty, so leading the family nurse to comment
that she is ' "just like one of the boys" ' (58). Even her name is
sexually ambiguous (it is actually short for Ethelred, and she is
sometimes nicknamed 'The Unready'). She is also intellectually gifted
and is able to compete with her elder brother, Norman, in his classical
studies, even though she receives no formal schooling outside the
home. Ethel chafes at being a woman and having to engage with
trifling duties instead of with larger and grander issues. She also
regrets the ideologies of femininity which curtail her freedom of
action, as well as the ever-increasing family responsibilities which
allow her almost no time of her own. When Norman decides to go
to New Zealand as a missionary, the disparity between male and
female opportunity is forcefully brought before her, as her exchange
with her brother reveals:

> "O Norman, it is the most glorious thing man can do! How I
> wish I could go with you!"
> "Your mission is here," said Norman, affectionately.
> "I know it is – I am contented with it," said Ethel; "but oh!
> Norman . . . you have found the more excellent way." (517)

Ethel's frustration and protest are powerful signifiers in the novel,
but she, like the other May children, relies on her mother's letter as
a kind of talisman or *aide-mémoire*, a constant reminder of the need
to note and eradicate personal failings. As each member of the family
seeks to develop his or her aspirations, their efforts are set against
a past of loss and other-worldly values; they all have to learn how
to bring their characteristics into accordance with a morality which
usually combines religious and secular goals, though with the former
predominant. Given this emphasis, it is hard to understand Yonge's
seemingly disingenuous comment that 'I am afraid the moral is

not good'[17] since there is never any question as to what ultimately constitutes right conduct. As with other mid-Victorian texts, the ethical precepts on which the text relies invite the readers into the shared communal value system of orthodox middle-class Christianity, specifically shaped here by Yonge's own Oxford Movement Anglicanism.

In this environment, personal ambition has to be subordinated to the more stringent demands of duty and humility. Norman must modify his early conviction that ' "Fame and glory – they are the spirit of life" ' (21) and suffer a temporary setback to his hopes of winning academic honour through an endowed scholarship to Oxford; the ostensible cause of his failure is a (false) accusation of misconduct, but the underlying lesson is clear – he cared too much about being first, as he himself realises, and his demise must be regarded as his punishment. Significantly, this new humility (he refuses to be reinstated either to the scholarship or to the head of the school, even when his name is cleared) is inspired in him by his reading of his mother's copy of Thomas à Kempis, given to him after her death; the text's emphasis on self-negation speaks to him as she would have spoken, thus foregrounding, as in several others of the texts under discussion, the potency of the mother's spiritual influence from the grave. Awareness of the dangers of self also leads Norman to choose a missionary life in New Zealand rather than a successful career as an Oxford academic. In a more secularized context, Tom also has to subordinate personal ambition to the higher demands of duty: having struggled to overcome his early moral cowardice and lack of openness, he must also curb his longings for widened opportunities abroad and undertake to follow in his father's medical footsteps, so that he can carry on the May practice and enable Norman to fulfil his high spiritual goals.

Of particular interest is the way in which female ambition has to be brought into line with a morality of self-sacrifice and dedication to higher goals, validating an ideal of womanly conduct already well established in the period. As Judith Rowbotham has shown, Victorian girls' stories aim to explain and justify the position of women in society, in class and gender terms, and to convince their readers to conform to conventional expectations of female behaviour.[18] Yonge's novel is no exception, and similarly seeks to present and teach a desirable femininity.

The gender implications of *The Daisy Chain* as a whole will be discussed in more detail below, but at this stage it is relevant to note how the narrative engages with the desires and self-images of the young female characters. The second May daughter, Flora, is in many ways an admirable young woman. About sixteen when the story opens, she is shown as being efficient, helpful, and a valuable steadying influence in the family. But as the narrative unfolds, it becomes clear that her besetting sins – as Mrs May's letter has indicated – are pride and self-esteem. Always clear-eyed about the best way to deal with crises or family problems, she is too fond of authority and dislikes being second; she also acts nobly to reinforce her own self-importance rather than from truly moral motives. When Dr May wishes Margaret to be left undisturbed with her suitor, Alan Ernscliffe, so that he can propose to her in peace, Flora resents being ordered about like a child and told to leave the house with Ethel; as her comments to her younger sister reveal, she seeks to challenge paternal authority:

"If he had done me the favour of speaking to me himself . . . I should have shown him that it is not right that Margaret should be left without anyone at hand in case she should be overcome. He is of no use in such cases, only makes things worse." (297)

Ethel's shocked reaction to this filial insubordination is reflective of her creator's profound reverence for her father and consistent deferral to his patriarchal supremacy (until well into middle-age, she consulted him about the tone and morality of her books, for instance).

Yonge, indeed, seems highly ambivalent towards the kind of female capability, driven by a sense of self-importance, which Flora embodies. This becomes even more evident when, having revealed herself as a highly successful diplomatist in managing the disharmonious group of women who constitute the local Ladies Committee, she furthers her social 'career' by becoming engaged to George Rivers, the son of a nearby wealthy landowner. George is not wholly unworthy, and turns out to have more virtues than are at first obvious, but he is solid and heavy, upsets the younger May children by laughing at them, and is described as 'shallow-brained and extravagant, and having been born in the days when Mr Rivers had been working himself up in the world, had not had so good an education as his little half-sister' (363). Yonge makes clear that Flora wants to marry George for the wrong reasons – that is, that he will bring her position and more chance to exercise her social skills –

although this is only indirectly hinted by Flora herself in her one anguished confession to Ethel just before her wedding: ' "Oh! what have I done? It is not worth it!" ' (405). This is the expression of a sentiment about which the narrator claims ignorance:

> Did a flash come over her then, what the father was, whom she had held cheaply? What was the worth of that for which she had exchanged such a home? She spoke not a word, she only clung tightly – if her heart failed her – it was too late. (407)

The moment is highly significant for several reasons. It strengthens the prioritization of home values in the novel and sets up a non-negotiable opposition between the inestimable blessing of domestic security and the unknown dangers for a woman of external commitment based on false premises. Even more importantly, it contextualizes Flora's conduct in terms of the primacy of father–daughter relations. Allegiance to the patriarchal – albeit here a source of affection and support – becomes the measure of true goodness and self-perfectibility. This standard of evaluation is not applicable exclusively to women, since Tom's moral improvement is signified by his willingness to devote himself to serving his father professionally, but it is foregrounded in the case of Flora and, as will be shown, even more with Ethel. Thus youthful female virtue is defined according to an emotional engagement which reinforces a pre-adult and self-negating relational state, disregarded only at peril.

Flora's marriage is not overtly unhappy, and when, much to everyone's astonishment, George is elected as the local Parliamentary candidate, she revels in the further fulfilment of her social ambitions. Modestly concealing herself behind her husband's identity, she writes his speeches and masterminds his political activities, empowering herself in all but name. Yonge, however, while not deploring female strength – in *Womankind*, she writes, 'A weak, narrow-minded woman, incapable of sympathy with the higher life, may be tender, kindly, affectionate, but she is the most fatal drag upon her husband or lover'[19] – cannot allow Flora to function as a model for *The Daisy Chain*'s girl readers. Not only is the sophistry involved in Flora's internalized argument that 'what could be a greater duty than to incite her husband to usefulness?' (489) made clear, but the erring daughter/wife is subjected to the most extreme punishment. Caught up in the frenzy of activity surrounding the forthcoming election, the young mother leaves her baby daughter

totally in the care of her nurse, who, through dosing her with large
quantities of opium to keep her quiet, causes the child's death.
Reduced to a state of anguished numbness, Flora learns too late
Yonge's dictum that for a wife, 'homemaking is from the time of
her marriage her paramount earthly duty, and as long as husband,
sons and daughters need her, all other good works . . . must be kept
subordinate thereto.'[20] Physical punishment for moral offences – an
intrinsic element of the tract literature whose extremes Yonge herself
claimed to disapprove – is a narrative strategy in several of these
juvenile texts, most notably *What Katy Did*, but in exploiting
motherhood as the arena of frightful mental suffering Yonge is
undermining the very gender positioning which she seems anxious
to maintain. Flora's deep remorse and realization that ' "I have never
set my heart right . . . He has let me destroy my child here, lest I
should have destroyed her Everlasting Life, like my own" ' (575) is
compounded by an additional bitter twist to the moral lesson. Flora
is unable to relinquish the life of social and political engagement
which she has carved out for herself, because George has come to
rely on her too much for her to abandon him; thus even though she
is morally chastened and enlightened, the effects of her wilfulness
continue to function as her punishment, chaining her to a continuing
existence of now-hated power and artificiality.

In reducing Flora to an example of unseemly – and therefore
threateningly subversive – female self-assertiveness, Yonge demonstrates most stringently her moral bias and also possibly her most
draconian treatment of character in the novel. With Ethel, she still
applies ethical criteria to female behaviour, but in a gentler way.
Though unavowed as such, Ethel is probably to a large extent an
authorial self-portrait. She shares with her creator high intellectual
ability, shyness and physical awkwardness, as well as a passionate
devotion to Church causes. The last is actually what 'saves' Ethel;
though she too is temporarily blind to where her true duties lie and
is impatient of interference with her plans, she is, unlike Flora,
wholly unworldly and free from all self-esteem. The most contentious
aspect of her subjection to an overriding moral vision concerns the
treatment of her mental capacities. Ethel is bookish and eager for
knowledge. Like Maggie Tulliver in *The Mill on the Floss*, she is intensely anxious to keep up with her brother in his studies, following
his Greek and Latin tasks and actually helping him with them;
indeed, Norman himself acknowledges her superiority to him in
some respects. But as with Flora, Yonge is uneasy about the exercise

of female talents outside the traditional arena. Not only does the family governess, Miss Winter, complain about Ethel's carelessness and slovenliness resulting from her preoccupation with her classical pursuits, but a familiar moral paradigm of sinfulness and subsequent punishment operates in her case too. Immersed in a book, she lets her baby brother, Aubrey, nearly burn himself to death; in his anger and shock, her father specifically links her neglect with her studies – ' "I'll put a stop to all schools and Greek, if it is to lead to this, and make you good for nothing" ' (136). This is not merely an attack on 'learned ladies', but on the nature and social role of woman; Ethel must cease to be a bluestocking, not because female intellectual activity is in itself undesirable but because it may detract from the primacy of domestic duties.

Significantly it is Margaret, submissive and self-negating, who, using the argument of their mother's wishes, persuades Ethel to relinquish the idea of keeping up with Norman, and substitutes an alternative model of girlhood:

> "You see . . . we all know that men have more power than women, and I suppose the time has come for Norman to pass beyond you . . . for that [studying Greek] would you give up being a useful, steady daughter and sister at home? The sort of woman that dear mamma wished to make you, and a comfort to papa." (181)

Her discomfiture compounded by Norman's lofty statement that ' "it is really time for you to stop, or you would get into a regular learned lady, and be good for nothing" ' (182), Ethel regretfully concedes and dedicates herself to being more useful at home as well as expediting her great ambition to build a church at Cocksmoor.

Yonge herself was not antipathetic to women's intellectual achievements, although she was mistrustful of girls' schools and refused to support proposals for a new College for Ladies at Girton:

> I have decided objections to bringing large masses of girls together, and think that home education under the inspection or encouragement of sensible fathers, or voluntarily contrived by the girls themselves is far more valuable. All the most superior women I have known have been thus formed, by home influence.[21]

No doubt the kind of educational liberty represented in the girls' school stories of Angela Brazil, half a century later, would have appalled Yonge. In *Womankind*, she suggests a programme of education for girls, which includes Latin, Greek, modern languages, arithmetic and history. But all this is always to be subordinate to home duties, a conviction she articulates in her novel by showing Ethel's gradual transformation as she becomes domesticated, and thus more womanly and attractive. Though she still occasionally helps Norman in his academic tasks – for instance she offers him assistance when he is composing the poem for submission for the Newdigate Prize at Oxford – she is now resigned to her role as household manager, after Flora's marriage. The narrative protects Ethel from the excesses of ethical insistence; as has been noted, her spiritual righteousness is never in question, and she is rewarded when the foundation stone of the Cocksmoor church is finally laid. But the curtailment of her intellectual freedom and fulfilment is an indication of Yonge's own ambivalence and reluctance to subvert the orthodox gendered codes on which her attitudes towards women were constructed.

If the moral framework of *The Daisy Chain* is all-embracing, it is not obtrusive. In keeping with the spirit of reserve which characterized the Oxford Movement, its teaching is offered implicitly rather than explicitly. As suggested earlier, Yonge herself deprecated juvenile tales in which pious little children talked openly about religion, and the word 'God' is never actually cited in the novel. The lessons of humility and selflessness which structure the narrative are not foregrounded to the extent that they close it off entirely to other possible ideologies or value-systems, either. Most important in this respect is its treatment of behavioural patterns in relation to gender. While essentially conservative in outlook, it is by no means inflexible or absolutist in the models it sets up for its young female readers. Many of the issues which it discusses – parenting, the exercise of individual talent, public versus private activity – introduce questions about gender-specific behaviour and role-playing which suggest that Yonge was able at least to contemplate, if not to endorse fully, alternative social categories.

Yonge's attitude towards gender was inevitably to a considerable extent conventional. Brought up to defer to male authority, and with no models of female intellectual achievement directly before her, at least in her early circles (later, one of her close friends was Elizabeth Wordsworth, first Principal of Lady Margaret Hall, Oxford, though she never wholly concorded with the latter's championing of college education for women), she remained firmly convinced of women's secondary status. Belying her own very considerable mental abilities, she always overtly supported the head/heart sexual dichotomy; in a letter of 1894 to Annie Moberly, for instance, she writes, 'I do think that a woman produces more effect by what she is than by a thousand talks and arguments.'[22] In the second paragraph of *Womankind,* Yonge states unequivocally, 'I have no hesitation in declaring my full belief in the inferiority of woman, nor that she brought it upon herself,'[23] and this belief underpins much of the work. Furthermore, in it she validates the traditional womanly virtues. For her, 'gentleness and modesty ... are the chief grace of womanhood,'[24] while a woman without refinement is 'a hateful unsexed creature.'[25] Girls have a responsibility to set good examples to their brothers, 'whose whole notions of womankind are formed on their mothers and sisters';[26] this sets up an almost impossible ideal of womanly superiority, with its accompanying moral burden. Similarly, the duty of parental care devolves supremely on daughters. In maintaining the female domestic ideal, Yonge is of course replicating the contemporary 'Angel in the House' mythology – the perfect lady 'is sure to make homes that radiate light and warmth from their glowing central hearth',[27] and her perfection is predicated on her self-forgetfulness, devotion to others, and acknowledgement of 'the utmost sacrifice of herself as simply natural'.[28]

Not surprisingly, much of this gender ideology is prioritized in *The Daisy Chain.* Domesticity is an important female attribute here. Despite her deficiencies, Flora has many admirable qualities, and her neatness and household efficiency are set against Ethel's untidiness, carelessness and practical ineptitude; a mark of the latter's spiritual progress is her physical transformation into a well-kept woman who can now make tea for the family without getting into a complete tangle over it. From a different starting point, the fairy-like little Meta Rivers, George's sister, who has never had to be other than merely ornamental, learns from the May girls to take a fuller participation in running the house and not to allow frivolous social activities to deflect her from her duty to her father and brother. Home affiliations must always take precedence over outside ones, as Margaret tells Ethel – 'If we are not just the thing in our niche at home, I don't think we can do much real good elsewhere' (87). As has already been shown, too, the chief crime of which Flora is guilty is her neglect of her supreme domestic responsibility, the care of her child; in permitting the nurse to undertake the role which she should be fulfilling, while she herself participates in public engagements, she is reneging on one of the primary functions of womanhood.

Flora's omissions highlight the novel's emphasis on motherhood, a significant aspect of its gender traditionalism. As in so many of the texts in this study, the figure of the mother is supremely important. She is the guide and exemplar, a role model for her daughters and a source of inspiration for the whole family. Mention has already been made of Mrs May's pervasive posthumous influence, beginning with the letter in which she sets out goals of improvement for her children to follow. All use her as a point of reference, as well as regarding her as an image of spiritual beatitude to which they must aspire. Appearing briefly at the beginning of the novel as 'a lady with a beautiful countenance of calm sweetness' (4), she quietens and soothes her unruly family just by her presence. After her death, she continues to shape their behaviour: Dr May tries to deal with the problems of Tom's deceitfulness and Margaret's engagement as she would have done, and Ethel struggles on short-sightedly, refusing to wear glasses because Mama did not like to see her in them; in each case, it is suggested that it is the maternal power of personal influence, rather than any direct intervention, which has the greatest effect on individual development and moral self-improvement. Indeed, Dr May himself is conscious of his own inadequacies without her guiding hand, now that he has to 'act the part of father and mother both' (299). Like Warner and Burnett, Yonge stresses the sympathetic and emotional essence of maternity, the loss of which not only threatens moral growth but also retards the ability to engage in emotional relationships with others.

Another familiar icon of female ideality which appears in *The Daisy Chain* is that of the blessed invalid. The carriage accident which kills Mrs May injures Margaret so badly that she is immobilized for the rest of her short life (she dies seven years later). Restricted, like Cousin Helen in *What Katy Did*, to a sofa existence, she lives vicariously, taking on the household management from her bedside and becoming a surrogate mother to the other children. She regards this curtailment of her activity as a sign of God's will to which she is content to submit – 'I have been thinking how well off I am, able to enjoy so much, and be employed all day long' (128). She also sees it as a salutary check to incipient ambition, a temptation now removed from her, as she tells Richard:

"... government, and management, and influence – you would not guess what dreams I used to waste on them, and now here

I am set aside from it all, good for nothing but for all you dear ones to be kind to." (411)

Even more importantly, as with Helen, Margaret's immobility signifies not only self-renunciation but also a denial of sexuality. In her case, romantic commitment is enacted as tokenism, not devoid of emotional feeling – she and Alan Ernescliffe genuinely love each other – but destined never to be fulfilled in the normal physicality of marriage. Although her engagement takes place, the narrative closes off all subsequent futures except that of union in an afterlife: Alan dies of fever in the Samoan Islands, and she herself gradually fades away to her own death not long afterwards, a 'white form, half-seen in the twilight, whose hopes had fleeted away from earth, and who was calmly, softly gliding after them' (614); significantly, her betrothal ring is set in the chalice for the new church at Cocksmoor, 'the "relic of a frail love lost" . . . becoming the "token of endless love begun"' (607). The unusually emotional writing with which her death-bed scene is described suggests Yonge's deep engagement with this symbolization of perfected female spirituality, for whom 'all was over; nothing left, save what they had rendered the undying spirit, and the impress her example had left on those around her' (646).

Yonge's conventionality with regard to gender roles is also evident in her presentation of masculinity. As has been shown, paternal authority, while its judgements may not be infallible, must always be deferred to. Schoolboy values of honour, truthfulness, decency, and respect for rules are the basis for future healthful manhood, and those who stray from them thereby signify their own betrayal of a male ethic. The text also validates the Victorian public/private gender division. Flora's disastrous incursion into the world of politics and Ethel's equally problematic involvement with the male arena of scholarship indicate a distrust of negotiation between the polarities of male and female roles, although, notably, it is the threat to the womanly ideal, rather than the potential emasculation of maleness which most seems to concern Yonge. As Rowbotham has argued, Yonge, like other mid-century writers such as Elizabeth Sewell and Emma Marshall, was anxious to present the reasons behind the establishment and maintenance of this duality, so as to convince girl readers of its necessity or desirability.[29] Flora's chastisement and Ethel's compromised ambitions would thus make them more acceptable as role models, young women who have been shown the folly of attempting to disturb the status quo.

Within this basically traditionalist framework, however, *The Daisy Chain*, as has already been suggested, questions the construction and implementation of images of masculinity and femininity within a highly ordered society. Like Coolidge and Montgomery later in the century, Yonge challenges essentialist notions of gender-specific qualities and roles. For her, the most important constituents of individual distinctiveness are moral ones, and these both sub-sume gender divisions and are common to both sexes. Many 'good' values (truthfulness, self-sacrifice, humility), like 'bad' ones (self-aggrandisement, vanity, deceitfulness), are not in fact depicted as gender specific, certainly in any biological sense. Through its articulation of possible role reversals, the novel teaches its adolescent readers that men and women can learn from each other and that, within certain parameters, selfhood can transcend the social (though not the religious) codes of conventional ideology. A discussion between Margaret and Mr Wilmot, the local incumbent, about whether or not Ethel should be encouraged in her Cocksmoor plans, reveals how Yonge problematizes, without resolving, the issues involved. In answer to Margaret's comment that ' "girls are told they ought to wait patiently, and not to be eager for self-imposed duties" ', Mr Wilmot is less confident about insisting on such gendered restrictiveness:

> "I am not saying that it is not the appointed discipline for the girls themselves . . . If they would submit, it would doubtless prove the most beneficial thing for them; but it is a trial in which they often fail." (151)

His uncertainty here seems to mirror Yonge's own reluctance to rigidify behavioural codes along strictly gender drawn lines.

In several respects, the novel formulates behaviour patterns which disrupt normal sexual categorization. Within the family as a whole, gender roles seemed blurred or reversed. Norman's confident masculine self-image is considerably undermined by the way in which he responds to his mother's death; his panic-attacks and fainting fits, brought on by confrontation with physical sickness, come close to that very female malady, brain fever, and he himself is contemptuous of what he considers to be his own fine-ladyish 'nerves'. In her letter about her children, noting Tom's 'girlishness and timidity' Mrs May ironically comments, too, that seemingly ' "Tom and Mary made a mistake . . . he is the girl and she the boy, for she is a rough, merry creature, the noisiest in the house" ' (49).

Such female vigour is not condemned; indeed, in *Womankind*, Yonge acknowledges the benefits of allowing 'tomboyism' in girls – 'a wholesome delight in rushing about at full speed, playing at active games, climbing trees, rowing boats, making dirt-pies and the like.'[30] Of course, the progression towards adulthood gradually re-draws the boundaries: Mary has to become more ladylike, while Tom learns to be more manly. But Yonge certainly offers versions of youthful characteristics which replicate 'real life' diversity rather than literary or ideological stereotypicality.

Most notable in this respect is her presentation of the eldest May boy, Richard. Richard lacks the traditional 'male' qualities of forcefulness, ambition and authoritarianism; instead, he embodies the 'female' ones of gentleness, self-effacement, and domestic skills. Overshadowed and somewhat awed by the superior intellectual abilities of Norman and Ethel, he has no confidence in himself, an image reinforced by his siblings' impatience with his 'slowness'. Yet he is valorized in the story for these very qualities. Notably, after Mrs May's death it is he, rather than Flora or Ethel, who fulfils the maternal functions for the family, 'watching over the little ones more like a sister than a brother' (45). He, too, helps Ethel to look neater, and even teaches her how to thread a needle so that she can repair her torn skirt. Of all the Mays, Margaret most clearly recognizes that for all his solidity (he dampens Ethel's initial enthusiasm for the Cocksmoor scheme) and absence of apparent cleverness he is a far better 'eldest' than Norman would be because he provides ' "a calm, cautious steady balance to the quick-silver heads some of us have got" ' (89). As they come to rely on Richard more and more, the rest of the Mays concur with Margaret's judgement; and when he becomes the new incumbent of the parish he is enabled to combine familial and parochial duties to the benefit of both spheres. Richard, of course, is a cleric, not a soldier or a robust sailor like Harry, for example, and hence his more 'female' virtues are appropriate to the sexually transgressive nature of his calling. But the feminine aspects of his maleness are paralleled in Dr May himself, who, although the unquestioned paternal authority, still has to undergo feminization in order to replace the qualities lost with Mrs May. He must now act as both father and mother, learning to identify and sympathize emotionally with his children; and though as a doctor he operates professionally within the female arena of nurturance and healing, he is called on to exercise these skills on a more intimate level of personal relationships.

Conversely, certain qualities more usually associated with maleness are, albeit within strictly defined parameters, presented as
female virtues. In excess, or when they imperil demands of family, as
in the case of Flora's public activities or Ethel's over-zealous scholarship, they are of course deprecated, but as Yonge's discussion of
'Strong-minded Women' in *Womankind* indicates, they form an
essential component of admirable femininity:

> Without a strong mind, a woman is nothing better than an
> intelligent bit of drift weed, driven hither and thither by force
> of circumstances, and totally dependent on her surroundings.[31]

The ability to make judgements, act independently, and stand
up for right, which for Yonge constitute true womanly strong-
mindedness, are, somewhat surprisingly, embodied in Meta Rivers,
the 'fairy' girl whom Norman marries. Seen at first as a light-hearted,
airy creature, more like an insubstantial romantic heroine than a
morally serious character, she comes to display much more solid
sense and toughness than her appearance would suggest. Changing
from a fine young lady, petted and indulged, to one who takes on
family and neighbourhood responsibilities, she proves a worthy
partner for Norman, despite his aunt's initial misgivings about the
match – ' "I am quite frightened at Miss Rivers' looks" ' (626). Indeed,
Meta's level-headedness provide a necessary ballast to Norman's
neurotic obsession with himself, as Dr May observes – ' "she has a
bright, brave temper and elastic spirits that would be the very thing
for him, poor boy, with that morbid sensitiveness . . . she would
brighten him" ' (428). Their union thus reverses some of the traditional dichotomies of sexual relationships (as of course does Flora's
and George's with less happy results). It is also significant that she
is accorded financial power, since it is her inheritance which pays
for Norman's passage to New Zealand.

The novel, then, is equivocal in its representation and confirmation
of gender roles, both validating orthodox ideologies and deconstructing them in the recognition that they are to a considerable
extent socially and circumstantially determined. The moral scheme
does not sexually compartmentalize, either; if women must be strong
and supportive, men must learn to be selfless and considerate, and
the lesson may be hard for both. Interestingly, the same feeling of
confinement which Ethel suffers on being excluded from the outer
world of male activity is experienced by Tom when he has to accede

to the demands of duty and remain in Stoneborough to help his father in his practice. In an image of entrapment, frequently found in women's texts to represent the female condition, he describes himself to Ethel as ' "racing about this miserable circuit, just like your gold pheasant rampaging in his cage" ' (599).

As has already been noted, the sharpest questioning of gender roles in *The Daisy Chain* occurs with the character of Ethel, probably the most directly accessible of the May family for girl readers. In this respect, the most equivocal aspect of her portraiture is her positioning with regard to sexual/romantic fulfilment. Early on, her closeness to her father is foregrounded: they look alike, she has inherited many of his characteristics (he admits to his own heedlessness in youth), and he comes increasingly to depend on her for companionship and support. Margaret's engagement to Alan Ernescliffe strengthens Ethel's resolve to dedicate herself wholly to Dr May; she vehemently counters Norman's laughing comment that girls have lovers – ' "I will never let papa or any of you be second to any one" ' (316) – and reiterates this determination when Flora announces her intention to marry George:

> Leave him who might, she would never forsake him . . . she . . . laid up her secret vow – that no earthly object should be placed between her and her father. (393)

Yonge apparently promised her readers that she would never let Ethel marry,[32] but the narrative does in fact negotiate between the notions of self-sacrificial asexuality and romantic involvement. While in Oxford to hear Norman's Commemoration poem, Ethel meets a distant cousin, Norman Ogilvie (the identity of names may be significant), and they are immediately attracted to one another. As the week goes on, however, Ethel becomes increasingly guilt-ridden, seeing her preoccupation with the young man as a temptation away from her true role in the family; she therefore decides to return home before her emotions get inextricably engaged.

Ethel's decision is clearly admirable in the context of the novel's moral coding – significantly, it is the worldly Flora who tries to argue her out of it – but the implications of the incident are not unambiguous. In resisting 'normal' female sexuality, and rejecting it for ethical criteria, is Ethel asserting her independence of conventional gendered behaviour or merely enacting another traditional female role, that of self-abnegation? A free indirect speech commentary describing Ethel's feelings on her return fails to establish a viewpoint:

If Ethel breathed more freely, there was a sense that tranquillity is uninteresting. It was, it must be confessed, a flat end to a romance, that all the permanent present effect was a certain softening, and a degree more attention to her appearance. (490)

Moreover, does Ethel's refusal to abandon her father, though a duty commonly assumed by Victorian daughters, indicate a refusal or inability to face the conditions, social and sexual, of mature adulthood?

At the end of the novel, a single life is triumphantly validated, and readers are assured that Ethel has fully got over any temporary feelings of disappointment about Norman Ogilvie:

She had never given away the depths of her heart, though the upper surface had been stirred. All had long subsided, and she could think freely of him as an agreeable cousin, in whose brilliant career she should always be interested. (637)

But the narrowness and lack of emotional fulfilment which the validation potentially endorses are recast in a religious contextualization which deflects from their negative signification:

Norman Ogilvie's marriage seemed to her to have fixed her lot in life, and what was the lot? Home and Cocksmoor had been her choice, and they were before her. Home! but her eyes had been opened to see that earthly homes may not endure, nor fill the heart . . . She felt that . . . she might look to becoming comparatively solitary in the course of years – then tried to realize what her lonely life might be, but broke off smiling at herself, "What is that to me? . . . My course and aim are straight on, and He will direct my paths." (666–7)

As in *The Wide, Wide World*, feminized spiritual values are encoded in the heroine, thus reinforcing the sexual and religious orthodoxy of the novel as a whole. Whereas Warner, however, allows for the possibility of negotiation between moral elevation and romantic fulfilment, albeit with subversive implications, Yonge's highest ideal must ultimately look beyond everyday life. For her, only by relocating womanly self-expression in other-worldliness can the tensions between varying alternatives to gender orthodoxy be resolved.

Notes

1. [Charlotte M. Yonge], *The Daisy Chain: or Aspirations* (tenth edition; London: Macmillan, 1870), p.v. All subsequent page references are to this edition and are included in the text.
2. See Chapter 1, p.3.
3. Christabel Coleridge, *Charlotte Mary Yonge: Her Life and Letters* (London: Macmillan, 1903), p.183.
4. Yonge apologizes in the Preface for the fact that the story may be considered too long and the characters too numerous (p.vi).
5. See Chapter 1, pp.11–12.
6. Charlotte M. Yonge, *Womankind* [serialized 1874–7; published in book form 1887] (new edition, London: Walter Smith & Innes, 1889), p.64. She makes the same objections to impossibly and obtrusively saintly children in her 'Children's Literature of the Last Century', *Macmillan's Magazine*, vol. XX, nos. 117–19 (1869), p.309.
7. Ibid., p.63.
8. Christabel Coleridge, op.cit., p.59.
9. Ibid., p.64.
10. Ibid., p.183.
11. E. Nesbit, *The Wouldbegoods*, (London: Puffin Books, 1958), p.190.
12. Margaret Oliphant, *Phoebe, Junior* [1876] (London: Virago, 1989), p.141.
13. Ibid., p.175.
14. Gillian Avery, *Childhood's Pattern* (London: Hodder & Stoughton, 1975).
15. See Gillian Avery, 'Home and Family: English and American Ideals in the Nineteenth Century', in ed. Dennis Butts, *Stories and Society: Children's Literature in its Social Context* (London: Macmillan, 1991). Avery makes the point that 'the complex Victorian social stratification . . . which was such a rich source of material for the adult novelist, had a deadening effect on children's books' (p.42).
16. Christabel Coleridge, op.cit., p.178. Also see Ethel Romanes, *Charlotte Mary Yonge: An appreciation* (London: A.R. Mowbray, 1908), p.17.
17. Christabel Coleridge, op.cit., p.301.
18. Judith Rowbotham, *Good Girls Make Good Wives: Guidance for Girls in Victorian Fiction* (Oxford: Blackwell, 1989).
19. *Womankind*, p.82.
20. Ibid., p.266.
21. Letter of 22 July 1868, to Emily Davies in Girton College Library, quoted in Georgina Battiscombe, *Charlotte Mary Yonge: The story of an uneventful life* (London: Constable, 1943), p.146.
22. Christabel Coleridge, op.cit., p.325.
23. *Womankind*, p.1.
24. Ibid., p.105.
25. Ibid., p.99.
26. Ibid., p.130.
27. Ibid., p.189.
28. Ibid., p.190.
29. Rowbotham, op.cit.

30. *Womankind*, p.10.
31. Ibid., p.232.
32. Amy Cruse records that Dr Moberly made Yonge promise that she would never allow Ethel May to be married or Dr May to die, in any of the sequels to *The Daisy Chain* that she might write. (Amy Cruse, *The Victorians and their Books*, London: George Allen & Unwin, 1935), p.54.

4

Louisa May Alcott:
Little Women

Louisa May Alcott's *Little Women* (1868) is probably the most famous of all the works discussed in this study, and of the nineteenth-century texts certainly the most enduring in popularity.
Although it is over a hundred and twenty years since its first
appearance, it remains a best-seller in both the United States and
in Britain. The original novel is available in both hardcover and
paperback editions on the permanent classics list of mainstream
publishing houses, selling alongside abridged, adulterated and car-
toon versions of the adventures, and even the further adventures,
of Meg, Jo, Beth and Amy. The book has been dramatized for stage
and screen, and television and radio adaptations continue to be
broadcast for audiences who, habituated to a cultural diet of comic
strips and soap operas, can have at best only a limited understanding of mid-nineteenth-century New England life. Elaine Showalter,
in an essay on the phenomenon of *Little Women*, has noted how a
number of twentieth-century women, as diverse in their origins
and achievements as Gertrude Stein, Simone de Beauvoir and
Adrienne Rich have all been prepared to admit to the impact of the
novel as a formative influence on their lives.[1]

A text with such an established and central position in the female
reading experience carries its own particular problems. Indeed
one of the difficulties encountered by recent critics of *Little Women*
has been the perceived disparity between emotional engagement
with the text and evaluative criteria. As Lavinia Russ observed,
it is difficult to view any text objectively when it has been deeply
embedded in early imaginative experience and the empathy with
characters and episodes has blurred the boundaries between fiction
and fact.[2] Going further, Catherine Stimpson suggests that the
problematics of reading *Little Women* highlight an important area
of concern for feminist criticism, a concern which, in the remit of
this study, has particular bearing on the reception of children's literature. As a child, Stimpson memorized and could quote whole

chapters of *Little Women*, a text she locates as central in the 'paracanon', that alternative but complementary literary hierarchy, composed of works whose 'worth exists in [their] capacity to inspire love', whether or not they are judged by the critical establishment to have literary value.[3] As Stimpson argues, *Little Women*, like *Huckleberry Finn* or *Tom Sawyer* (the male equivalents with which it is often compared), is indubitably a work that makes an indefinable but fundamental appeal to a collective readerly imagination. In the years since its original publication it has acquired mythic status, occupying a special place in American culture as '*the* American female myth, its subject the primordial one of the passage from childhood, from girl to woman.'[4]

British audiences are not immune from responding to this story of female progression: in the first survey of the most borrowed 'classic' authors in British libraries, undertaken by the Public Lending Rights Office in 1993, Alcott was placed twentieth, just below Shakespeare and above Conrad and the Brontes.[5] Certainly *Little Women* is the childhood text most frequently analysed by feminist critics for its reflection and exploration of female culture and for the complicated narrative tensions it reveals. The story of the four March sisters and their mother, Marmee, during a year when their father is away at the American Civil War, provides a paradigm of female struggle whose literary influence can be seen in texts as dissimilar as Susan Coolidge's *What Katy Did* and E. Nesbit's *The Railway Children*, works which also explore the processes of growing up in fictional frameworks that reinforce the problematic nature of specifically female adolescence. Stories for children frequently stress their protagonists' ability to survive in a world without adults. When such a narrative also focuses on girls who are removed from obvious patriarchal influence, the emphasis on possibilities of female autonomy becomes intensified. Yet *Little Women* is by no means a simple text to interpret in the revised feminist critical framework of the enterprise undertaken in this study. In addition to the issues of critical evaluation referred to above, it raises questions about ideologies of the feminine, their impact on women's roles in both domestic and professional spheres, and literary reception. Close analysis of the text elicits unresolved tensions in the depictions of girlhood and the narratives available to women, whether realized or projected, and in turn this poses intriguing lines of enquiry about the requirements for women authors to produce work in prescribed genres and with strictly controlled subject matter.

Little Women is one of the first fictional texts for children to convey the difficulties and the anxieties of girlhood, and which suggests that becoming a 'little woman' is a learned and often fraught process, not an instinctual or natural condition of female development. In its ability to promote a double set of value systems, the book maintains a precarious balancing act, simultaneously providing for its readers a positive image of the values of home and female domesticity *and* arguing for the importance of creative independence for women. Indeed it is the very coexistence of these apparently conflicting elements that has contributed to the novel's continued appeal, and that more recently has exposed it to the rigorous critical scrutiny of feminist literary scholars, who find in the text evidence of teasing contradictions about female authorship and consequent ambivalent messages as to its conformist or subversive intent. The use of Jo March as a projection of her creator's aspirations further serves to emphasize the frustrations that women's imaginative creativity encounters. Jo is perhaps the first of the heroines in this study who act out their own psychic fragmentation through adopting the role of author, and who figure prominently in fiction for girls, and whose uncertainties provide scope for readers' empathetic response. As Stimpson has observed:

> Possibly . . . both female and male readers love any text that gives an experience of division and self-division. . . . the female reader's love of *Little Women* becomes a synechdoche for both a female and a male love of a textual escape from any psychological and ethical coherence that seems as pre-formed as a slab of concrete.[6]

In its portrayal of adolescence as a transitional period from girlhood to womanhood, the novel registers a crucial point of tension in many women's lives. The March girls are encouraged to develop their distinctive talents as separate individuals, and readers are invited to engage imaginatively with the challenge that Jo offers to certain traditional modes of female behaviour. Her longing for action and her careless disregard for passive and decorative femininity is visualized as both desirable and natural, and adolescence is perceived as the period of opportunity for self-expression and acceptable rebellion. At the same time, however, the women's world which Marmee and her four daughters inhabit is offered as a positive model of the civilizing and the necessary, a feminizing and thus taming influence on the harsh rationalism of the coexistent but non-intrusive all male Laurence household. In addition, the little women's struggle to please, to conform simultaneously to several incompatible demands, reflects the pressures placed on women in a society that made personal independence into a political manifesto, while clearly establishing a demarcation of gender roles that excluded women from decision-making processes. In a review of recent Alcott scholarship, Ann B. Murphy has usefully summarized the possible polarized critical positions: 'Is *Little Women* adolescent, sentimental, and repressive, an instrument for teaching girls how to become "little", domesticated and silent?' Alternatively, is it 'implicitly revolutionary, fostering discontent with the very model of female domesticity which it purports to admire?'[7] It is the refusal of the book ultimately to resolve the intractable questions it raises that creates it anew as a dynamic text for modern readers, who recognize in Jo March's confusion about her gendered identity and the pull between the demands of family and those of individualism a withdrawal from the overarching sentimental structure that apparently controls the novel's narrative direction.

Little Women was a book written to commission by an author who was intensely professional in her attitude to what she saw only as an uncomfortable and difficult task. 'I don't enjoy this sort of thing', Alcott confessed to her diary, in the process of struggling with the story for girls she had been asked to produce so as to fill what her publisher saw as a profitable gap in the market. 'Never liked girls', she admitted revealingly, 'or knew many, except my sisters; but our queer plays and experiences may prove interesting, though I doubt it.'[8] Filled with misgivings, she plodded on with the work, her distaste for the enterprise undoubtedly a major contributory factor in its ultimate success. For it is important to recognise the innovatory calibre of *Little Women* as a 'girls' story'. Although produced specifically for a female juvenile audience, it is a text that deliberately avoids many conventional features of contemporary American children's fiction by substituting comic incident for sentimental pathos, and by rejecting the paradigms of female fictional propriety (such as were found in Susan Warner's Ellen Montgomery) for the vital, androgynous Jo March and the talented if overexuberant Amy. Despite the clear moral directive of *Little Women*, Alcott refused, as Ruth K. MacDonald has noted, to follow the conventional format of didactic literature for children. Neither did she use the novel to advance political and ethical causes, such as the temperance movement, abolition of slavery or progressive education, all issues taken up in the reformist tendency that characterized much children's writing of the period.[9] Recoiling from the fashionably sentimental structures of juvenile narrative, Alcott relied instead on the genre of domestic realism which she had exploited so successfully in her earlier *Hospital Sketches* (1865), a work firmly rooted in her personal grim experience of nursing at a field hospital in Georgetown during the Civil War. Despite her initial reluctance for the task, her decision to base the work for girls on her own family was to be a major turning-point, not just in her own career, but in the history of children's literature, and when in August 1868 Alcott read the proofs of *Little Women*, she was surprised by the power of its immediacy: 'Not a bit sensational, but simple and true, for we really lived most of it; and if it succeeds that will be the reason of it.'[10]

Alcott's open acknowledgement of her own departure from the sentiment and the didacticism of contemporary fictional practice is present throughout *Little Women*, where she makes explicit comparative reference to the difference between her heroines and their literary counterparts. 'If she had been the heroine of a moral storybook', the narrator observes about Jo, bereft of companionship after Beth's death in the second section of the novel,

she ought at this period of her life to have become quite saintly, renounced the world, and gone about doing good in a mortified bonnet, with tracts in her pocket. But, you see, Jo wasn't a heroine; she was only a struggling human girl, like hundreds of others.[11]

Alcott's quasi-satirical treatment of religious sentimentality and moral sententiousness effectively promotes her own stance as realist. In contrast to the idealized portraits of heroines in conventional novels, Meg, Jo, Beth and Amy are no paragons of perfection, but adolescent girls sensitive to their own personality deficiencies and for whom social gaucherie and the lack of new clothes are very genuine concerns. The intertextual dimension of *Little Women* indicates its degree of literary sophistication in its response to well-established genres: the evangelical, sentimental and heroic narratives that were characteristic of popular literature. References to other fictions in the novel include, among others, Bunyan's *The Pilgrim's Progress*, Scott's *Ivanhoe*, Goldsmith's *The Vicar of Wakefield* and, significantly, Warner's *The Wide, Wide World*, classic examples of respectively, a moral allegory, a historical romance, a sentimental comedy and what had already become a highly influential story of female self-development. These are the literary models which both serve as inspiration for Alcott's heroines and expose their realist foundation.

For, as Jo points out, the economic materialities that determine the March family's existence are far removed from the fantastic scenarios of popular romantic fictions, where

> "some rich relative [would] leave you a fortune unexpectedly; then you'd dash out as an heiress, scorn everyone who has slighted you, go abroad and come home my Lady Something, in a blaze of splendour and elegance." (213)

The inclusion in the novel of parodies of clichéd scenes from contemporary children's literature also enhances the distinction between *Little Women* and its predecessors. During the account of Beth's first, almost fatal, attack of scarlet fever for instance, as the illness approaches its crisis Alcott shifts the focus of attention from the sickroom to Aunt March's house. Here Amy has prepared her childish and misspelled Last Will and Testament, a comic foil which undermines the potentially sentimental excesses of the stock deathbed tableau. And when Beth's death does occur, in the second volume of *Little Women*, later to be retitled *Good Wives*, the authorial voice draws attention to the dying girl's refusal to fade away according to type, for:

> Seldom, except in books, do the dying utter memorable words, see visions, or depart with beautified countenances.[12]

Similarly the March sisters' deviation from standard conduct book behaviour is a pronounced feature of episodes which could have been used as exemplary. At the smart New Year's Eve party at the Gardiners' house, Meg sprains her ankle dancing in high heeled shoes that are too tight, and Jo spills coffee on a dress that she has already ruined with a scorch mark. The incidents offer a striking contrast to Ellen Montgomery's Christmas visit to Ventnor in *The Wide, Wide World*, where the heroine functions as an exemplar of decorum and moral superiority.

It is, however, *The Pilgim's Progress* which provides the most explicit model for the narrative and the spiritual schema of the novel. Receiving the book as a gift from their mother on Christmas morning, the girls are encouraged to see themselves as unworthy pilgrims on the symbolic journey towards self-improvement, and the naming of episodes in *Little Women* after Bunyan's own chapter headings reinforces the analogy at every stage of the story. Yet the male text offers no easy solutions for female adaptation, as Marmee, herself a victim of patriarchal control, is prepared to admit. As a literary construct *The Pilgrim's Progress* presents a behavioural ideal which in the literal absence of the father takes on the power of the Logos, the all-powerful word which carries the authority to determine female conduct and which negates female identity. Struggling to obey the dicta of this fictional text, the sisters succeed only partially in conforming to its template of spiritual perfection, and the existence of alternative literary identities within *Little Women* indicates the inadequacy of Bunyan's powerfully simple ideal in resolving the contemporary problems which the girls encounter.

This is conveyed most tellingly through the conceptualization of Jo March as author, a role which embodies Alcott's ambitions and forms an eloquent comment on women's position in the literary market place. Like Alcott, Jo's first literary inclination is towards the Gothic, the sensational genre that liberates her fantasies of violence, aggression and cross-dressing. The sexually transgressive implications of their context and the latent subversion they encode are, however, not allowed to flourish in the world that is dominated by a patriarchy which represses the unacceptable female text. Her encounters with publishers and later with Professor Bhaer force Jo to confront the tension between commercial practice and conventional family values, and she ultimately tones down her exotic taste for thrillers to the more domestic, acceptable mode of moral fables for children. Jo's hopes for her future echo those of her creator. '"I want to do something splendid before I go into my castle"', she declares, '"something heroic or wonderful, that won't be forgotten after I'm dead. I shall write books, and get rich and famous"' (196). The remark makes explicit the connection between personal ambition, literary practice and the parameters of achievement for women. Although for both Alcott and her heroine the dream was to materialize, it was in a dimension which Alcott certainly saw as compromising her early idealism.

As discussed in the introductory chapter, children's writing in the nineteenth as in the twentieth century lacked literary prestige, and writing for girls in particular, largely the province of women, ranked even lower in status than other forms of children's literature.

In part this has been used as evidence of the campaign to trivialize women's literary achievement, what one feminist critic has called a general 'belittling . . . of women and women's culture.'[13] In this context it is highly significant that Jo's ultimate professional destination is as an author of books for boys, not for girls, a sphere where she can continue to allow her boisterous imagination to have free rein, and where her subjects will not be tied to domestic or matrimonial affairs. Alcott's personal resistance to stereotyped categorization as female novelist continued well after she had recognized the need to satisfy market forces. Working on the sequel to the first section of *Little Women*, she was infuriated by the public demands for the expected romantic conclusion to the narrative. 'Girls write to ask who the little women marry, as if that was the only end and aim of a woman's life. I *won't* marry Jo to Laurie to please anyone,'[14] she declared passionately, almost wilfully providing her dynamic heroine with a deliberately anti-romantic lover, twice her age. Alcott's disaffection from the literary niche in which she found herself was profound, and despite the financial triumph of *Little Women*, she could not rekindle the sense of exhilaration she had experienced after her first appearances in print. *Little Women* ensured the family's economic security but it consigned Alcott to a career path which fractured her sense of artistic integrity as she became bitterly aware of the treadmill to which she had committed herself. In April 1869, just after the publication of *Little Women*, she confessed to her journal, 'Feel quite used up but the family seem so panic-stricken and helpless when I break down, that I try to keep the mill going.'[15] The frustration and self-division which Alcott personally experienced and which is a running theme throughout her personal writings, her journal and her letters, surfaces most provocatively in her most famous work. As noted earlier, it is this refusal to be easily codified or to be reduced to any single or simple interpretation that forms a significant factor in understanding why *Little Women* has acquired its 'classic' status.

Alcott's four heroines, and in particular her self-portrait, Jo, the unruly second daughter of the March family, embody the anxieties of female adolescence and social insecurity at a time when such problems went formally unacknowledged. The March sisters span the ages from twelve to sixteen, the period of female puberty, each sister a discrete component in the exploration of the processes of women's acculturation. Amy, the youngest and the nearest to childhood, has apparently the simplest lessons to learn, those closest to the conventional moral tutelage of the time: the need to subdue vanity, to work in harmony with others and to control selfish impulses. The educational precepts that are exemplified through her story recur in more developed form with Meg, the daughter at the other end of the age spectrum, and the one who at the conclusion of *Little Women* has to embark on her own domestic career, the goal that implicitly she and the others are working towards in their preparation for adulthood. Although Marmee tells her two eldest daughters that it is better to ' "be happy old maids than unhappy wives, or unmaidenly girls, running about to find husbands" ' (141), she also makes it plain that spinsterhood comes a poor second to the main purpose of a woman's life. ' "To be loved and chosen by a good man is the best and sweetest thing which can happen to a woman" ' (40), she advises Meg and Jo in direct opposition to the author's privately declared opinions. It is this definitive statement of Marmee's which signposts most strikingly the critical contradictions of the text, for her injunction seems to undermine the novel's sympathetic identification with the issue of female independence and the importance of the creative life for women.

Despite Marmee's insistence on the passive roles that women must adopt as they wait for 'a good man', the March household, as it functions in the first significant section of *Little Women*, is presented as a self-contained and self-supporting female unit and all four daughters must address the need to earn their own living. Creativity, whether perceived as a conventionally feminine or as a transgressive act, is a central ingredient in the text's conceptualization of female autonomy. Each sister realizes her individuality through artistic self-expression: Meg's embroidery, Jo's writing, Beth's music and Amy's drawing and sculpture are not merely leisure pursuits for bourgeois young women who wish to occupy their time, but serious activities which double in providing vital imaginative sustenance and, in Meg's and Jo's case, a practical source of income. Marmee, as the focus and the guiding spirit of this all-female household, thus paradoxically encodes both the traditional values of domesticity *and* the more progressive move towards female self-sufficiency and individual fulfilment.

The contradictions are made more forcibly apparent with the portrayals of Beth and Jo, who are paired as twinned but antithetical extremes of the growth to womanhood. Beth, the third sister, although at one level seemingly a stereotype of female virtue, is also used by Alcott to address the complex issue of compatibility

between image and reality. Conforming to the traditional iconography of the 'angel in the house', delicate, frequently compared to a
rose, with large, soft eyes, self-effacing and tranquil, Beth must
learn to overcome her natural timidity in order to achieve full social
integration. Her blushing shyness and feminine modesty operate as
both positive and negative attributes, for, while her fragility and
gentleness encourage masculine protection (she is the automatic
recipient of largesse from the Laurence menage), her failure to cope
with external community structures results ultimately in her death.
The spiritual perfection that she embodies, whilst offering an inspirational source of guidance to her sisters, is doomed in a world
which demands that women must ultimately function outside the
family which has nurtured them.

Beth's reluctance to integrate is complemented by Jo's boisterous-
ness and sociability, qualities which she must learn to curb or at
least channel into appropriate outlets. Jo's energy must be subdued
because, as the book demonstrates, it can lead to moral unruliness:
her inability to control her temper for instance results in an accident
where Amy nearly drowns skating on thin ice. And her longings to
chat with boys and men as equals carry dangerous overtones of
sexual freedom: at the Gardiners' party, Meg has to restrain her
sister from joining a group of 'half a dozen jovial lads [who] were
talking about skates' (50), because of the impropriety involved.

At fifteen, Jo is the sister who most powerfully projects the
physiological and psychological disturbances of adolescence, and
for virtually all readers she is the character in whom the emotional
substance of the novel is invested. Yet, as Anne Scott MacLeod has
argued, Jo as a fictional creation merely extends the reality of the
experience that many American girls encountered in their journey
from girlhood to womanhood, when the childhood licence they had
enjoyed was brought to an abrupt end by the realization that the
time had come to embark on adulthood.[16] As noted in the introduction, the nineteenth-century American experience of growing
up for girls was significantly different from the Victorian insistence
on silence and inactivity that English middle-class children were
expected to submit to, and this difference becomes apparent in the
alternative scenarios that American and British authors contrive for
their heroines. Even Ethel May in Yonge's *The Daisy Chain* is allowed only a brief, temporary excursion into tomboyhood. The point
is reinforced emphatically in *Little Women* in the scene when the
free and easy demeanour of the March sisters is contrasted with the

formality of Laurie's English visitors, whose reliance on rigid class division is seen as 'starched-up' and inhibiting. The inhibitions are not merely manifestations of outward codes of dress and behaviour but relate crucially to a revised ideology of girlhood that problematizes conventional notions of the feminine. '"Young ladies in America love independence as much as their ancestors did"' (193), says John Brooke in defence of Meg, with a consciousness of the separate origins of the two cultures that is implicit throughout the novel. It is this very sense of liberation, the 'psychic as well as physical freedom' as MacLeod notes,[17] that Jo March is so reluctant to relinquish as she moves inexorably towards the position of maturity that society demands of her.

In a cultural climate where, as Warner's *The Wide, Wide World* demonstrates, fictional literature for girls most frequently emphasized the growth of a perfectible moral sensibility and seemed to provide role models of femininity that could go unchallenged, Alcott broke with the prescriptive barriers of her age in order to articulate her own uncertainties about gender relations and the latent power structures of family life. As critics have pointed out,[18] such uncertainties were to a certain extent a reflection of the current debate about women's nature as well as symptomatic of nineteenth-century American economic concerns about the sexual division of labour. *Little Women* contributes in part to this debate by dramatizing the difficulties of establishing clear gendered identities in the pre-adult stage of development. Alcott's own upbringing had been highly unconventional, and *Little Women* as an autobiographical, if somewhat sanitised, text is based upon its author's own childhood experience of repression and a consciousness of difference in a family that was ostensibly progressive in its social and educational practice. As the second in a family of four girls, Louisa May Alcott was continually reprimanded by her father for her failure to live up to his ideal of the pattern of feminine behaviour, and in particular to be like her sisters, especially her older sister, Anna, who was mild-mannered, docile and naturally home-loving. 'I don't care much for girls' things', she wrote pathetically in her diary in March 1846, at the age of thirteen, as she imagined her mind to be 'a room in confusion, and I was to put it in order',[19] a task at which she failed miserably.

Like her creator, Jo's inability to keep tidy exhibits itself most noticeably in her excess of physical energy, her body refusing to behave decorously, 'her long limbs . . . very much in her way' and 'a fly-away look to her clothes' (23). References to Jo's appearance characterize her resistance to conventional femininity, and the opening pages of *Little Women* portray her as a classic study in physical awkwardness, a 'colt', 'uncomfortable' with 'large hands and feet'. Jo is a character who is unwilling to acknowledge the changes that are taking place in her own body and who is reluctant to leave behind the androgynous world of childhood, where boys' games and wild energetic play are permissible pursuits for New England pre-adolescent girls. She is torn between the attractions of the female role, as represented by Marmee, and evident in her own spontaneous mothering of the sick Laurie (whose disorderly room she is able to transform with a few quick feminine touches) and her distaste for adult sexuality to which her adolescent awakenings uncomfortably alert her. She is shocked by the fact of Meg's romance with John Brooke and the physical intimacy she witnesses between them provokes in her a reaction of disgust. Similarly, despite the obvious mutual attraction between them, Jo is appalled by the suggestion that she and Laurie might become lovers.

This confusion about her own gendered identity is further illustrated in the hair-cutting episode, when she sells her long chestnut locks to a wig-maker as her contribution to the family finances. Proud of her independence and defiant about the social solecism she has committed by displaying herself with cropped hair, Jo is nonetheless deeply disturbed at the sacrifice of 'my one beauty', the symbol of her femininity. The incident is recounted in images of violence and mutilation. ' "Didn't you feel dreadful when the first cut came?" ' asks Meg, 'with a shiver', and Jo, despite her pose of indifference, is forced to confess that, ' "It almost seemed as if I'd an arm or a leg off" ' (223). Weeping in bed at night for the loss of her hair, she cannot understand the reason for her tears. The episode can be read in Freudian terms as a re-enactment of the experience of female castration. Jo's recognition of lack is commensurate with her loss of innocence and exposes her fear of initiation into adult sexuality, a fear that continues to be manifest throughout both *Little Women* and its sequel, *Good Wives*. There are also interesting auto-biographical correspondences between the character's and the author's condition of deprivation. In 1862 when she was nursing at the military hospital in Georgetown, Alcott's own hair was shorn during her attack of typhoid. The projection of the experience in such graphic detail onto her fictional persona hints at the psychological damage inflicted by such an act and the anxieties that underlie the bravado which characterizes the tomboy awkwardness of both Jo and her creator. The scene suggests too the polarization within the text between a desire for independence and a need to express femininity, an opposition that Jo negotiates with only partial success.

A reading of the diary, which Alcott was encouraged to keep by her parents as a necessary adjunct to self-scrutiny and improvement, provides some insight into the context of Jo March's creation. Early entries in the diary suggest how the difficulties Alcott confronted as a child were internalized to produce a fraught individual whose only way of coming to terms with her own psychic tensions was to redraw their boundaries through artistic means. According to Bronson Alcott's interpretation of Puritan doctrine, with which his daughter was instilled, the rigid demarcation of gender characteristics made it impossible for her desire for action to be contained within the remit of condonable female behaviour. Her wish for masculinity became an imaginative and expressive retreat and her diary, reticent in style, indicates the close correlation between psychological and linguistic control. 'I long to be a man', wrote Alcott at the outbreak of the Civil War, while in 1865 she confessed dispiritedly that, 'I was born with a boy's spirit under my bib and tucker.'[20] Both statements are private but desperate testimonies to her discomfort with the straitjacket of adult female propriety, a dictate which was at odds with the passionate energies which she could only interpret as freakish and incompatible with womanhood.

It is a masculine discourse to which Alcott reverts in order to articulate Jo March's rejection of the feminine. From the opening chapter of the book, where she vigorously asserts that ' "I like boys' games and work and manners! I can't get over my disappointment in not being a boy" ' (22) and claims the right to be ' "the man of the family now papa is away"' (24), Jo echoes Alcott's own strategies of evasion in her refusal to be formed into the mould of adulthood prepared for her. Whistling, sprawling, untidy, and full of ambitions that transcend her domestic destiny, Jo March reflects the self-assertion and the self-doubt that characterize adolescence in its search for an individual identity. Without clear examples of strong, independent women to follow, Jo, like her creator, is forced back on male role models for inspiration. As Elaine Showalter has observed, as girls, 'both Jo and Amy measure themselves continually against the most towering and unapproachable models of male genius: Shakespeare for Jo, Michelangelo for Amy.'[21] Lacking any comparable female sources of inspiration outside the home (Aunt March provides only a negative image of singleness, as a woman who has repressed her capacity for love), they turn to the male fields of action and achievement for stimulus, and in measuring themselves against inappropriate standards of excellence, become conscious only of their own inadequacy. Personal and artistic creativity in *Little Women* is thus without any appropriate female yardstick and the debate about woman's nature which Jo enacts is extended through the discussion of her artistic practice which forms a complement to her self.

The division that manifests itself in *Little Women* and in the Gothic tales of power, revenge and dark desire that Alcott wrote effortlessly for contemporary magazines is indicative of her personal experience of repression, an experience that speaks tellingly to her female audience. Both Jo's literary productions, and the roles she creates for herself in the family's amateur theatricals, suggest subversive tendencies and the need to enact fantasies of power. In the plays the children perform and in male disguise, Jo can release the aggressive impulses that would otherwise be unacceptable. In a perfect illustration of the personality split she embodies, she can cast herself as both hero and villain simultaneously, taking on adventurous and romantic parts in her home-made dramas, while her alternative persona engages in deeds of murder and violence.

The same fantasies of the forbidden are projected in her commercial literary life, where, like her progenitor, Jo writes sensational thrillers of madness, eroticism, death and despair, subjects of which she is taught to be ashamed, her very knowledge of them reprehensible because it encourages her to 'desecrate some of the womanliest attributes of a woman's character'. '"They are trash, and will soon be worse than trash if I go on; for each is more sensational than the last"', Jo is forced to acknowledge, looking at her stories in a bitter moment of self-assessment, when Professor Bhaer has shown her the error of her ways with his 'mental or moral spectacles'. '"I can't read this stuff in sober earnest without being horribly ashamed of it; and what should I do if they were seen at home?"'[22] In *Little Women*, the tension between masculine precepts of morality that determine behavioural codes, and female imaginative energy and expressive resources creates a problem for the woman artist that can only be resolved through compromise. Literary creation is Jo's only outlet for the passionate and rebellious elements in her nature, and while the writing of thrillers is seen as acceptable as a stage in adolescent development, or a genre that is appropriate for men rather than women, once Jo approaches adulthood she must cast aside such delinquent tendencies. As Marmee makes abundantly clear, the subversive impulses that Jo satisfies through her writing are incompatible with the contemporary versions of selfhood for women, where anger must be kept hidden and a silent conformism cultivated.

For, as Mrs March admits, the image of unruffled saintliness that she presents to the world is an illusion, and one acquired with the help of her husband's insistence on female self-control:

"I am angry nearly every day of my life, Jo; but I have learned not to show it; and I still hope to learn not to feel it, though it may take me another forty years to do so." (118)

The model that Jo March yearns to emulate is thus closer to her own nature than she at first realizes, and as a source of inspiration consequently more powerful. In Jo's ultimate union with Professor Bhaer she, like her mother, exchanges her father's moral instruction for that of her husband, unable to function independently in a patriarchal world without the guidance of a male authority figure.

Little Women then maintains an uneasy equilibrium between the fantasies of rebellion it dramatizes and the moral message it claims to promote. Whilst on the one hand it endorses Jo March's defiance of the womanly, and invites support for a reinterpretation of women's roles generally, it also reinscribes the traditional myths of femininity in its valuation of the ideals erected by the patriarchal order: motherhood, marriage and the values of home. The uneasiness which exists between Alcott's own deeply felt feminism and the conventional models of family which the text promotes thus reflects the contemporary political and cultural debates of mid-century American society. The progressive theories about women's nature and the move towards political emancipation contend with economic requirements which rely on the maintenance of a strict sexual division of labour, the production of children and the consequent centrality of the domestic role for women.

In the March household which acts as the magnetic power centre of *Little Women* the concept of womanliness is explored in ways which only serve to perpetuate the ambivalence that marks the novel as a whole. The home, with Marmee as its symbolic centre, functions as a matriarchy within the overriding patriarchal system. As such it facilitates an examination of female strength and the mutual support network that women are seen to construct but without finally allowing that strength any political influence. During the first part of the narrative Mr March is conveniently absent from home, his shadowy but prevailing presence making its impact through the medium of his letters and through the moral legacy he has left behind which continues to direct the women's behaviour. Even after his return, he remains a vague figure, officiating at Meg's wedding and providing fatherly advice when necessary, but barely registering as a character on the reader's sensibilities.

By removing Mr March as a major focus of interest from *Little Women*, the novel limits the possibilities of marital discord and parental tyranny in its analysis of the power structures of family life. Any acknowledgement of the existence of potential tensions between husband and wife is reserved for the depiction of Meg's marriage to John Brooke where it can be presented as suitably educative. As well as underplaying family difficulties that its author found particularly painful to confront, the novel develops a strategy which left Alcott free to focus her domestic history on mother/daughter relationships and on the interactions of sisters, relationships which had more positive significance for her than the failures in marital harmony to which she had personally been witness. As Nina Auerbach has argued,[23] Mr March's removal from the main action of *Little Women* results in a celebration of the primacy of the female family and in turn this foregrounds the special qualities of womanhood which male outsiders, such as Laurie and Professor Bhaer covet. The women's close knit and self-sufficient society is presented as culturally and psychologically necessary both for the girls whose identity it shapes and for the men for whom it provides the elements that are missing in their otherwise sterile lives. Laurie, the isolated boy next door, gazing wistfully through the window at the illuminated tableau of women, in what Auerbach has pointed to as a reverse of the fictive norm, can only long for entry into the privileged feminine world, with its symbolic referents of flowers, light and fire, the magic circle of women representing the family support network which he has been denied. Similarly Jo, despite her impulses towards independent action and the freedom of masculine role-play, finds solace and sustenance through her identification with Marmee as mother figure, the prime source of nurturing and psychological protection.

To some extent the debate about female values which *Little*

Women enacts reiterates the Victorian intellectual dilemma of 'the woman question', the quandary as to whether women were capable of functioning independently, equal to and competing with men, or whether their strengths were something other, a natural complement to masculine qualities. In *Little Women,* Jo and Marmee posit two extremes of the ideological spectrum, through Jo's self-assertiveness and her transgression of gender boundaries, and through Marmee's undeviating adherence to the iconization of womanhood. Ultimately, because Jo is in a transitional stage of development and irresistibly bound by the psychological ties of family (and because Alcott was sensitive to the responsibilities of her position as children's author and driven by the need to find success in the market place), she does conform to Marmee's strictures, but not before her challenge to that behavioural model has been made the imaginative heart of the novel. At the same time, the identification between mother and daughter is emphasized so as to highlight the inner conflicts surrounding female development in a society which harboured profound contradictions in its teachings. Marmee's confession to Jo of her own feelings of rage and her efforts at self-control bring the two women together, and Jo's aspirations for self-assertion are tempered by her wish to emulate the role model her mother provides her with. Jo's confusion has its source in this psychic split between 'masculine' and 'feminine' norms, a split that her mother too has experienced in a revealing insight into generational patterning. The two warring impulses, between the aggressive independent self and the mothering instinct, are perceived as irreconcilable in the contemporary culture that Alcott depicts. Marmee's role and Jo's eventual decision to adopt a version of it is, however, at one level fully satisfying, for it allows Jo to remain in the childish state she does not want to relinquish, finding approval by being seen to adhere to her parents' criteria.

As in a number of more conventional texts of the period, motherhood remains a sanctified institution in *Little Women* and the values of family that Alcott presents as irresistible ultimately reinforce the return to the conservative model as propounded by Bronson Alcott and which in its denial of women's individuality informed his daughter's upbringing. Recent feminist psychoanalytic theory, in its deconstruction of Freudian models of infant development, has emphasized the centrality of the mother both in psychological and in cultural terms. As Ann B. Murphy has argued, the mother is seen:

not as scapegoat or saviour, but as the primary, if inadvertent, enforcer of patriarchal values as well as their victim, and thus as fulcrum of the private and public. . . . The institution of motherhood in a patriarchal culture achieves not only the reproduction of mothering but the perpetuation of patriarchy.[24]

Aware of the importance of women's work within the home and the essential psychological framework that the family creates, Alcott's investigation of female identity formation and family structures in *Little Women* can find no practical solution to Jo's problem in the prevailing ideological and literary climate.

In its concentration on women's culture and its values, *Little Women* stresses the significance of sisterhood and female bonding in a male world that is cold, commercially oriented and ignorant of female value systems. An example of an unmediated patriarchy is to be found in the Laurence household with its luxurious environment and its prioritization of individual achievement, a household which is inhabited by men who are unable to communicate their deepest feelings to one another. Old Mr Laurence, after the death of his daughter, retreats into himself and becomes a crabby, quick-tempered old man, while his grandson, Laurie is, at the beginning of *Little Women*, an emotionally repressed adolescent, hungry for tenderness and expressions of love. In contrast, the relationships between the sisters, although not without occasional disagreements and jealousies, are intimate and mutually supportive. Through Marmee's inspirational presence, the March women are seen to have a transforming effect on the lifeless palace of the Laurences, constructing a sleeping beauty myth in reverse as they reinvigorate the dormant male emotional territory.

In contrast to the isolated male establishment next door, the female community, materially poor but spiritually wealthy, is grounded on principles of sharing, mutual support, self-sacrifice and generosity. The first actions in which the little women engage are those of self-denial and communal charity, banishing thoughts of personal Christmas presents, preparing the parlour to welcome Marmee home from work, and, on Christmas morning, giving up their breakfast to help a poor family in need. The sisters' interdependence is constantly emphasized, and the dangers of uncaring individualism are made apparent in the episode where the girls are too absorbed in their own activities to notice Beth's plea for help in visiting the suffering Hummel family. Their indifference results in

Beth's attack of scarlet fever, which is caught from the Hummels, and which proves almost fatal (an incident which also suggests Alcott's acquiescence in contemporary literary forces and their moral lessons). From Laurie's perspective, the March sisters continually form a composite, symbolic portrait of womanhood, a work of art in which each girl takes her place in the collective illustration of femininity: whether they be gathered around the parlour fire, or setting out on a picnic, each girl has her allocated task. The sisters' individual identities are thus succoured by the communal experience, which they carry with them to the male world of rationalism and paternal authority, a world which, apart from Beth, they must learn to negotiate to their advantage.

In what could be interpreted as a return to a dangerously essentialist view of gender, *Little Women* ascribes domestic skills to women only: even Jo can exercise a positive feminizing influence on Laurie, and, later, on Professor Bhaer, tidying Laurie's sickroom and helping Professor Bhaer sew on buttons and darn socks, tasks at which he proves to be incompetent. Despite the fantasies of independence that the novel licenses, self-assertion ultimately cannot prosper. The disasters of Jo's dinner party where the oven won't light, the bread burns and she serves strawberries with salt instead of sugar form a salutary lesson on the organizational and cooperative skills necessary for a smooth domestic life. The promise of an autonomous childhood world which *Little Women* offers its readers is an illusion which fails to materialize in the practical domestic environment in which girls are inevitably positioned. Marmee in *Little Women* consequently becomes a model of practical as well as symbolic maternity, capable in the domestic sphere, charitable in her deeds outside the home, the repository of wisdom and tact. In the examination of the development of female identity which the novel conducts, Marmee is invested with the primary twin functions of psychological prop and cultural role model for her daughters. Perfect because she has contained and controlled her impulse for autonomous life, she is thus created as the emblematic centre of the multi-dimensional metaphor of home.

In contrast to this dramatization of female strength, Alcott's men form a revealing, if separate, study in gender relations. Neither in *Little Women* nor in her other domestic fictions does Alcott portray men as virile or exhibiting traditional attributes of masculinity. Their power is either economic, as in the character of Mr Laurence, or moral, as in the conception of Mr March and Professor Bhaer. Even

Laurie, the most dynamic male figure in *Little Women* and the potential romantic lead, is described from Jo's perspective as atypically masculine. Indeed he is compared with Jo herself, an indeterminately gendered figure:

> "curly hair; brown skin; big, black eyes; handsome nose, fine teeth, small hands and feet; taller than I am, very polite for a boy." (54)

His features effectively combine the exotic and the delicate. As Madeleine Stern has pointed out, this description itself is a modification of the original version of the manuscript where Laurie is not 'taller than' but the same height as Jo and suggestions of his effeminacy are more pronounced.[25] And although, as a boy, Laurie can get into scrapes and display a natural physical athleticism, this is always tempered by a sensitivity and a yearning to be loved as he seeks the girls' company. In what most readers find a disappointingly inadequate alternative to Laurie's vitality and charm, Professor Bhaer, Jo's ultimate lover and husband, lacks any suggestion of sexual dynamism. A deliberately anti-heroic character, he is introduced through a series of negative characteristics, being 'neither rich nor great, young nor handsome, in no way what is called fascinating, imposing or brilliant.'[26] His redeeming personality traits are benevolence, wisdom and an unerring moral sensibility, all qualities which Jo can respect intellectually, but, more significantly, which can provide her with a moral touchstone in her own dealings. Her difficulties in coming to terms with her sexual identity are resolved in fictional terms as Professor Bhaer becomes a father-substitute for a woman whose reluctance to mature can it seems only be satisfied through alliance with a paternal surrogate.

Little Women forms a fascinating study of gender politics in a society which established strict guidelines for women's roles in the domestic sphere. Although the novel formally accedes to these conventional guidelines, for reasons that are complex both professionally and personally on Alcott's part, it also projects a profound mistrust of the principles and practices that confined women to roles of wives and mothers and that led to the apotheosis of femininity as a cultural icon. Through the story of Jo March and her fraught adolescence, Alcott suggests the complexities that underlie essentialist concepts of definitive gendered identity, and the consequent difficulties which girls experienced in their attempt to conform to clear-cut behavioural models. In addition, the admitted autobiographical correspondences between Jo and Alcott reflect the discordance of the woman artist with her society and the pressures on her to conform to public requirements in her choice of genre and subject matter. Jo's move from sensational to realistic fiction does not merely replicate Alcott's own career change. It also has important implications for thinking about *Little Women* as a response to the demands from a male publisher for books for girls which perpetuate the prevailing ideology that would continue to dictate their artistic and behavioural limits.

Notes

1. Elaine Showalter, *Sister's Choice: Tradition and Change in American Women's Writing*, (Oxford: Clarendon Press, 1989), p.42.
2. Quoted in Ann B. Murphy, 'The Borders of Ethical, Erotic and Artistic Possibilities in *Little Women*', *Signs: Journal of Women in Culture and Society*, vol. 14 (3), Spring 1990, p.564.
3. Catherine R. Stimpson, 'Reading for Love: Canons, Paracanons and Whistling Jo March', *New Literary History*, 21, 1990, p.958.
4. Stimpson, p.967.
5. Reported in *The Guardian*, 7 January 1993.
6. Stimpson, p.970.
7. Murphy, p.564.
8. Louisa May Alcott, *Life, Letters and Journals*, ed. Ednah D. Cheyney (London: Sampson, Low, Marston; Searle & Rivington, 1889).
9. Ruth K. MacDonald, *Louisa May Alcott* (Boston: Twayne, 1983), p.15.
10. Cheyney, p.199.
11. Louisa May Alcott, *Little Women* (London: Puffin Books, 1953), p.231. All subsequent references are to this edition and will be included in the text.
12. Louisa May Alcott, *Good Wives*, (London and Glasgow: Blackie, n.d.), p.136.
13. Stimpson, p.967.
14. *Life, Letters and Journals*, p.201.
15. Ibid., p.202.
16. Anne Scott McLeod, 'The Caddie Woodlawn Syndrome: American Girlhood in the Nineteenth Century', *A Century of Childhood 1820–1920*, ed. Mary Lynn Steven Heininger, (Rochester, NY: Margaret Woodbury Strong Museum, 1984), pp.98–119.
17. McLeod, p.104.
18. See particularly Sarah Elbert, *A Hunger for Home: Louisa May Alcott's Place in American Culture* (New York: Rutgers University Press, 1987) for a full discussion of this issue.
19. *Life, Letters and Journals*, p.48.
20. Ibid., p.127.

21.   Showalter, op.cit., p.58.
22.   *Good Wives*, p.136.
23.   Nina Auerbach, *Communities of Women: An Idea in Fiction* (Cambridge, Mass: Harvard University Press, 1978).
24.   Murphy, p.574.
25.   Madeleine B. Stern, *Louisa May Alcott* (University of Oklahoma Press, 1971), quoted in Showalter, p.56.
26.   *Good Wives*, p.137.

5

Susan Coolidge:
What Katy Did

If Louisa May Alcott can be credited with pioneering the American family story, Susan Coolidge may certainly be counted as another important early contributor to the genre of domestic narrative. *What Katy Did* (1872), the first of her five family sagas which she wrote between 1872 and 1886, has much in common with *Little Women* and the later chronicles of the March family. Essentially episodic in structure, it depicts the everyday activities of the six Carr children – their games, their schooling, their interaction with friends and relatives; even the climactic event of the novel, Katy's fall from the swing and subsequent injury, is placed in a domestic setting. The narrative gives considerable attention to what the children do when they are alone. As with *Little Women*, where although Mrs March is a constant influence she is not actually present for much of the time, the originality and appeal of Coolidge's work lies in its exploration of juvenile behaviour isolated from direct contact with adults. Unlike Susan Warner, or even Charlotte Yonge, in whose The *Daisy Chain* (1856) the young Mays interact largely within an adult context, both Alcott and Coolidge write to a considerable extent from a child or adolescent-centred perspective, creating the illusion of a free world of youthful experience, albeit a temporary one. Coolidge's characters, indeed, are children in a way that Alcott's are not: whereas the reader is constantly reminded that the March girls are incipient 'little women', in *What Katy Did*, at least in the earlier part, the Carrs are able to disregard the world of adult closures towards which they are moving. Though both novels, too, share a simplicity of outline, concentrating on a relatively narrow range of characters within a restricted environment, Coolidge's more unsophisticated language – as illustrated in the already-discussed opening paragraph – confirms the impression that this is more unequivocally than its predecessor a work for a juvenile audience.

To categorize *What Katy Did* thus is not, however, to suggest that it has no wider significance or relevance to the cultural ideologies

of its time. Like all the texts treated in this study, it both replicates
and questions prevailing social and gender role-models. In connection with this it can also be linked with *Little Women* in that the
representation of family structure prioritizes female behaviour.
Although there are two boys among the Carrs, their parts are minor
compared with those of the girls (and, as will be shown, the narrative presents some interesting gender reversals), and as *Little
Women* does with Jo, the novel places greatest emphasis on Katy
herself, the exuberant scapegrace who finds the womanly ideal so
troubling. The centrality of the heroine and her disturbed sense of
gendered identity highlights each novel's concern with femininity,
both as a cultural construct and as a socio-psychological state towards which every female adolescent must inevitably progress. As
stories for girls, these novels then are not just entertaining narratives
but are also explorations of gendered social and spiritual development, inviting reader identification with the main characters and
the dilemmas and trials they experience.

In its mode of behavioural exploration, *What Katy Did* follows a
pattern already laid down by girls' fiction in America and England
in the mid-nineteenth century. Like *The Wide, Wide World* (1850), *The
Daisy Chain* (1856) and *Little Women* (1868), it is built on the framework of a moral pilgrimage. Depicting the passage through trial
and endurance to the goal of perfected selfhood, it feminizes and
domesticates the models of Bunyan's *Pilgrim's Progress* and the
Bildungsroman, combining the former's ethical preoccupations with
the latter's concentration on the achievement of personal maturity
in a way that has particular relevance to a young female readership.
Its narrative structure enacts a progression towards an ideal of female
conduct, according to which the achievement of happiness and self-
satisfaction is dependent not upon material or intellectual success
but upon self-discipline and the learning of a moral code through
suffering and the example of others. This, as Nina Baym has pointed
out, is a basic plot of much popular women's fiction in America in
this period – including Harriet Beecher Stowe's *Uncle Tom's Cabin*
(1852), Maria Cummins's *The Lamplighter* (1854), and Augusta Evans
Wilson's *St Elmo* (1866), to name but a few – and provides an important source of the typology of feminine characteristics and ideals of
the time.[1]

Within this essentially didactic structure, however, *What Katy Did*,
like many of its predecessors, simultaneously upholds and challenges
contemporary ideals, questioning rigid stereotypes of gendered

behaviour, and thus reflecting the gradual shifts in attitudes towards female roles which occurred from mid-century onwards. Even while implementing an apparently definitive and ideologically orthodox narrative closure, it offers a revisionist view of certain aspects of female conduct and assumptions about femininity.

It also encapsulates an openness towards female experience, in common with many nineteenth-century American girls' novels. As has already been noted in the introduction to this study, American juvenile texts tend to allow their heroines a considerable degree of freedom, certainly in a social and physical sense. Even Warner's Ellen Montgomery, morally constrained by the religious imperatives which rule her spiritual life, roams the countryside alone and mixes socially in a way that would be impossible for Charlotte Yonge's or Elizabeth Sewell's heroines. Katy's girlhood is similarly unrestricted, and she too enjoys an ethos in which the exercise of female energies is not necessarily viewed with abhorrence or wholly stultified by proprieties. Indeed it is because of this that her 'punishment' in being immobilized for four years is so harsh and traumatic. When Margaret May in *The Daisy Chain* is likewise immobilized (and through no fault of her own), she accepts her lot patiently and without question; the American Katy, however, suffers from a far deeper sense of frustration at the curtailment of her free movement.

Another important element of the work which links it to its contemporaries is the closeness of its author/subject relationship. Like so many nineteenth-century women writers for children, Coolidge relies heavily on autobiographical material, reproducing in all her books about the Carr family details drawn from her own background and experiences. Yet, ironically enough, she seems to have been unwilling openly to acknowledge this identification. Following a female literary convention of the time – also adopted by Susan Warner – she took refuge under an assumed name. Born Sarah Chauncey Woolsey, she purportedly took on the pen-name Susan Coolidge for her first published work in joking emulation of her younger sister, Jane, who had already written fiction under the pseudonym of Margaret Coolidge. One biographical source quotes her as saying, 'I will be a sister of the famous Margaret Coolidge.'[2] The reason for this strategy is not obvious. Reference has already been made to the low status of children's writers at this time, and it could have been that Coolidge did not wish to be publicly associated with an unprestigious area of literary activity. She came from a distinguished New England family with notable academic connections: earlier Woolseys included Jonathan Edwards and Theodore Dwight; her uncle, Theodore Dwight Woolsey, was president of Yale; and one of her cousins became dean of the Yale Law School. In the company of such intellectual eminence, she possibly felt that juvenile writing was best offered via a fictional identity. It is certainly significant that her other, more 'serious' works – volumes of poetry, editions of *The Autobiography and Correspondence of Mrs Delany* (1879), *The Diary and Letters of Frances Burney, Madame D'Arblay* (1880), and *The Letters of Jane Austen* (1892), and a book of historical sketches, *An Old Convent School* (1895) – were issued under her own name.

After the success of her first literary effort, a series of stories written for a little boy, called *The New Year's Bargain* (1871) (praised by English writers for children such as Jean Ingelow and Christina Rossetti), it was clearly in Coolidge's interests to stay with her persona, but her unease about contemporary literary evaluations may have continued. Though she wrote many more children's books, in late middle age she claimed to feel quite distanced from her earlier juvenile fiction, writing to a (male) literary admirer:

> I am glad you liked Katy as a boy and like it still. I reread the story for the first time in years . . . and found it unexpectedly interesting. It is odd how one can come freshly to one's own books after a long interval and judge them somewhat as a stranger might.[3]

Indeed, if anonymity as an autobiographical children's writer was Coolidge's aim, she seems to have succeeded. Despite the popularity of the *Katy* series, especially among English readers (the books remain standard items in the Puffin classic list), there is little available critical material on Coolidge's work. There are no biographical studies except an article (a shortened version of a lecture) by Frances Darling in the *Horn Book Magazine* in 1959; nor has her work been taken up by recent feminist criticism as is the case with Warner and Alcott. It also seems that today, particularly in the United States, the *Katy* books are far less widely known than Alcott's or Montgomery's novels. Yet, as has already been suggested, her work has much in common with theirs in its adaptation of the popular sentimental and domestic tradition for young readers and in its depiction of American girlhood, and it deserves equal recognition and critical attention.

The available biographical information makes clear the close parallels between life and art which Coolidge was apparently anxious to conceal. The large rambling house and garden, the localized neighbourhood, and the school are all drawn from her early years in the outskirts of Cleveland, where she lived from her birth in 1835 to 1855. The Carr children are the four daughters and one son of the Woolsey family, plus an adopted boy cousin who lived with them; as in *Little Women*, the characteristics and appearance of each real-life child are reproduced in the fiction, with Sarah as Katy, the untamed eldest girl. These autobiographical elements continue in Coolidge's later novels. In *What Katy Did at School* (1873), the account of boarding-school life which forms its narrative centre replicates the time that Sarah and her younger sister, Jane, spent at the Select Family School for Young Ladies in Hanover, New Hampshire; the mischievous Rose Red is a composite portrait of two of Sarah's schoolfellows. And *What Katy Did Next* (1886) is little more than a thinly-disguised rehearsal of the two years which the Woolsey sisters and their mother spent in Europe between 1870 and 1872, after their father's death. Coolidge's biographer suggests that all the stories about the Carr family are 'a mixture of truth about the Woolsey children and fiction so well blended that it was never quite possible even for Susan herself to separate the one from the other.'[4] Whether or not this was the case, the reliance on personal details certainly suggests that, at thirty-five, Coolidge started to look back on her own experiences and reassess them in the light of her maturer reflections.

Taking its narrative impetus from the basis of personal experience, *What Katy Did* restructures autobiographical material within an archetypal didactic framework: the volatile and wayward heroine badly injures herself as a result of disobedience, and is restored to physical and moral health only after a long period of penitential suffering. On one level, this constitutes the novel's central theme, the validation of an overriding vision which reinforces ethical and social orthodoxies. The story literally reproduces the traditional Christian patterning of fall after sin, succeeded by a gradual painful rise to a transformed selfhood. This enacts the conversion theme, a consistent feature of nineteenth-century children's stories of an evangelical cast, which, despite their uncompromisingly stern didacticism, remained so popular (Katy's younger brother, Dorry, for instance, wants Maria Edgeworth's *Harry and Lucy* for Christmas). There seems, moreover, nothing self-parodic about Coolidge's use of the device here: Katy's accident on the swing, the result of wilfulness, lays her low spiritually as well as physically, eventually enabling her to achieve a more purified womanhood and to act out the roles which that state demands.

This central didactic formulation is not dislocated from the novel as a whole. Katy's fall is anticipated in accordance with the narration's realistic mode: her recklessness and defiance of authority have already been demonstrated in the book's preceding chapters, and it is therefore not unlikely that eventually she will have to pay a heavy price for her shortcomings. More importantly, the novel's engagement with moral concerns is foregrounded, albeit not overobtrusively, from the beginning. An interpretative narrative voice evaluatively contextualizes the children's behaviour, thus establishing the work's ethical orientation. In the first chapter, for instance, the reader is told that Katy 'was a dear, loving child, for all her careless habits, and made bushels of good resolutions every week of her life, only unluckily she never kept any of them.'[5] Her traumatic progression towards moral improvement is also foreshadowed: of her plans to be as good as an angel, the narrator remarks, 'A great deal was to happen to Katy before that time came' (9). This evaluative function is sometimes accorded Dr Carr who reprimands Katy after her 'scrapes' and reminds her that major disasters are often caused by only a little thing – ' "for the want of a nail the shoe was lost" ' (35) – a reminder that he repeats after her accident, this time telling her that the small horseshoe nail is 'Obedience' (132).

The novel's moral figuration also depends on the use of role models, characters whose function is to suggest admirable or undesirable modes of conduct. Most important here are the female protagonists – indeed, Dr Carr is the only adult male in the story, apart from a few extremely minor characters. These models can be divided roughly into two groups, those to be emulated and those to be rejected, although they are not entirely distinct. Of the first, the clearest examples are the dead Mrs Carr and Cousin Helen.

Mrs Carr introduces into the novel a familiar type in nineteenth-century sentimental fiction, the mother who although physically absent (usually through death) continues to exert a powerful influence for good on her family. In Harriet Beecher Stowe's *Uncle Tom's Cabin* (1852), for example, St Clare has a redemptive vision of his mother on his death-bed, and even the vicious Legree is temporarily halted in his atrocities by the recall of maternal love.

The maternal orientation of almost all the texts discussed in this study is notable: Ellen Montgomery's mother all-encompassingly effects her daughter's early spiritual development; Mrs March acts as constant guide and confidante to her four girls; the dead Mrs May continues to function as a point of reference for the large family she has left behind; Mother in *The Railway Children* is her children's central support throughout adversity; and the dead Mrs Craven is the spiritual force that animates the secret garden. For the young Carrs, their mother is now only a memory and 'a sad, sweet name, spoken on Sunday, and at prayer time' (2). This ritualistic invocation of the Mother carries obvious Christian associations, and, in the religious ethical framework of the novel, reference to her can produce important changes in behaviour. After Katy's defiant initiation of the forbidden hide-and-seek game, Dr Carr reminds her 'of the time when her mamma died, and of how she said, "Katy must be a mamma to the little ones, when she grows up"' (51), drawing her inescapably into the adult female world through the matriarchal role. After her accident, Katy herself recalls her mother's request that she take care of the younger children. And significantly, she first walks downstairs again on her mother's birthday. Mrs Carr, like the other mothers mentioned above, contributes to the book's participation in what Ann Douglas has called the feminization of American culture in this period,[6] embodying an ideology of womanhood which prioritizes service and self-forgetfulness. At the same time, however, she represents female power, a pervasive influence in a predominantly woman-centred environment.

Cousin Helen has a similar role and one that is perhaps more provocative for the feminist critic. She is another archetypal fictional figure of the period, the sofa invalid who becomes an icon of gendered moral excellence. In almost constant pain, she serves not only as a specific mentor to Katy but as a model of true womanhood, imaged in terms of a persistent iconography in mid-nineteenth century literature. Most notably formulated in Coventry Patmore's epic poem of married bliss, *The Angel in the House* (1855–6), the figure of woman-as-angel sanctifies the female virtues of self-abnegation and redemptive power. This figure appears as the blessed relative or friend who advises and comforts the erring or suffering, operative in texts as diverse as Sewell's *Amy Herbert* (1844), Dicken's *David Copperfield* (1850), and George Eliot's *Adam Bede* (1859). In *What Katy Did*, the ideology is confirmed by patriarchal approval. As Dr Carr tells his eldest daughter:

"Cousin Helen is half an angel already, and loves other people better than herself. I'm very glad she could come here for once. She's an example to us all, Katy, and I couldn't ask anything better than to have my little girls take pattern after her." (106)

Helen, like her namesake Helen Burns in *Jane Eyre*, teaches lessons of resignation and self-forgetfulness, giving meaning to Katy's own entry into the female world of passivity and helplessness by instructing her in the concept of God's School of Pain ' "where He teaches all sorts of beautiful things to people" ' (137). She also influences Katy through her own shining example, showing her that suffering will enable her, too, to act as guide and mentor to others. Helen does not accord with the literary images of saintly heroinism which the children have imbibed from their reading. (Katy, for instance, in anticipation of Helen's visit, imagines that she will be like a character out of Elizabeth Sewell's highly moralistic and somewhat maudlin *Amy Herbert* and for all the Carrs 'there was a sort of mixture of Sunday-school book in their idea of her' [94]). In fact Helen turns out to be fun-loving and full of entertaining ideas, is not obviously saintly, and thinks it is not inconsistent with illness to enjoy pretty things.

Cousin Helen nevertheless embodies the self-abnegation central to contemporary ideologies of womanhood. Herself denied participation in married life because of a crippling accident, she has nobly relinquished her fiancé to another woman and now has a vicarious existence, watching the domestic joys of the couple who are her 'dearest friends' (106) and who have named their daughter after her. This apparently willing renunciation of sexual fulfilment has fascinating implications. Helen seems to accept her lot without repining – when Dr Carr asks after her ex-fiancé, she replies 'with one of her brightest looks' (104). But her inability to engage in the normal activities of her own sex symbolizes the suppression of desire inherent in the 'angel' image. The polarization of woman into angel or demon in nineteenth-century art and literature, discussed in an excellent study by Nina Auerbach,[8] has obvious relevance here. Helen's effectiveness as a mentor is predicated on the negation of threatening and morally disruptive female physicality. As with those other angelic figures, Beth March and Helen Burns, it seems that ideal femininity cannot combine the spiritual and the corporeal. In Helen's case, the difference is that she has actually moved beyond adolescence and into full potential sexuality. Such an ideology of femininity, though spiritually exemplary, nevertheless is not the pattern for all women, and the text does not prioritize the kind of excellence which Cousin Helen represents. Katy's pre-adolescent physical curtailment may be suggestive of arrested sexual development, but eventually she is allowed re-entry into the world of physical normality and, it is implied, she will not be fated to live life permanently at such a remove.

Set against these angelic mentors are those women who function as anti-models. Each represents a different type: the spinster, the sentimental heroine, and the browbeaten wife. The first type is figured in Aunt Izzie and Miss Pettingill; the former, as already indicated, is well-intentioned and kind at heart, but cannot understand or sympathize with nonconformity; the latter is endearingly eccentric, but, living in a familial past and linked to the outside world only through her role as community seamstress, has allowed herself to become a parody of self-obsessed singleness. Imogen Clark, at the other extreme, is the self-creation of her own febrile imagination, acting out, like Maria Edgeworth's Angelina, the fantasies which she has imbibed from romantic literature. A 'naturally' bright girl who has 'read so many novels that her brain was completely turned' (81), she fascinates Katy who regards her as a beautiful being from another planet. When Imogen arrives to spend the day with the Carrs, dressed in incongruously glamorous but shabby clothes, Katy comments delightedly, ' "Oh, Imogen, you look just like a young lady in a story!' " (82). That is indeed how Imogen sees herself, as is clear from her rehearsal of her romantic adventures to the enthralled children in the darkened parlour:

> "Oh, it was lovely, girls, perfectly delicious! I suppose I did look well, for I was all in white, with my hair let down, and just one rose, you know, here on top. And he leaned over me, and said in a low, deep tone, 'Lady, I am a Brigand, but I feel the enchanting power of beauty. You are free!' " (86)

The didactic force of the humour here is directed as much at Katy as at Imogen. If the latter's reading has produced an absurd self-image, the former's more dangerously has encouraged the construction of a wholly unrealistic feminine ideal. Imogen temporarily carries Katy with her into this glamorous world, but her absurd posturing and self-centredness are eventually seen in their true light. Masculine wisdom proves right: Dr Carr's prediction that ' "two or

three years hence she won't seem so nice to you as she does now" '
(89) is borne out when Imogen reappears during Katy's convales-
cence, as vulgar and self-dramatizing as ever and quite unconcerned
about her friend's health. In its demolition of sentimental stereotypes, the text not only shatters romantic distortions of womanhood
but also insists that the imagination must be contained within clear
boundaries. As her father tells Katy, ' "Make-ups are all very well
. . . as long as people don't try to make you believe they are true" '
(89). As for Montgomery's Anne Shirley, Katy's education includes
the lesson that fantasy must be tempered by contact with the real.

Katy's encounter with the last type of woman also illustrates how
her imagination constructs people according to the models of literary
romance. In this instance, however, the novel's reductive methodology is directed by a far more humanitarian concern. Mrs Spenser
is one of Katy's previous 'intimate friends' (69), one who appears
only referentially in the text and who is not herself the object of
irony. She is a source of romantic mystery for the whole neighbourhood, a reputed invalid whose husband, 'a handsome, rather
bad-looking man' (76), is frequently absent from home. When Katy,
fascinated by the 'romance of the closed door and the lady whom
nobody saw' (76) boldly enters the house, instead of a dramatic
victim figure she finds a frail, sick woman, neglected and in disarray.
As the girl's curiosity gives way to a more genuine desire to help
the poor creature, so Mrs Spenser herself becomes less the focus of
literary subversion and more the means of social comment. Her
suffering symbolizes womanhood oppressed by patriarchal tyranny.
Eventually Mr Spenser, who, it is discovered, is a forger on the run
from the police, returns and carries off his wife to some unknown
destination. Though Katy is too young to understand the social and
sexual implications of all of this, Mrs Spenser is a reminder of how
women may be annihilated in marriage. She functions as a warning
of what the alternative to a single existence may really be like; if
Helen's vicarious sexual fulfilment seems psychologically suspect,
Mrs Spenser's helplessness and total abandonment to her husband's
will seems considerably worse.

The intertextuality which suffuses *What Katy Did* also functions
as a means of indirect didacticism. The books which the Carr children
read or mention give some indication of the popular and influential
literature of the time, and foreground – though not uncritically –
value-systems which operate in the novel. All the texts mentioned
have in common some element of moral purpose, encouraging their

readers to learn from the behavioural models which they depict. Though the good little heroine of Maria Edgeworth's *Harry and Lucy* – which Dorry requests for Christmas – is distinctly *not* the fictional prototype of Cousin Helen, the ethical imperatives of obedience and reasonableness promoted in Edgeworth's tales for the young are valorized in Coolidge's work. Similarly, Katy's pleasure in Warner's *The Wide, Wide World* and Sewell's *Amy Herbert* may be dismissed as the sentimental taste of an adolescent girl, but the books' emphases on female long-suffering and self-abnegation, as well as their portrayal of the close relationship between a pious, ailing mother and her daughter, clearly have an intertextual referentiality whose moral significance contemporary readers would be expected to pick up. Also of significance is Cousin Helen's gift to Cecy – Charlotte Yonge's *A Book of Golden Deeds* (1864), a work which foregrounds children's heroism in terms of Christian ideals, especially self-sacrifice. Literature is never a substitute for life in *What Katy Did*, but some of the lessons it teaches are prioritized in the novel's moral framework, even if these have to be adapted to the more robust world the family inhabits.

The focal point of *What Katy Did* is of course the heroine's fall and subsequent rise, in terms both of its centrality as a moral signifier and its meaning for feminist criticism today. As has already been argued, the narrative structure itself creates the textual 'message'. Katy sins, is punished, and achieves full recovery and redemption only after much suffering and painful self-examination. The simple moral framework which surrounds this act of disobedience is, however, more complex in terms of an exploration of gendered codification than it first appears. Of what sin is Katy really guilty? Her disobedience in using the broken swing is an act of defiance against authority. Although the narrator does suggest that it would have been more reasonable of Aunt Izzie to have explained to Katy why the swing was forbidden territory, the implication is that adult authority must be respected unquestioningly. It is thus a moral transgression which must be atoned for. But her punishment seems disproportionately harsh in purely ethical terms. Though her changed behaviour indicates Katy's spiritual transformation (she becomes more tolerant and understanding of others, sympathizing with Elsie and tolerating Dorry's well-intentioned ineptitude), nearly four years of pain-ridden immobility is a high price to pay for a moment of ill-tempered rebelliousness.

Katy is, however, also guilty of transgressing gender codes, and it is this subtextual didacticism which is more troubling for a modern reader. Her exuberant energy and impetuousness defy her society's standards of true womanliness. So while in the earlier part of the book her disruptions of gender ideologies remain relatively free of narrative control, they cannot be allowed to predominate or seriously to challenge sexual orthodoxies. The potential iconoclasm of Katy's disobedience is figured in the description of her short-lived but exhilarating ride on the banned swing:

> Now she was at the top of the high arched door. Then she could almost touch the cross-beam above it, and through the small square window could see pigeons sitting and pluming themselves on the eaves of the barn, and white clouds blowing over the blue sky. She had never swung so high before. It was like flying, she thought, as she bent and curved more strongly in the seat, trying to send herself yet higher, and graze the roof with her toes. (119–20)

The articulation of power and control, the enactment of the strong upward movement of the swing, and the metaphor of flying, reminiscent of Hélène Cixous' notion of anarchic feminine *jouissance*, all voice an energy and aspiration which challenge narrow boundaries of female expression. Like Edna Pontelier's triumphant achievement of swimming skills, in Kate Chopin's *The Awakening* (1899), Katy's daring threatens the status quo. Also as with Edna, the subliminal sexual liberation of the act is an important element in the physical achievement as Katy goes beyond the boundaries of acceptability. Her offence, then, is cultural as well as moral, and order must be restored on both counts. Significantly her punishment involves bodily repression. Paralysed below the waist for the four years of her adolescent development, Katy symbolizes female entrapment, confined to her room, imprisoned within her own body, to emerge as a subdued adult. Suitably chastised, she thus finally fulfils her mother's dying request, herself becoming a mother figure, humbled and fully effective within the domestic sphere.

It would be wrong, however, to see this apparent crushing of female self-expression as the novel's sole and final statement. The narrative conclusion certainly enacts an ideological conformity which seems to close off possibilities for more radical readings of the text. It may also seem inappropriate to consider *What Katy Did*, in the terminology of Gilbert and Gubar, as a palimpsestic work, whose overt message conceals a more radical subtext.[9] But as Susan K. Harris has suggested with reference to many of the mid-century sentimental/domestic novels, it may be necessary to 'read beyond the ending', as contemporary readers themselves did. In other words, the closure does not have absolute meaning, isolated from the rest of the book, but derives significance retrospectively in the context of those signifiers which have preceded it and with which it contrasts or conflicts. Harris's proposal that such novels may have functioned as a means of testing possible alternative modes of womanhood through the deconstruction of the narrative's formulaic covering could be applied here, as to Warner's fiction.[10] *What Katy Did* is not a revolutionary text, nor does it positively anticipate an era of less constrained female roles (although it is notable that in the last of Coolidge's *Katy* series, *What Katy Did Next*, the heroine not only travels to Europe but takes on all the emergency organization when her companion's little daughter catches Roman fever). But neither is it an evangelical tract, for all its recall of the type. It challenges or questions some of its age's assumptions about ethical imperatives and gender roles, disrupting in various ways the orthodoxies which it seems finally to validate and representing social and sexual disorder within the microcosmic context of the private, domestic world. It suggests coexistent power structures and alternative modes of female conduct; it deconstructs family hierarchies; it enacts fantasies of female power and heroism; it formulates a Utopia of childhood autonomy; and it enacts genre subversion.

Right from the beginning, conventional familial structures are dislocated. The family life which Coolidge depicts in the opening chapter is, like Alcott's representation of the March family, notably skewed. As in much nineteenth-century sentimental/domestic fiction, the parental patterning diverges from the norm of the nuclear family. The Carrs' mother is dead, and though their father is still alive and influential, he is most characterized by physical absence.

> Dr Carr, their papa, was a dear, kind, busy man, who was away from home all day, and sometimes all night, too, taking care of sick people. The children hadn't any mamma. She had died when Phil was a baby, four years before my story began. (2)

Although a substitute mother exists in the figure of their well-meaning and pious Aunt Izzie, she lacks any understanding of children and exerts control chiefly through her sharp tongue and constant nagging. In a sly authorial dig at the unrealism of moralistic children's books, the narrator comments that 'the young people she liked best, and understood most about [were] the good boys and girls in Sunday-school memoirs' (3).

Already there are interesting hints of role reversal here. Dr Carr, as a physician, acts out through his profession the qualities usually associated with women – tendance of the sick – while the aunt, unmarried and the power who must be placated before the childhood Eden of unrestraint can be enjoyed, to some extent represents patriarchal authority. Moreover, in the Carr household, it is the father who seeks to modify conventional gender divisions, wishing all his children to be 'hardy and bold' (3) and allowing his daughters a large degree of physical freedom. Distinctive sexual characteristics, with their accompanying behavioural coding, are also blurred within the family. Conventional patterning is undermined in the vignette with which Coolidge introduces the reader to the children. Thus the two youngest seem to reverse biological gender: Dorry (Theodorus), pale, fat and querulous, looks 'like a girl who had got into boy's clothes by mistake', while Joanna – always known as Johnnie – is 'a square, splendid child [who] had big brave eyes . . . and [was] like a boy who, in a fit of fun, had borrowed his sister's frock' (7). Even their names are sexually confusing.

There is a similar deceptiveness, though of a subtler kind, in the case of Clover, ostensibly a model of young girlhood: 'a fair, sweet dumpling of a girl, with thick pigtails of light brown hair and shortsighted blue eyes, which seemed to hold tears, just ready to fall from under the blue' (4–5). But like that other misleadingly adorable heroine of romance, Rosamund Vincy, in George Eliot's *Middlemarch*, Clover's innocent image conceals a determined will and manipulative skills. She knows how to get her own way, and, unlike the good little girl of pious juvenile fiction, she exploits her appearance of virtuous femininity which is to some extent self-created – her adorable dimples are partly 'the result of a pointed slate-pencil with which Clover was in the habit of deepening them every day while she studied her lessons' (62). Significantly, too, conventional femaleness has to be forced on her in the shape of the weekly hair-curling which she so detests.

The most interesting member of the family is of course Katy herself, the eponymous heroine. She is clearly in some degree a self-portrait. Coolidge's biographer notes the likeness: 'Susan . . . was uncommonly tall, as she describes Katy Carr, quick-witted, impulsive and full of imagination'.[11] Katy's inventiveness and gift for story-telling also reflect her creator's own talents. The portrait, however, is not self-indulgent. In presenting her, Coolidge oscillates between authoritarianism and licence, both seeking to confine her within the ethical framework and allowing her to escape it. In common with those other tomboy figures, Ethel May and Jo March, Katy experiences a constant battle between intention and deed, as her disruptive qualities – carelessness, untidiness, impetuousness – threaten the womanly ideals set before her, and as her imagination overturns the established stability of daily existence. Though she tries to console herself for her failings 'with planning how, by and by, she would be beautiful and beloved, and amiable as an angel' (9), the traditional image of female perfection is not powerful enough to impel her towards significant improvement.

Katy's rebellious unconventionality embodies both her own and her creator's resistance to nineteenth-century notions of ideal womanhood. Coolidge herself by no means replicates her age's model of her sex. She never married, and though she does not appear to have had a specific career other than writing, she acted for many years as reader and adviser to her publishers, Robert Brothers of Boston. She was 'crisp and decisive' in her business relations with them, not hesitating to object when she felt she was being financially disadvantaged.[12] She was also physically adventurous: in 1872, she and her close friend, Helen Hunt (later Helen Hunt Jackson, who became well known for her work on behalf of native Indians), took a trip out West, not a soft option at that time since it involved horse-riding on rough trails and camping in remote wilderness areas.[13] Much of this unorthodox spirit is reflected in her central character, albeit within a narrower sphere.

Katy also functions to deconstruct the idea of the romantic heroine. In the chapter entitled 'Paradise', the children each give their version of what they will do when they are 'grown up'. In contrast to their friend, Cecy Hall, who envisages herself as a beautiful, pious, do-gooding lady, resisting the blandishments of all 'the young gentlemen' (17), Katy has goals which are both more heroic and more sexually aware. On the one hand, she means 'to *do* something grand', positing as role models women who challenge conventional femininity – Grace Darling, Florence Nightingale, female artists; on the other hand, she has a very realistic attitude towards virtuous idealism – ' "it would be nice to go and ride with the gentlemen *sometimes"* ' (19), she announces. Her choice of reading is also a significant element in her iconoclasm. Enthralled by Tasso's *Jerusalem Delivered*, she responds physically to the images of male heroism which it presents, feeling 'hot and cold by turns as she read, and as if she must rush at something, and shout and strike blows' (45). There is a strong suggestion of gender reversal in Katy's behaviour and ideals. Her tomboyishness, though represented only as high-spirited heedlessness and effervescence, is an unconscious resistance to the restrictions of female propriety which await her in adulthood and for which Clover and Cecy, 'a neat, dapper, pink-and-white girl, modest and prim in manner, with light shiny hair, which always kept smooth, and slim hands, which never looked dirty' (8), are clearly preparing themselves. Unlike Jo March, Katy never actually expresses the wish that she were a boy nor does she share Jo's sexual ambiguity; she does not refer to herself in masculine terms and is not described in male-gendered language. And, as has been seen, her move into incipient womanhood seems to be accomplished without trauma or protest. But her unconventionality is certainly foregrounded over the more 'correct' images of girlhood embodied in Clover and Cecy, and offers a challenge to patriarchal essentialist notions of the feminine.

Katy is also the central motivator for much of the novel, and it is through her that potentially subversive notions of female power are articulated. Firstly, she is the chief initiator of action, and all the 'delightful schemes' (9) in which the Carrs participate are thought up by her. The children defer to her decisions, acknowledging in her a quality of leadership which is not solely due to her age. More importantly, she exerts control through the power of language, both by speaking from the 'wild zone' of female discourse, in which Showalter locates feminine 'difference,'[14] and by usurping the male privilege of naming. Like many of the other heroines in the texts under discussion, Katy is a verbal manipulator, a story-teller who creates new worlds of the imagination exempt from the dominant order's reason and common sense, represented here by Aunt Izzie. This exacting and unimaginative pseudo-parent (her only creative skills are exercised negatively in inventing dreadful stories about children who injure themselves by climbing posts and ladders, in a vain attempt to curb the Carrs' wildness – an ironic foreshadowing of Katy's future fall), on discovering Katy's highly romantic story, 'The Blue Wizard, or Editha of the Hebrides', commits it to the fire as a 'mass of trash' (59); she is unable to engage with the discourse of the fantastic irrational which empowers her niece. Katy, like

Scheherezade, entrances her companions through words (the children beg her to continue the tale she began long ago), seizing on the only area in which women can exert subversive influence. Even on her sick-bed, she functions as the master-magician who transforms the common-sense realm. For the festivities of St Nicholas she acts as secret gift-giver, and on St Valentine's Eve she engineers the trick in which the Valentine verses she herself has written are distributed to her unsuspecting audience.

Katy is further empowered through her assumption of the right to name – a power which in her hands becomes anarchic. Exploiting the Law of the Father, the Logos from which women are excluded, she leads her fellow-pupils in a challenge to the established order when she invents the lunch-time Game of Rivers. Not only is each girl renamed after a mighty river and instructed to run her own course round the schoolroom, but Katy herself becomes 'Father Ocean', the male progenitor of natural forces and the controller of their movements. Of course such disruption, bringing literal destruction in its wake, is only temporary: according to institutionalized authority this is a punishable offence, and Katy is finally dethroned by the gentle admonitions of the 'tender-hearted' teacher, Mrs Knight (34), who appeals to her conscience – the ultimate arbiter in the prevailing ethical system. Nevertheless, the incident represents a feminine subversion of the status quo, an act similar to that which immediately precedes it when Katy, having lost her sun-bonnet in the yard of the neighbouring rival school, defends her honour by climbing into the forbidden territory to retrieve it, thus becoming for her class-mates a symbol of triumphant daring and iconoclasm.

The novel also explores 'difference' through its depiction of separate spheres or Utopias, realms accessible to the socially subdominant and in which adults are denied participation. One such place, imaged as an arcadia where weekly rules cease to apply, is 'Paradise', a marsh thicket full of wild flowers which has been given Edenic status by the children themselves and to which they escape on summer Saturdays – 'to them it seemed as wide and endless and full of adventures as any forest of fairy land' (11). Like Mary Lennox's secret garden in Burnett's novel, it is an autonomous magic world where nature flourishes and imagination has free rein. Significantly, the first demonstration of Katy's inventive skills occurs here, as she tells the younger children her fairy story about the wild rose bush. Within the bower of ropes and branches which they have constructed, they enjoy a picnic which is much more fun than any 'grown-up dinner party' (15). Later, there is an even more specific recall of the biblical/Miltonic myth of pre-lapsarian freedom before inevitable entry into the symbolic order:

> it was comforting to remember that Paradise was always there; and that at any moment when Fate and Aunt Izzie were willing, they had only to climb a pair of bars – very easy ones, and without any fear of an angel with flaming sword to stop the way – enter in, and take possession of their Eden. (22)

A similar retreat is provided by the corn-loft which, again to the incomprehension of the matter-of-fact Aunt Izzie, affords the children a place of entertainment on rainy days. Here, too, Katy regales them with more of her stories as well as organising recitation sessions to which all contribute. In this Utopia, the children possess their own discourse, not only creating a literature of their own but also exercising their imaginations by transforming their mundane liquid refreshment (weak vinegar and water) into far more glamorous sounding concoctions. Interestingly, this escape has paternal approval; temporarily at least the patriarchal acknowledges the 'Other's' right to its own mode of self-expression.

Even the portrayal of Katy's corrective invalidism contains an element of subversive questioning and suggestiveness. Prostrate and immobile, Katy cannot effect physical change but she can indirectly challenge the notion of womanly passivity. On St Valentine's Day, for example, holding court as Queen Katherine, she not only acts as the ruler who plays the tricks, but she also rewrites the tale of Red Riding Hood: in her version, Red Riding Hood triumphs over the wolf and she and her grandmother live in comfortable security, unthreatened by annihilation, thus defeating masculine tyranny. When Aunt Izzie dies, still physically powerless Katy becomes the female head of the family, holding 'the threads of the house firmly in her hands' (186). While this is in some respects a vindication of the female domestic role, it is worth noting that Katy is only fourteen and that her initiation into household management is also entry into the politics of adulthood, where recalcitrant personalities as well as puzzling recipes have to be brought to order. Virtually in sole charge, she now controls – not as the patriarchal Father Ocean who brought destruction, but as the enthroned Queen, loving but strong, who has, in Helen's words, become 'The Heart of the House' (219).

What Katy Did, then, like *Little Women*, rewrites the sentimental-evangelical novel of earlier decades in such a way as to suggest, if not to recommend, gender roles and codes of behaviour which subvert contemporary hegemonies. Centring on the activities of the pre-adolescent sphere, it shows that acceptable womanliness and a spirit of female enterprise are not incompatible. While never actually denigrating the ideals it builds on, it does recontextualize them in a more liberal environment, opening the way to a more overtly radical representation of girlhood later in the century.

Notes

1. Nina Baym, *Woman's Fiction: A Guide to Novels By and About Women in America, 1820–1870* (Ithaca, NY: Cornell, 1978), and 'Portrayal of Women in American Literature, 1790–1870' in ed. Marlene Springer, *What Manner of Woman: Essays on English and American Life and Literature* (Oxford: Basil Blackwell, 1977).
2. Frances C. Darling, 'Susan Coolidge, 1835–1905', *Horn Book Magazine*, June 1969, p.232.
3. Ibid., p.244.
4. Ibid., p.239.
5. Susan Coolidge, *What Katy Did* (London and Melbourne: Ward, Lock, n.d.) pp.8–9. All subsequent references are to this edition and will be included in the text.
6. Ann Douglas, *The Feminization of American Culture* (New York: Alfred A. Knopf, 1977).
7. An oblique satiric reference to the fictive model established by Helen and developed by Katy after her fall occurs in Nesbit's *The Railway Children* (1905), when Peter attacks the idealization of female martyrdom as a fantastic pose that his sister must avoid:

   > "If you're not careful you'll turn into a beastly little Sunday-school prig, so I tell you."
   > "I don't mean to be a prig. But it's so hard not to be when you're really trying to be good."
   > (The Gentle Reader may perhaps have suffered from this difficulty.)
   > "Not it," said Peter; "it's a jolly good thing it wasn't you was hurt. I'm glad it was *me*. There! If it had been you, you'd have been lying on the sofa, looking like a suffering angel and being the light of the anxious household and all that. And I couldn't have stood it." E. Nesbit, *The Railway Children* (London: Puffin Books, 1960), p.172.

8. Nina Auerbach, *Woman and the Demon: The Life of a Victorian Myth* (Cambridge Mass. and London: Harvard University Press, 1982).

9. Sandra M. Gilbert and Susan Gubar, *The Madwoman in the Attic* (New Haven: Yale University Press, 1979), p.73.

10. In her *19th Century Women's Novels: Interpretive Strategies* (Cambridge: Cambridge University Press, 1990), Susan K. Harris discusses various sentimental/domestic novels, including Warner's *Queechy*, suggesting that even the most apparently conservative allowed contemporary women readers to discover a hidden, alternative plot in addition to the surface one. She derives her idea of 'reading beyond the ending' from Rachel Blau DuPlessis, *Writing Beyond the Ending: Narrative Strategies of Twentieth Century Women Writers* (Bloomington: Indiana University Press, 1985).

11. Darling, op.cit., p.233.

12. Ibid., p.243.

13. Coolidge first met Helen Hunt Jackson early in 1856 in New Haven, shortly after the birth of the latter's second son. Coolidge became one of her closest friends, especially after the death of Helen's husband, Major Edward Hunt, in September 1863. Their trip together out West in the summer of 1872 included visits to San Francisco, the Pluto Canyon Geysers, Yosemite, the Big Trees, and Lake Tahoe. Conditions were often rough: they travelled by open wagon, mule, horseback, and on foot, and they sometimes slept at dingy camp towns; in Yosemite they followed the trail to the Great Fall on their own, without a guide.

14. Elaine Showalter, 'Feminist Criticism in the Wilderness', *Critical Inquiry*, vol. 8, no. 2 (Winter, 1981), p.201. Showalter's thesis is discussed in more detail in Chapter 1 of this study.

6

E. Nesbit:
The Railway Children

In April 1905 Edith Nesbit wrote disconsolately to J.B. Pinker, her literary agent, 'I wish you could get me an order for a serial for grown-up people – something like the *Red House*. I don't think it is good for my style to write *nothing* but children's books'.[1] Her remarks expose not merely her personal frustration with the genre of which she was a supremely talented exponent but also her sense of relegation to the ranks of second-class literary citizenship, a danger to which she was keenly alive. Wary of being permanently classified as a literary lightweight, Nesbit constantly tried to diversify her output, continuing to produce adult novels, short stories and poems which failed to match either the financial rewards or the popularity of her juvenile fiction. By 1905 she had published some of the most successful children's novels of her day, including *The Story of the Treasure Seekers* (1899), *The Wouldbegoods* (1901), *Five Children and It* (1902) and *The Phoenix and the Carpet* (1904), the last of which had inspired H.G. Wells to write to her prophetically, 'You go on every Xmas, with a book like this, and you will become a British Institution in six years from now. Nothing can stop it.'[2] The promise of becoming a cultural fixture could not, however, prevent Nesbit's conviction that she was underrated as a serious writer and that the rapturous reception given to her work for children somehow impeded her artistic development. Her reaction provides a revealing insight into women's aspirations and their role in the contemporary market place. Like her American predecessor, Louisa May Alcott, and other writers in this study, Nesbit remained dissatisfied with the medium that brought her success, ironically sensing that the increasing celebrity of her work was in inverse relation to her ambitions to be taken seriously as an artist.

In addition, the renewed critical attention being paid to the novel in England from the 1880s onward, with the concomitant attempts to develop a theory of fiction, insisted on the reclamation of the genre for intellectuals, a category which inevitably excluded women and children. The result was, as Felicity Hughes has suggested, that 'novelists in a bid for critical respectability, tried to dissociate the novel from its family readership and redirect it toward what was seen as art's traditional elite audience of educated males.'[3] As Hughes points out, Henry James's essay 'The Future of the Novel' (1899) recommends very different standards for literary evaluation from those implicit in his earlier essays for *The Nation* when he referred to Alcott and Warner as authors to be admired. In 'The Future of the Novel', a piece which anticipates the beginnings of modernist literary criticism, James argues strongly and influentially for the preservation of such a division between the intellectual and the popular market as a prerequisite for the survival of the novel as a serious art form:

> The high prosperity of our fiction has marched very directly with another "sign of the times", the demoralisation, the vulgarisation of literature in general, the increasing familiarity of all such methods of communication, the making itself supremely felt, as it were, of the presence of the ladies and children – by whom I mean, in other words, the reader irreflective and uncritical.[4]

As an author writing for readers designated as 'irreflective and uncritical' on both age and gender counts, Nesbit was an automatic victim of the move towards literary exclusivity. Although when she began working on juvenile fiction, she was convinced of her own work's superiority to current children's stories, and refused to be deterred by publishers' reluctance to accede to her demands for proper remuneration (she asked the relatively high sum of a £50 down payment plus a $16\frac{1}{2}$ per cent royalty for *The Story of the Treasure Seekers*), she gradually acquiesced in the contemporary assessment of the genre itself, and, like a number of other women writers for children, became complicit in the process of her own self-devaluation, accepting without question the cultural premise that held that popularity and 'art', children and literary quality, were mutually incompatible.

Although Nesbit, like other female authors in this study, may have resented the market in which she found her success, it paradoxically facilitated her release from imposed traditions of canonical writing and allowed her to situate herself in radical relation to establishment practice. For Nesbit's novels are not merely pieces of childish entertainment nor unthinking inventive fantasies but highly sophisticated productions which continue to enact the tensions shared by a number of nineteenth-century texts by women writers and which we have explored with particular reference to children's literature. In common with other women writers of the period, Nesbit found in fiction a convenient vehicle for articulating dissident opinions in an acceptably packaged form. Like Alcott's *Little Women*, the narrative of *The Railway Children*, as in several of her other novels, masks potentially radical undercurrents by its reassuringly conventional framework of a return to the norm. Family life as it is ultimately envisaged in the resolution to this text presents parents and children in a stable and orthodox interrelationship, with adult authority providing the ethical and behavioural guidance thought necessary to educate and socialize innocent pre-adolescents. Within this formal narrative scheme, however, Nesbit, once described by Noel Coward as 'the most genuine Bohemian I had ever met',[5] uses children's literature as a political and proto-feminist tool. All her books explore the anarchic potential of childhood and in their identification with a juvenile perspective gain a licence to satirize adult mores and expose the disabling effects of a patriarchal and capitalist establishment. Julia Briggs has commented on Nesbit's

> creative use of child's play as a potentially critical imitation of the adult world, a device echoed at the stylistic level by her travesties of the literary techniques of her predecessors, and their aspirations to high-minded conformity.[6]

Nesbit discovered this creative use of the child's perspective only after a lengthy career in journalism, during which she had worked in collaboration with her husband, Hubert Bland, one of the influential forces in the Fabian movement. Her first full-length novel for children, *The Story of the Treasure Seekers*, did not appear until she was forty-one by which time she was familiar with the dual pressures of supporting a family and being allocated the subsidiary role of wife in the marital and professional partnership. Yet behind the facade of loyal and acquiescent supporter of a charismatic husband was a deeply unconventional woman. Nesbit had married Bland at the age of twenty-one, when seven months pregnant with their first child, Paul, and despite Bland's inveterate womanizing, they remained together until his death in 1914. Alice Hoatson, Bland's mistress and Edith's closest friend, shared their household in a tacit *ménage à trois*, and her two children by Bland were brought up by Edith as her own. Yet the Bohemianism which Coward had recognized and which manifested itself outwardly in Nesbit's eccentric dress, in her cigarette smoking, in her disorderly housekeeping arrangements and in her diverse circle of artistic friends, remained at variance with her continual need for a harmonious family. This ideal persists as a central motif in her novels despite their recasting of traditional domestic roles, and it forms a source of tension in her writing which the discussion of *The Railway Children* will further develop.

The story of *The Railway Children* deals simply with the changes in fortune that beset a family whose father is wrongfully imprisoned on a political charge. Moving from London to a small country village, where their mother supports them through writing stories and magazine articles, the three children discover the attractions of the local railway line, and this becomes the focus of a series of adventures. With the help of an elderly gentleman, a regular passenger on the line, they procure the release and return of their father, and the family fortunes are restored. This uncomplicated narrative structure conceals, however, a complex engagement with concepts of family and sibling relationships. It also enacts teasing oppositions in its representation of exemplars of female behaviour.

Indeed, in its consideration of separatist notions of gender, Nesbit's work addresses issues similar to those which have become the subject of more recent feminist literary debate. Is the representation of difference a perpetuation of conventional attitudes to women's roles in its foregrounding of the maternal feminine principle as a civilizing source? Or does it recognize the limitations of such a stance by showing female articulacy in a context of restricted power? The following discussion of *The Railway Children* will consider the essential ambivalence at the heart of Nesbit's writing and its significance in relation to shifting ideologies of girlhood at the turn of the century. In addition it will show how Nesbit simultaneously draws on and subverts traditional gendered models of reading for children, both through her representation of girl characters and through the stylistic interplay of her writing.

Although the use of intertextuality is most prominent in Nesbit's earlier humorous novels, *The Story of the Treasure Seekers* and *The Wouldbegoods*, which together form a sophisticated critique of clichéd juvenile literary convention, the parody of heroic discourse in *The Railway Children* also establishes a dialogue between fictive models of gender that is crucial to this discussion. All Nesbit's work exposes a profound concern with ideas of gender-specific identity and with investigating concepts of female nature. As Oswald Bastable remarks in *The Wouldbegoods,*

> "It's no good. You may treat girls as well as you like, and give them every comfort and luxury, and play fair just as if they were boys, but there is something unmanly about the best of girls. They go silly, like milk goes sour, without any warning."[7]

In its focus on a heroine who at the age of twelve is poised between childhood and the awakening sexuality of full adolescence, and its use of a traditional sentimental structure, unusual for Nesbit's work, *The Railway Children* forms an extensive examination of the concept of 'unmanliness', in both its social and literary dimensions, which Oswald Bastable views with such contempt. The ironic portrait of Oswald in *The Wouldbegoods* depicts him as a classic representative of male establishment standards, measuring girls against a norm of masculine behaviour from which they diverge. Taking as its starting point the position of Other to which girls and women are relegated by this establishment, *The Railway Children* both satirizes the essentialist approach to gender (largely through the characterisation of Peter), and explores the notion of difference more seriously so as to reconstitute and reaffirm a positive notion of the feminine. At the same time the novel reveals uncertainties in Nesbit's own authorial positioning. Through its foregrounding of maternal strength and its ambivalent portrayal of Roberta, the enterprising young heroine, *The Railway Children* functions as a site for negotiation between conflicting ideologies of femininity.

It is not solely the narrative content of *The Railway Children,* however, which raises important questions for the feminist reader. The novel also provides a good example of how establishment standards (such as those articulated by the fictional Oswald Bastable) have worked to demote girls' fiction and to invalidate the investigation into femininity that they frequently constitute. In this context it is worth considering the view given of the text by Humphrey Carpenter, in *Secret Gardens* (1985), a sustained study of children's literature of this period. Carpenter, while valuing contemporary texts produced by male authors, such as Richard Jeffries' *Bevis: The Story of a Boy* (1882) and Kenneth Grahame's *The Wind in the Willows* (1908), dismisses *The Railway Children* as constructed around a 'series of soap-opera crises'.[8] The judgement exposes his reliance on formalist critical criteria that ignore the psychological levels on which the text operates and that implicitly disparage the sustained nature of its appeal to generations of (mostly) female readers. Over fifty years after its first publication, *The Railway Children* was named in a *Sunday Times* survey as one of the hundred best books for children written in English or translated into it. Nesbit was one of only six authors whose work was mentioned twice and the only woman. In the 1960s the book was made into a hugely successful feature film, and in the 1990s it has no difficulty retaining its place in the list of best-sellers in the Puffin classics series.

In some ways, as has been suggested, *The Railway Children* has much in common with the sentimental and domestic tradition of girls' literature that flourished in nineteenth-century American writing, and, despite significant cultural differences, it shares crucial narrative stratagems with those works. In particular the motifs of the fragmented family, the absent parent and the affirmation of female strength which *The Railway Children* employs to powerful effect are also central to classic American texts, such as *The Wide, Wide World*, *Little Women* and *What Katy Did*. In its use of the device of the lost or absent father, the novel reveals its debt to the type of evangelical and sentimental literature which *The Story of the Treasure Seekers* and *The Wouldbegoods* systematically debunks. It does, however, make a more positive statement on the reinstatement of the father at the end of the novel than do the earlier texts discussed in this study. The importance attached to father/daughter relations, emphatically endorsed in Roberta's attempts to get justice restored and in the final reconciliation scene, develops the latent psycho-sexual undercurrents which can also be perceived in *The Daisy Chain* and more overtly in *Little Women*, and which pervade Nesbit's later *The House of Arden* (1908). In *The Railway Children*, Roberta's need to construct a self-image on the maternal model, a pervading feature of her search for a feminine identity, adds to the ambivalent nature of the closing embrace between father and daughter. Indeed this passionate reunion scene in the final chapter of the novel is one whose mythic dimension has been recognized by a number of critics more sympathetic than Carpenter to Nesbit's achievement, including Nesbit's biographer, Julia Briggs, who notes that it 'shares its emotional intensity with some of the greatest discovery scenes in literature – Iphigenia and her brother; Lear and Cordelia; Leontes and Hermione.'[9] Its effect is produced not through any analytical process of judgement but through a response to the fundamental dynamic of archetypal structures. As father and daughter clasp each other fervently, the act of restoration is realized in a graphic moment of emotional and physical intimacy which is played out in the presence of a textual audience, whose choric function serves to stylize and freeze the act of mutual repossession:

"Oh! my Daddy, my Daddy!" That scream went like a knife into the heart of everyone in the train, and people put their heads out of the window to see a tall, pale man with lips set in a thin close line, and a little girl clinging to him with arms and legs, while his arms went tightly round her.[10]

As Briggs points out, that fictional moment of reclamation not only has significant parallels in classical dramatic scenarios, but is just one of a number of narrative strategies which Nesbit exploits as part of a developed investigation in her writings into wish-fulfilment and its psychological mechanisms. Its recurrence in *The House of Arden*, where the father/daughter attachment resurfaces more obsessively, endorses its primal and enduring quality, and it is important to recognize its similarities with the obsessive attachment present in *The Daisy Chain* in Ethel May's symbiotic relation with her father. It is in part this unashamed reliance on the formulaic nature of fabular narrative which invests both classical literature and much children's literature with its vital ritualistic dimension. Yet it is precisely this that has also provoked censure. Carpenter, for instance, dismisses the scene as 'tear-jerking',[11] ignoring the powerful dramatic impact that cuts across hierarchical critical methodologies. His view of the episode reduces it to the status of a sentimental trick glibly pulled off by a facile practitioner who knows how to manipulate her audience, and indicates an inbuilt resistance to reading processes which diverge from established formalist criteria.

Moreover, as a male response to a work which has found its most ardent admirers among girls and women, Carpenter's indifference, and even hostility to Nesbit's achievement, indicates that a novel such as *The Railway Children*, which on the surface might appear to give equal attention to its male and female characters, has marked gender affiliations in terms of the response it evokes, speaking particularly to female readers.

It is easy to understand why earlier critics have ignored the gendered dimensions of Nesbit's writing. For unlike her transatlantic contemporaries, L.M. Montgomery or Gene Stratton Porter, who reject the family structure in order to scrutinize their heroines' displacement and consequent struggle with issues of selfhood, Nesbit places girls within a family unit that contextualizes them both socially and educationally. Whereas American texts of the period frequently consider ideologies of isolated girlhood as one important element in the exploration of the emergent North American consciousness, Nesbit more often examines the cultural implications of femininity from the perspective of the norm of the nuclear family. Girls are thus seen, not apart from, but alongside their brothers and boy cousins, as they are in the earlier English text, *The Daisy Chain*.

Significantly, however, the respective treatments of boys and girls evident in these texts reinforce rather than diminish their subversion of gender stereotyping. Although Nesbit's girls are almost invariably more sensitive and intuitively sympathetic than boys, their ambitions and interests are not seen as necessarily distinctive. Indeed the influence of new educational objectives and Fabian ideals of sexual egalitarianism merge in the portrayal of girls in Nesbit's later fiction. *The Railway Children* to a large extent dismantles conventional expectations of female passivity and assumptions about philosophies of difference by the simple device of selecting a railway line as providing the main narrative thread, and establishing it as the focal point of interest for girls as well as boys. It is by no means coincidental that trains in this novel (as is the case with ships conventionally) are of the feminine gender.

In a further inversion of normal literary practice, it is Roberta's ambition to be an engine driver which is satisfied in *The Railway Children* rather than her brother's, when as an 'Engine-burglar' she rides in the cabin and learns how to operate the controls. Peter's doubts about the appropriateness of his sister's mechanical bent are dispelled in the opening chapter of the novel, when Roberta wants to join in mending his broken toys:

> "Can girls help to mend engines?" Peter asked doubtfully.
> "Of course they can. Girls are just as clever as boys and don't you forget it." (13)

It is worth noting that it is the father who provides the moderating voice here, and that it is in his absence that Peter, attempting to assume the patriarchal role, reverts to a travesty of masculine authoritarianism in his treatment of his sisters. The family which embodies the ultimate ideal of harmonious relations in *The Railway Children* also disrupts conventional gendered hierarchies and concepts of difference. Father's admirable attempts to re-educate his son's assumptions about female technical skills are, however, somewhat undermined later in the novel when the Doctor explains to Peter (a future leader of the Empire no doubt) that:

"Men have to do the work of the world and not be afraid of anything – so they have to be hardy and brave. But women have to take care of their babies and cuddle them and nurse them and be very patient and gentle . . . Boys and girls are only little men and women. And we are much harder and hardier than they are" – (Peter liked the 'we'. Perhaps the Doctor had known he would.) – "and much stronger, and things that hurt *them* don't hurt us." (216)

It is difficult to read this as innocent or devoid of irony, or to reconcile the functionalist philosophy with the dramatization of Bobbie's superior strength, intellect, and courage in the central section of the book, or indeed with the satire of masculine complacency that is directed through Oswald Bastable in Nesbit's earlier work. The two episodes quoted, however, reflect the uneasy tension between radicalism and conformism that is latent in Nesbit's writing. Significantly, the essentialist assumptions about gender, as articulated by the Doctor and propounded most insistently by Peter, are foregrounded during the father's absence. While it is difficult to locate any consistent authorial stance towards such assumptions, it could be argued that the undermining of inflexible 'masculine' discourse in *The Railway Children* is integral to the novel's revisionist perception of the family and the prioritization given to the 'feminine' principle. As will be discussed subsequently, the father's reintegration into the family unit at the end of the book shows his acceptance of this principle rather than any resumption of patriarchal domination.

Peter's initial scepticism about girls continues to be exhibited in behaviour that, in its assumptions of male superiority, is openly satirized. His ineffectual stance as leader – ' "I'm the head man of the family when Father's away" ' (131), he asserts unconvincingly – merely exposes him to ridicule, and his efforts to support Mother only occur when he is following Roberta's example. Similarly, although he is inspired to claims of valour by male heroic archetypes, these are revealed as having no substance beyond their rhetorical positioning:

> Phyllis and Bobbie remembered how the boys on the canal-boats had thrown coal at them, and they said so.
> "Oh, nonsense," said Peter. "There aren't any boys here now. If there were, I'd fight them."
> Peter's sisters were kind enough not to remind him how he had *not* fought the boys when coal had last been thrown. (134)

Indeed throughout the novel, the girls' level of awareness and understanding continually exceeds their brother's, but in a parody of adult feminine strategies, they pretend to ignorance in order to feed the male ego. Even when he is caught stealing coal in what he thinks of as an iconoclastic act of heroism, Peter is not allowed to take sole responsibility, but to his chagrin learns that Roberta and Phyllis have known all along of his secret. ' "We knew where he got it" ', says Bobbie.

> "No, you didn't," said Peter.
> "Yes, we did," said Bobbie. "We knew all the time. We only pretended we didn't just to humour you."
> Peter's cup was full. He had mined for coal, he had struck coal, he had been caught, and now he learned that his sisters had 'humoured' him. (42)

It is worth noting that Peter's act of theft, the only reprehensible act the children commit, derives its inspiration from his readings of boys' fiction. Peter tries to evade the ethical issues implicit in his crime by finding analogies for his role in classic adventure narratives. He thinks of his exploit as 'a lone adventure'(39), envisages himself as 'a dauntless leader', and constructs his identity according to the model of the hero in a tale of daring and mystery. When discovered *in flagrante delicto*, however, his fictive status is exposed, and from being the glamorous bandit of his fantasy he is reduced ignominiously to, 'something small and dark . . . scrabbling and rattling furtively among the coal' (40).

In their childish play, the children envisage for themselves divergent subjectivities, and their games frequently re-enact traditional versions of gender roles in contrast to the subversive identities which the narrator ascribes to them. Making a bandit's lair in the attic, they rely on literary precedents for imaginative stimulus. 'Peter was the bandit of course' (37) comments the narrator with restrained irony, while Phyllis, the more docile of the sisters, is allocated the part of captured maiden, and Bobbie, flexible and self-denying, takes on all remaining supportive parts, including that of the parent who must pay a ransom for her daughter. The subsequent events of the novel both confirm and question this allocation of stereotypic roles: Peter's banditry is inappropriate in a realistic context and his failure to demonstrate real strength is in marked contrast to Bobbie's resistance and courage; Phyllis is bound by the captivity of the feminine – always tearing or dirtying her dresses, she finds her clothing a constant encumbrance; Bobbie, sensitive, supportive and altruistic, experiments during the course of the narrative with different female identities, including those of both parent and child.

The questioning of concepts of gender difference that informs the representation of the sibling relationship is perhaps most explicitly formulated in the children's views of marriage. While Phyllis, the youngest child, in a conventional formulation idealizes marriage as a condition where she will be the object of permanent love and affection, and Roberta sees herself continuing the role of wife as practised by her own mother, Peter reluctantly accepts the fact that marriage is a social necessity:

"I suppose I shall *have* to be married some day", said Peter, "but it will be an awful bother having her round all the time. I'd like to marry a lady who had trances, and only woke up once or twice a year." (118)

His approach to marriage as obligation, and to the idea of a wife as awkward encumbrance comically exposes a male ideal of woman as passive object, emerging from her hypnotic state at rare intervals and at his convenience. As Elisabeth Bronfen has argued, woman has been most valued as aesthetic object when all her capacity for action has been nullified.[12] So Peter, ignoring a parental example that actively reassesses this model, finds the idea of marriage only acceptable when the female lacks consciousness and the male is allowed an independent existence untroubled by her demands.

The implicit critique of a society which relies on a hierarchical model of gender relations is further developed in *The Railway Children* through the dialogic structure of male/female discourse that emerges in the examination of gendered concepts of childhood.

Peter's 'boyishness' is expressed in his typically aggressive and con-
frontational style, a contrast to his sisters' tactical and tactful use of
both language and non-verbal communication. He is fond of issu-
ing orders in a peremptory fashion – ' "Stand firm . . . and wave like
mad! . . . Don't stand *on* the line, Bobbie . . . Keep off the line, you
silly cuckoo!" ' (108–9) – while the girls rely on the more strategic
use of suggestion. And whereas girls and women are associated
with the creative imagination, Peter's observation is unequivocally
literal. The children's first sight of a train, for instance, evokes sharply
divergent responses, from the girls' metaphoric perception of 'a
great dragon tearing by', to Peter's factual, 'It's awfully tall isn't it?'
(33–4). Slang expressions, too, feature prominently as a part of Peter's
discourse but absent from his sisters'. The designation of slang as
distinctively male is, as already noted, used to telling effect by Alcott
in the portrayal of Jo March, and as will be shown later, by Angela
Brazil, who appropriates slang to designate the modern schoolgirl,
in her challenge to traditional gender boundaries.

Male linguistic codes in *The Railway Children* are proved to have
their limitations. Peter, required to make a speech at the public
award-giving ceremony at the station, finds that the formal conventions of oratory are inadequate as an expressive medium in
comparison with his own childish words, however incoherent.
Similarly the child-centred language in which the novel is written
functions as an ideological alternative to restrictive establishment
linguistic codes. As Julia Briggs notes:

> In adopting the voice of the child, Edith Nesbit had, ironically,
> found a way of articulating her feelings of rebelliousness and
> subversiveness as a woman. Adopting the child's voice allowed
> her not only to locate her own position as a woman in a male-
> dominated society, but also to escape from the pressure to write
> like a man.[13]

The Railway Children provides an opportunity for challenging
received communication both in its own literary practice and in
episodes which reveal the value of alternative strategies. On numerous occasions in the novel it is the non-verbal aspects of communication, as instinctively used by the girls, that prove more
effective than speech. Bobbie makes contact with the Russian
refugee through 'the touch of the hand she thrust into his' (88), and
Phyllis kisses both Perks and the signalman in spontaneous

gestures of sympathy to assuage feelings of resentment. Only when hurt or damaged do boys resort to these same female tactics. Jim, although 'like most boys of his age . . . called all such things "pawing", and detested them' (200), finds that when he is wounded and awaiting rescue, holding Bobbie's hand is a surprising comfort.

The critique of patriarchal discourse and the dominant ideology it encodes is developed most interestingly in the episode with the Russian émigré. Enclosed and isolated by his alien language, the Russian cannot make himself understood by the villagers, who, in their insularity, assume he must be either mad or a criminal. Yet, like Mother, the Russian is a writer, able to deploy the talents of imagination and creativity that are more normally associated with girls and women in this text and that stand in opposition to male economic power. It is Mother with whom he shares a common language (they converse together in French), although it is the children, led by Bobbie, who break through the language barrier, via non-linguistic signs. Closely identified with the realm of the feminized other and the linguistic semiotic, unintelligible in the symbolic order, the refugee transgresses the boundaries of conventional masculinity. The children consequently are forced to reassess their notions of gendered difference. They bring him flowers, and are surprised when he weeps: ' "I never saw a man cry before" ' (91), says Bobbie. As noted earlier in this study, tears are characteristically an expression of feminine emotion, exploited most pervasively in fictions for girls such as *The Wide, Wide World*. Moreover Peter, imbued with false ideals of militarism, charges the Russian with cowardice on learning that he has deserted the army after being conscripted as a political prisoner. His over-prescriptive definition of courage is symptomatic of his limited thinking, an attitude that Mother has to redress.

The Russian's situation as an innocent victim of political injustice echoes that of the children's father, wrongfully condemned by an establishment system that relies on palpable evidence, and that is consequently open to abuse. His location in the zone of non-establishment discourse finds further parallels in the emphasis in the novel on female silence and secrecy. Mother's refusal to discuss the circumstances of Father's plight to the children for instance confines her to a world of internalized emotion, while Bobbie's initiation into adulthood is also characterized by the internalization of grief and the consequent retreat into silence. The episode when she learns of her father's disgrace shows her movement into the female world of knowledge and secrecy as she replicates her mother's behavioural patterning, repressing her own misery for the sake of others.

Within the framework of family life in Nesbit's novels, girls are frequently depicted as stronger than their brothers and having a greater degree of insight, and they tend to provide the behavioural models to which boys must aspire. Roberta is the undeclared heroine of *The Railway Children*, and in the licensed world of childhood that the father's absence releases, she has the freedom (albeit temporarily) to explore divergent subjectivities, as both androgynous child and burgeoning adult woman. Her equivocal position is reflected in the dialogue she conducts with herself during her vigil with Jim in the dark railway tunnel:

> "Don't be a silly little girl," she said. She was always very angry when anyone else called her a little girl, even if the adjective that went first was not 'silly' but 'nice' or 'good' or 'clever'. And it was only when she was very angry with herself that she allowed Roberta to use that expression to Bobbie. (197)

The dual identity, realized through the dramatization of the split persona in this extract, focuses on the problem of the adult/child division and its accompanying discourse. Seeking validation as an adult and a female, Roberta divides herself into male/female. The girl is the mature self: the 'boy' child the fantasy self who must be admonished. The episode occurs towards the end of the novel, when Bobbie has already endured trials that have caused her to adopt the maternal role and to anticipate the responsibilities of adulthood. There is a clear contrast between this stance and the careless freedom that she shows in the early stages of the book, when, gay and irresponsible, she leaves the kettle to boil dry and is complicit in her brother's theft of coal. It is one further instance of the ambivalence regarding radical and conventional positioning between which the text is poised.

This negotiation between the tomboy and the developing feminine consciousness is reflected in the narrative models applied in the text as Roberta switches between male heroic narratives of rescue, where she is required to demonstrate qualities of leadership and initiative, and female sentimental plots which denote the little woman in training. Yet the relative value ascribed to each remains unclear. The ambivalence over the signification of the feminine can be seen in the episode when the children prevent a serious rail accident by alerting the driver of the oncoming express train to an obstruction on the line. Realizing that they are too late to run back to the station and warn the signalman, the girls discover that the clue to salvation ironically lies in their oppressive clothing. They remove their red flannel petticoats, tear them into strips and make flags which are effective in averting the disaster. The very signs of their femininity, which at first appear to impede their progress and sap their energy – they cannot run as fast as their brother, and they perspire uncomfortably and feel faint from the heat of the flannel – become the instruments of their power and influence. The liberation that ensues from removing their underwear is a deliberate affront to the standards of propriety they have been brought up to respect:

> "You're not" – Phyllis faltered – "you're not going to *tear* them?"
> "Shut up", said Peter, with brief sternness.
> "Oh, yes", said Bobbie, "tear them into little bits if you like . . ."
> She took the red flannel petticoat from him and tore it off an inch from the band. Then she tore the other in the same way. (107)

Bobbie, readier than her younger sister to break with convention, finds a heroic role by divesting herself of girlish clothing and transforming it into a symbol of danger. The petticoat (white this time) recurs in a subsequent episode with very different effect. Supporting Jim in the railway tunnel while waiting for help, Bobbie uses her underclothing to make a soft cushion of folded flannel in order to alleviate the boy's discomfort:

> "Oh, what useful things flannel petticoats are!" she said; "the man who invented them ought to have a statue directed to him." (198)

Tellingly, Roberta assumes that invention is a male prerogative. On separate occasions and put to different purposes then, the feminine can be variously a signal of danger, a heroic symbol and a source of tenderness and support.

The impact of traditional ideologies of womanhood and authorial unease about them is also fully visible in *The Railway Children*, which has been compared to *Little Women* in the presentation and discussion of the value attached to domestic stability, and in the conceptualization of female character, with marked similarities

between Roberta and Jo March.[14] Like Jo, Roberta has a name that
is easily shortened to a masculine diminutive, and, on the verge of
adolescence, she too finds a source of anxiety in the tension between
the attractions of carefree childhood and the appeal of womanliness,
between the desire to run wild and the need for an ordered, secure
environment. The works also share the motif of the absent father
and the consequent weighting of responsibilities impressed upon
the children. Like the March family, the Railway Children rely on
the services of an old gentleman of the Mr Laurence type. In the
received fairytale tradition, he becomes their benefactor, showering
them with material gifts in recognition of their spiritual generosity.
In turn, his grandson is a subdued version of Laurie, the privileged
boy who appreciates the simple pleasures of family warmth and
psychological succour provided by the woman-centred household
which shelters him during his illness.

The most significant point of comparison between the two texts,
however, and one that raises provocative questions for the feminist
psychoanalytic critic, is in the iconization of motherhood. Mother in
The Railway Children, like Marmee in *Little Women*, functions as a
model of self-sacrificial maternal perfection, battling against economic and emotional pressures to maintain a home for her threatened family. Her guiding principle is devotion to her children and
it is this need for the continuous maternal presence that initially
defines motherhood, realized from the childhood perspective. The
true mother figure is 'almost always there, ready to play with the
children, and read to them, and help them to do their home-lessons'
(9). The awful consequences of parental neglect (already seen in *The
Daisy Chain* with Flora May's child) are made evident in the episode
with the bargeman and his wife, whose baby almost dies in a fire,
after having been left unattended. The insistence on the psychological dimension of mothering is reinforced by the momentary visual-
ization of Mother in the role of child, when even as an adult she
re-experiences feelings of abandonment and loss:

> "No one", she said at last, "ever loved anyone more than my
> mother loved me." Then she was quiet again. . . . It seems so easy
> and natural to run to Mother when one is in trouble. Bobbie
> understood a little how people do not leave off running to their
> mothers when they are in trouble even when they are grown up,
> and she thought she knew a little what it must be to be sad, and
> have no mother to run to any more. (55)

The fear of loss of maternal support, a subliminal force in virtually all Nesbit's stories of children whose family security is threatened, is potently realized in this momentary role reversal, where Bobbie's level of understanding marks a stage in her transition from child to woman. The permanence of the maternal image as a force in the realization of the daughter's identity suggests the importance of archetypal patterning in the construction of the gendered self. Bobbie's perception undergoes a subtle change as she reflects on the continuity of female selfhood, perpetuated in terms of mother/daughter relations. As her subsequent position with regard to her siblings makes clear, in her adoption of the nurturing role, her command of household skills during Mother's illness, and her instinct for family solidarity, she dramatizes the process that Nancy Chodorow has termed 'the reproduction of mothering'.[15] Indeed the mother/daughter role reversal that occurs during Mother's illness provides a premature illustration of this process. In her delirium, Mother calls,

"Mamma, mamma!" and Bobbie knew she was calling for Granny, and that she had forgotten that it was no use calling, because Granny was dead. (58)

During Mother's reversion to infantilism with its consequent loss of the capacity for coherent speech, Bobbie becomes empowered as the surrogate mother in control of the household domain.

The role of the mother in providing a positive behavioural model for her daughter indicates the fundamental power of the maternal myth in determining the direction of girlhood narratives. Like Jo in *Little Women*, Bobbie finds in Mother an embodiment of female virtue and a source of inspiration which helps her to formulate her own code of conduct. The code in part perpetuates the Victorian projection of the Angel in the House, incorporating domestic strength, caring for others, self-abnegation, and stoicism in the face of adversity. The woman's duty as home-maker is literalized graphically in *The Railway Children* when the family, uprooted from their London home and arriving at their rented cottage, appears to be in danger of fragmentation. As the children gaze dispiritedly on the bleak, unlit, unheated house, hear the rats scurrying inside the walls and find that the promised meal has not been prepared to welcome them, Mother is transformed into a creative force, producing harmony from chaos, food from scraps, light from darkness and cheerfulness

from disillusionment. This energizing process is repeated subsequently by Bobbie, who during her mother's illness acts as her
substitute. In the period of crisis which threatens the family's sense
of equilibrium, Bobbie becomes housekeeper, nurse, manager,
charitable worker in a temporary version of the roles she could
expect to appropriate as an adult. Accidentally learning the secret
of her father's disgrace, she identifies closely with her mother's
efforts of emotional renunciation and keeps the truth from the
younger children. As discussed above, it is female silence which
emerges as a crucial signification of the transition to mature womanhood, and a strategy of female power.

The uncertainties of the novel's stance, however, are problematized
by the ways in which, in contrast to earlier and more traditional
texts, such as *The Wide, Wide World*, Nesbit's work secularizes
motherhood and extends its scope to embrace all aspects of
parenting. As Noel Streatfeild has observed, *The Railway Children*
has a strong autobiographical foundation, and Mother, like the
author, can achieve the double feat of being both father and mother,
simultaneously economic provider and symbol of domestic continuity.[16] Through Mother's combination of literary and maternal
talents, Nesbit validates the power of the female imagination, a
concept which Alcott's Jo March found so troubling. *The Railway
Children* acknowledges and celebrates women as professionals, as
Mother's hobby, which began as an extension of her maternal role
in writing stories for her children's entertainment and 'funny pieces
of poetry for their birthdays' (9) is proved to have commercial value.
At the same time the author makes clear that female 'cleverness'
and the role of provider are incompatible with traditional maternity.
As Peter admits to the doctor, Mother, although a focus of general
admiration for her superwoman qualities, 'used to play with us
more before she had to be so clever' (51).

The ambivalence that the text expresses in its examination of
female roles is continued in the degree of scope allowed to the
woman-centred household. While it is Roberta who ultimately
manages to procure Father's release, and whilst the home in his
absence is a focus for creative talents to flourish, this fantasy world
is framed by a more sober and realistic awareness. The liberated
world in which children can run wild and indulge in adventures is
never completely free from restraint and the holiday atmosphere is
tempered by a social realism which exposes its limitations. So although self-sufficient within its own limits, the household is shown

to be without real power. Struggling to survive on Mother's erratic income, the family finds its resources stretched to breaking point in an emergency, and during Mother's illness the children are forced to seek support from exterior, male agencies. Both the doctor and the old gentleman come to the family's aid, wielding their superior worldly influence, which comprises material wealth, medical expertise, and political contacts. It is these which effect the miracle which will restore Mother to health and engineer the release of their father. Ultimately Mother's earning-power is shown as fragile and Roberta's energy and good sense, which have been celebrated in the main action of the novel, become directed not towards acts of rebellion but in conventional channels where patriarchal hegemony can once again exert its authority. In her childhood condition, Bobbie might experiment with a variety of gendered subjectivities, but the novel's conclusion admits a return to the conventional that signals the unreal and fantastic element of the girlhood adventures she has engaged in.

However, unlike certain other texts considered in this study, *The Railway Children* does not allow the power of the mother to be diminished by the father's return. In *Little Women* for example, Marmee retreats to the margins of the text once Mr March resumes his place at the centre of the household, and Jo's unruliness is subdued in order to gain her father's approval for her new-found womanliness. More problematically perhaps, in Frances Hodgson Burnett's *The Secret Garden* (1911), Mary Lennox noticeably recedes from the narrative focus after the return of her uncle, Mr Craven. In what can only be defined in feminist terms as a retrogressive plot movement, the position of control Mary has won is almost totally negated as Colin's restored energy signals his supremacy as future master of the house. *The Railway Children*, however, in its concluding episode, stresses the reconciliation between father and daughter as a harmonious completion, a prelude to the needful reconstitution of the fractured family controlled by the feminine principle, as discussed earlier. The final page of the text portrays Father waiting patiently outside the house that Mother has rented, waiting to be called and allowed entry to her domain:

But his eyes keep turning towards the house. And presently he leaves the garden and goes to stand outside the nearest door. It is the back door, and across the yard the swallows are circling. They are getting ready to fly away from cold winds and keen

frost to the land where it is always summer. They are the same
swallows that the children built the little clay nests for.

Now the door opens. Bobbie's voice calls:

"Come in, Daddy; come in!"
He goes in and the door is shut. (239)

This image of closure reinforces rather than denies female power.
Bobbie, having acquired womanly status, is now the doorkeeper,
facilitating entry to the feminine domestic territory. The woman is
not written out of the text but retains her authority over the home
in a newly formed realistic world, and the flight of the swallows to
a land of permanent summer signals the end of the narrative fantasy. The nesting images, however, also complete the picture of
harmony and unification with the replacement of the missing element in the psychoanalytic jigsaw. Retaining her position within
the Lacanian region of the Imaginary, Mother functions as necessary complement to the patriarchal order, which on its own has
proved fallible. Father's feminized move into the Imaginary as part
of Nesbit's presentation of a familial norm thus validates female
power in this context. The fact that such an interpretation also conforms to the Ruskinian vision of the restorative function of womanhood merely adds to the problematic dimension of the essentialist
nature of such apparent iconoclasm.

Kimberley Reynolds, as has already been noted, in her study of
patterns of children's reading in the late Victorian period, has remarked on the divisions between gender-specific texts and their
assumed readers' responses. Girls' literature, she argues, exhibits a
conservatism that was considered appropriate for encouraging
female submissiveness but that was largely absent from stories for
boys. As she suggests,

> girls' stories drew readers into ideological and discursive posi-
> tions which encouraged them to accept as right and natural the
> existing social structure, with its profoundly inconsistent, fre-
> quently perverse, and prohibitive attitudes towards women.[17]

Boys on the other hand were steered away from girls' fiction and
towards texts that attempted to instil into them 'a new, more manly
version of masculinity', challenging, active and removed from the
potentially dangerous zones of feminized domesticity. As the

preceding discussion indicates, *The Railway Children,* as shown for example in the satire of Peter's 'manly' attributes derived from his reading, opposes the two narrative positions.

While some critics can still argue that Nesbit's books are 'on the face of it directed to boys rather than girls'[18] because of the balance they retain between male and female protagonists, a sustained analysis of *The Railway Children* exposes a dependence on certain traditional motifs and narrative ploys characteristic of girls' fiction rather than boys', with all its inconsistencies. Both Nesbit's domestic adventure stories and her magic fantasies repeat patterns of juvenile experience which emphasize domestic and familial security, the centrality of mothering, the values of participation and the creative potential of imaginative play, all features of much of the girls' literature examined in this study. In their recurrent portraits of strong heroine figures, often supported by subsidiary male characters, the books also reveal a tendency towards gender role reversal and a revisionary approach to girlhood that strengthens their equivocal attraction for female readers. Invited to adopt a creative subject position in relation to the models of the feminine that Nesbit's texts promote, girls can thus align themselves with the imaginative and political possibilities that the novels disclose, while gaining reassurance from the overriding conservatism of their narrative direction.

Notes

1. Julia Briggs, *A Woman of Passion: The Life of E. Nesbit 1858–1924* (London: Penguin Books, 1987), p.260.
2. Ibid., p.297.
3. Felicity A. Hughes, 'Children's Literature: Theory and Practice', *English Literary History* 45, (Baltimore: Johns Hopkins University Press, 1978), p.554.
4. Henry James, 'The Future of the Novel', in *Henry James: The Future of the Novel. Essays on the Art of Fiction,* ed. Leon Edel, quoted in Hughes, p.549.
5. Briggs, p.338.
6. Julia Briggs, 'Women Writers and Writing for Children: From Sarah Fielding to E. Nesbit', eds Gillian Avery and Julia Briggs, *Children and their Books* (Oxford: Oxford University Press, 1990), p.248.
7. E. Nesbit, *The Wouldbegoods,* (London: Puffin Books, 1958), p.240.
8. Humphrey Carpenter, *Secret Gardens: A Study of The Golden Age of Children's Literature* (London: George Allen & Unwin, 1985), p.135.
9. Briggs, *A Woman of Passion,* p.1.

10. E. Nesbit, *The Railway Children* (London: Puffin Books, 1960), p.239. All subsequent references are to this edition and will be included in the text.

11. Carpenter, p.126.

12. Elisabeth Bronfen, *Over her Dead Body: Death, Femininity and the Aesthetic* (Manchester and New York: Manchester University Press, 1992).

13. Briggs, in Avery and Briggs, p.248.

14. Noel Streatfeild, *Magic and the Magician: E. Nesbit and her Children's Books* (London: Ernest Benn, 1958), p.125.

15. Nancy Chodorow, *The Reproduction of Mothering: Psychoanalysis and the Sociology of Gender* (Berkeley and Los Angeles: University of California Press, 1978).

16. Noel Streatfeild, *Magic and the Magician*, p.118.

17. Kimberley Reynolds, 'Girls' Own Stories', conference paper given at History Workshop Conference, Ruskin College, Oxford, June 1991.

18. W.W. Robson, 'E. Nesbit and *The Book of Dragons*', in Avery and Briggs, p.259.

7

L.M. Montgomery:
Anne of Green Gables

In August 1907, a few months after *Anne of Green Gables* had been accepted for publication, Lucy Maud Montgomery wrote joyfully in her Journal:

> Well, I've written my book. The dream dreamed years ago in that old brown desk in school has come true at last after years of toil and struggle. And the realization is sweet – almost as sweet as the dream![1]

The novel, which appeared in June 1908, was, like most of the other books discussed in this study, an overnight success, despite its modest beginnings. As Montgomery herself explains:

> Two years ago in the spring of 1905 I was looking over [my] notebook in search of some suitable idea for a short serial I wanted to write for a certain Sunday School paper and I found a faded entry, written ten years before:- "Elderly couple apply to orphan asylum for a boy. By mistake a girl is sent them." I thought this would do. I began to block out chapters, devise incidents and "brood up" my heroine . . . Then the thought came, "Write a book about her." (I, 330)

Initially, the expanded story seemed doomed to failure: after it had been rejected by four publishers in succession, Montgomery put the manuscript in an old hat-box, intending at some later date to cut it back to its original proportions. But she changed her mind when she rediscovered the forgotten work in the winter of 1906, and decided to try it out once more. This time she offered it to L.C. Page & Co. of Boston, who not only accepted it, but immediately suggested that "if you are not otherwise at work, it might be a good idea to write a second story dealing with the same character."[2] The novel straightway established itself as a best-seller: by mid-September

1908 it had gone through four imprints and through another two by the end of November. It was published concurrently in England, and had reached a fifth English imprint by May 1909, justifying the enthusiastic early review in the Montreal *Herald* which applauded it as 'a book which will appeal to the whole English speaking world'.[3] Its huge success continued: in May 1914 it reached its thirty-eighth American imprint, and since then it has been constantly reissued both in Britain and the United States, as well as being widely translated and adapted for stage, screen and television.

The novel's extensive popularity is partly due to its combined adult and adolescent appeal. But like so many women writing in this genre, Montgomery underplayed the status of her work, specifically categorizing it as one of her many 'juvenile yarns' (I, 236). She was amazed and gratified by the unexpected triumph of what she considered such an unpretentious work:

> My strongest feeling seems to be incredulity. I *can't* believe that such a simple little tale, written in and of a simple PEI farming settlement, with a juvenile audience in view, can really have scored out in the busy world. (I, 339)

With a self-deprecation characteristic of many children's writers, she was anxious to point out the book's limited scope. To Ephraim Weber, her pen-friend in Alberta, she declared:

> It is merely a juvenilish story, ostensibly for girls . . . I did not dream it would be the success it was. I thought girls in their teens might like it but that was the only audience I hoped to reach.[4]

She reiterated her amazement to George MacMillan, her other long-standing pen-friend in Scotland – 'I am surprised that they [the reviews] seem to take the book so seriously – as if it were meant for grown-up readers and not merely for girls'[5] – and expands on her 'surprise' in a letter to her cousin, Murray MacNeill, in July 1909:

> It has been a great surprise to me that Anne should have taken so well with "grown-ups". When I wrote it I thought it would be an amusing and harmless little tale for Sunday School libraries and "kiddies", but I did not suppose it would appeal to older readers.[6]

Montgomery's professed amazement may have been justified: certainly, it might have seemed unlikely that a story about an orphan girl in the rural Canadian Maritimes would capture a large adult public. The figures, however, proved the contrary. The novel's admirers included Earl Grey, the Governor General of Canada, and two English Prime Ministers, Stanley Baldwin and Ramsay MacDonald. Mark Twain also enjoyed it, though it is significant that his delight in Anne herself – 'the dearest, and most lovable child in fiction since the immortal Alice'[7] – foregrounds the work's juvenile quality. It was this aspect of the book that invited the patronizing responses of other of Montgomery's adult readers. Damning with faint praise, her former Literature professor at Dalhousie College, for example, considered that:

The . . . book just misses the kind of success which convinces the critic while it captivates the unreflecting general reader . . . The conclusion to be drawn from Miss Montgomery's achievement is that the great reading public on this continent and in the British Isles has a great tenderness for children, for decent, and amusing stories, and a great indifference towards the rulings of the critics.[8]

Nearly fifty years later, the critic A.L. Phelps echoes this judgement in a deceptively bland appraisal of the novel's merits – 'The unpretentiousness and innocence may be the kind of honest simplicity that does have life and even art in it.'[9]

Such attitudes are exemplary of the kind of critical stance frequently taken towards juvenile literature, especially from the later nineteenth century onwards when the generic separation between writing for children and that for adults became more marked. As with many of the other novelists examined here, Montgomery's fiction was produced in the context of a literary world in which it was impossible to be both a 'serious' and a 'juvenile' author. Her disclaimers of merit and her artistic devaluation of her work are, therefore, not surprising, though they may sound suspiciously disingenuous. They may indeed be self-protective strategies, a means both of forestalling hostile criticism and of coming to terms with a system which persisted in narrow and rigorous definitions of artistic excellence. As her biographer stresses, and as her Journals reveal, Montgomery was in fact extremely ambitious and confident of her ultimate literary achievement: 'I have . . . a belief in my power to succeed (I, 249) . . . never, at any time had I any *real* doubt that I would succeed at last . . . deep down, under all discouragement and rebuff I knew I would "arrive" some day' (I, 261), she asserts. More-over, she certainly wanted to enter the ranks of more sophisticated writers. Not only did she find the writing of sequels to *Anne* very tedious (the heroine became to her 'that detestable Anne', settling on her like an incubus[10]), but she attempted to break new ground with *The Story Girl* (1911), a novel representing 'a step on the way toward the more "mature" books she still hoped to write.'[11] She also knew how easily a novelist could become generically stereo-typed, as her comments on another new story, *Kilmeny of the Orchard* (1910), indicate:

> [It is] a love story with a psychological interest – very different from my other books and so a rather doubtful experiment with a public who expects a certain style from an author and rather resents having anything else offered it. (I, 362).

The fact remains that Montgomery's reputation rests on her *Anne* and *Emily* books; indeed the bulk of her fiction is directed primarily to a young female audience, even though she takes both of these heroines into wifehood and motherhood in later works in each series. She wrote only two novels specifically for adults, *The Blue Castle* (1926) and *A Tangled Web* (1931) (ironically, the former was repub-lished in 1972 as a children's book), perhaps more affected than she cared to acknowledge by her early doubt that 'I'll ever be able to write stories for mature people.'[12]

To imply, however, that *Anne of Green Gables* is not for 'mature people' is to over-simplify it. Though its major attraction may be the way in which it draws the reader into the immediacy of child-hood experience, it is misleading to suggest that it is merely a straightforward and unsophisticated representation of a pre-adolescent world. The subtlety of the novel's narrative technique, relying on the juxtaposition of Anne's own viewpoint and a more objective voice reminding the reader that the Edenic state of girl-hood is only temporary, presupposes an intellectually mature reader-ship. The novel's width of appeal also depends on the two main impulses which inspired it: Montgomery's desire to write a story for girls, which, while drawing on earlier examples of the genre, develops away from and challenges them in various respects; and her urge to re-enact her youthful experiences, dramatizing – and fictionally transforming – a past with which she was constantly preoccupied. The former dictates a strategy of literary subversion, in which familiar patterns are deconstructed and the main character herself is allowed an iconoclastic role. The latter produces a narrative which both recreates many of the events and emotions of Montgomery's own life and socially and psychologically reassesses them. The novel thus functions on two levels, exploring contemporary ideologies of girlhood and female behaviour, and textually enacting therapeutic recall.[13]

In many ways *Anne of Green Gables* replicates the narrative framework of earlier girls' fiction such as *The Wide, Wide World* (1850), and *The Lamplighter* (1854), in which an orphan is cast into a seemingly unwelcoming and uncongenial environment and has to adapt to the new circumstances. Three contemporary best-sellers which exploit this motif of orphanhood – Alice Rice's *Lively Mary* (1903), Kate Douglas Wiggin's *Rebecca of Sunnybrook Farm* (1903), and Gene Stratton Porter's *Freckles* (1904) – may well have also been influential on *Anne*. The first two have particular elements in common with Montgomery's novel, since they deal with a young heroine who, learning to find a place in an initially alien sphere, moves towards social, moral, and psychological maturity; at the same time, she has an effect on her surroundings, producing a change of heart or outlook in those who began as her antagonists. Within this pattern, the fiction asks gender-oriented questions and offers a revisionist view of male and female roles. Anne, brought from the orphanage to Avonlea to be adopted by Marilla Cuthbert and her brother Matthew, is thrown into a world which at first seems antipathetic to her unconventionality and independence of spirit. Like Rebecca and Mary, Anne enters an adult-centred and spiritually rigidified environment whose values she cannot understand. Through her encounters with the local community, she gradually discovers new dimensions to her own life and also helps to enlarge those of her mentors and companions, awakening them to a more sympathetic attitude towards girlhood as a fragile and complex stage on the way to mature womanhood.

Montgomery, like many of the other writers in this study, exploits the archetypal model in order to subvert some of the ideologies it embodies. One of her chief strategies is literary referentiality. *Anne of Green Gables* is both covertly and implicitly allusive. Like her creator, whose Journals constantly express a delight in books, Anne has an obsessive love of reading which feeds her relentless demand for 'scope for the imagination'.[14] Her intensely literary romanticism

is evident in her first eager outpouring to the bewildered Matthew
Cuthbert on their way to Avonlea:

> "It was pretty interesting to imagine things about them [the other
> asylum orphans] – to imagine that perhaps the girl who sat next
> to you was really the daughter of a belted earl, who had been
> stolen away from her parents in her infancy by a cruel nurse who
> died before she could confess." (17)

This fantasizing, a pervasive source of the novel's humour, echoes
Montgomery's own avowed passion for 'escapist' literature ('I would
like realistic and philosophical novels in spells, but for pure, joyous,
undiluted delight give me romance. I always revelled in fairy tales'
[I, 235]). It is also a characteristic shared by other heroines: Jo March,
Katy Carr, and Mary Lennox are all avid readers whose literary
passion transforms the mundane realities of their everyday lives.
In these works, as in *Anne*, not only is the literary imagination empowering for the characters but through its exploitation the novelist
herself is enabled to challenge codified established values.

At the most simple level of plot, *Anne of Green Gables* enacts its
subversion by rewriting the conventional format of the moral/
domestic tract-type literature offered to girls in the nineteenth century. That Montgomery found this kind of writing both compelling
and absurd is clear from various Journal entries. She ironizes her
early voracious appetite for the 'Pansy' books (stories of child life
by Mrs G.R. Alder, popular during the 1870s and 80s, and all
preaching the virtues of mission, temperance and prayer), for example, with the comment that, as a Sunday School teacher, 'I did
not feel at all like a Pansy heroine!' (I, 37). She also mocks another
early enthusiasm, the sickly sentimental *Memoir of Anzonetta Peters*,

> a type now vanished from the earth fortunately – but much in
> vogue at that time. It is the biography of a child who at five
> became "converted", grew very ill soon afterwards, lived a marvel-
> lous patient and saintly life for several years, and died after great
> suffering at the age of twelve. (I, 376)

In one of her later novels, *Emily of New Moon* (1923), Montgomery
satirically replays her own attempts to follow this saintly example
when Emily tries to impress her severely commonsensical aunts by
emulating Anzonetta's hymn-singing propensities.[15] Despite her

liking for Gothic romance, too, Montgomery is fully aware of its deficiencies: she calls Regina Maria Roche's *The Children of the Abbey* (1796) 'the mushiest, slumpiest book I have ever read', its central character

> a most lachrymose heroine who fainted in every chapter and cried quarts of tears if anyone looked sidewise at her. But as for the trials and persecutions which she underwent, their name was Legion . . . (I, 236)

Within *Anne* itself, a dual process of literary reversal and contrast both deflates the prototype and establishes a more realistic standard of girlhood behaviour. Anne is definitely not a conventional saintly heroine: thin, gawky, freckled, and red-haired, she falls far short of ideal female beauty, unlike her 'bosom friend', Diana Barry, who is 'a very pretty little girl, with her mother's black eyes and hair and rosy cheeks' (75). Neither does her conduct conform to that of the model heroine of sentimental literature. Anne is outspoken and bouncy, and, without sharing the tomboyish characteristics of Jo March and Katy Carr, she frequently demonstrates her lack of gender-specific attributes, especially in the traditionally female context of domesticity. She puts liniment instead of vanilla into the cake she makes for the new minister's wife; she serves Diana cherry-brandy in mistake for raspberry cordial, and makes her friend disgracefully drunk; she starches Matthew's handkerchiefs; and she lets pies burn in the oven. The fact that two of these disasters are due to Marilla's carelessness in forgetting to relabel the bottles only emphasizes Anne's volitionless aptitude for getting into trouble. At the same time, the mishaps are not given exaggerated significance or made the focal point of a weighty moral message as they would have been in their literary predecessors.

Montgomery also effects her literary subversiveness by offering a more humorous version of the familiar themes of loss, deprivation and isolation. An early scene in the novel in which Anne waits at the station with 'a shabby old-fashioned carpet bag' (16) to be collected by Matthew, both stresses her vulnerability and provides a comic perspective on it. Matthew is looking for a boy, not a girl, and he is so frightened of females that he can hardly bring himself to speak to her when he realizes she is the expected orphan. Anne, on the other hand, has already asserted her own independence by insisting on remaining outside the ladies' waiting-room. The

potential pathos of the situation is thus diffused, a reminder that
the experience of parental loss may not be quite as melodramatic as
some fiction would have it. The 'cruel stepmother/aunt' pattern of
earlier works is also disrupted. Marilla, though old-fashioned and
set in her ways, is not unsympathetic or heartless; at first unable
even to contemplate adopting a girl, she gradually warms towards
Anne and learns to understand her. Under her guardianship, Anne's
life is far from miserable, and indeed Green Gables becomes her
true home in both an earthly and a spiritual sense.

This deconstruction of generic prototypes is reinforced by a more
overt intertextuality. Anne's description of her early years of
orphanhood spent with the struggling Mrs Thomas and her drunken
husband naively but effectively challenges the platitudes of conventional discourse:

> "Do you know if there is anything in being brought up by hand
> that ought to make people who are brought up that way better
> than other people? Because whenever I was naughty Mrs Thomas
> would ask me how I could be such a bad girl when she had
> brought me up by hand – reproachful-like." (38)

Dickens was one of Montgomery's favourite novelists and the direct reference here to *Great Expectations*, that classic story of
orphanhood, both foregrounds the wretchedness of Anne's previous situation and puts an ironic gloss on it. There are also suggestive recalls of two of Montgomery's more recent literary ancestors.
In the ironically-entitled chapter, 'Anne comes to Grief in an Affair
of Honour', Anne is 'dared' at a party to walk along the ridge-pole
of the kitchen roof; not surprisingly, she slips and crashes to the
ground. The accident results in a broken ankle and seven weeks of
inaction. Echoes of *What Katy Did* are unmistakable here, but the
significant differences suggest that this is a deliberate reversal of
Coolidge's text. Anne's injury is a minor incident in the narrative,
and is not focalized as a necessary step on the way to moral maturity,
as it is with Katy. Anne's own account of the minister's wife's
response to her misfortune – ' "She is such a cheerful person to have
visit you . . . She never tells you it's your own fault and she hopes
you'll be a better girl on account of it" ' (158) – also functions to
deflate the kind of pious moralizing which Cousin Helen offers
to the prostrate Katy. Similarly, Montgomery comically rewrites
a key episode in *Little Women* in which Anne, having turned her

offending red hair green instead of black with a defective dye, is forced to have it cut off. As she says to Marilla:

"This is such an unromantic affliction. The girls in books lose their hair in fevers or sell it to get money for some good deed . . . But there is nothing comforting in having your hair cut off because you've dyed it a dreadful colour, is there?" (182)

Montgomery was in fact an admirer of Alcott's stories, which she first read in her teens. Indeed in one of her own early tales, 'Her Pretty Golden Hair' (1898), the heroine, like Jo March, sacrifices her one beautiful feature to help the family finances. But later in her career, she became more critical of such sentimentalization of female virtue, and in Anne's case the incident has an iconoclastic function designed to highlight the text's realist affiliations.

In this novel, intertextuality also becomes a self-referential device. Following a tradition already established by earlier didactic writers such as Maria Edgeworth and Elizabeth Sewell, Montgomery ironically dramatizes the deleterious effect on an impressionable mind of reading too much highly romantic literature. Interestingly, it is not *The Lurid Mystery of the Haunted Hall* (which Anne's teacher, Miss Stacy, tells her is a 'very silly, unwholesome book' [200]) that over-stimulates her imaginative tendencies, but Tennyson's *Idylls of the King*. Anne and her friends act out the death of Elaine, but the former, as the 'unfortunate lily maid' (187), nearly drowns on the leaky flat board which substitutes for the Arthurian heroine's barge. While the novel as a whole validates the imagination as an important vivifying power, this particular incident, like the one in which Anne becomes paralysed with fear of the ghosts with which she herself has peopled the Haunted Wood, serves as a reminder that fantasy becomes absurd, even dangerous, if it is too far disengaged from the real world.

In dismantling the more absurd elements of earlier literary types, Montgomery also substitutes alternative ethical priorities. *Anne of Green Gables* certainly has lessons to teach, but they are neither the narrowly religious ones of Warner and Cummins, not the more secularized but still Puritan-oriented ones of Alcott and Coolidge. The shift of emphasis is made clear in Montgomery's description of how the incipient Sunday School story was transformed into a novel: 'I cast "moral" and "Sunday School" ideals to the winds and made my "Anne" a real human girl' (I, 331). Making Anne a 'real human girl' means that Montgomery validates a female goodness divorced from traditional ethical strictures. Her own dislike of the grim Presbyterianism fed to her by her grandparents, which caused her so much psychological suffering, may have inspired a resolve to permit her heroines a freer spiritual existence than she herself enjoyed. Recounting in her Journals her gradual progression from a 'belief in the fine old hell of literal fire and brimstone' (I, 197) and from a conviction of sin to a more transcendental and organic spiritualism, she describes her ideal of religious worship, currently impossible in her own society:

> to go away . . . to the heart of some great solemn wood and sit down among the ferns with only the companionship of the trees and the wood-winds echoing through the dim moss-hung aisles like the strains of some vast cathedral anthem. And I would stay there for hours alone with nature and my own soul. (I, ·162).

This kind of natural religious impulse finds an echo in Anne, who shocks Marilla with her lack of biblical and doctrinal knowledge and takes a disturbingly unorthodox approach to Divine truth. For her, if Jesus is the lover of little children as depicted in the sentimental pictures, then He should not look so sad. Likewise, instinctively recoiling from the harsh doctrines and rigid discipline of church and Sunday School, her ideal mode of devotion is to ' "go out into a great big field all alone or into the deep, deep woods, and . . . look up into the sky . . . then I'd just *feel* a prayer" ' (47); like her creator, she refuses to believe 'that *religion* and *beauty* were antagonists and as far as the poles asunder' (I, 378). Such sentiments anticipate the pantheism of Burnett's *The Secret Garden* (1911) in which Colin and Mary are spiritually as well as physically rejuvenated through their contact with the natural world. As with Burnett's characters, Anne's selfhood, unlike that of Ellen Montgomery and other pious girl heroines, develops from outside the narrow parameters of religious orthodoxy.

While rejecting the doctrinaire didacticism of much children's literature, Montgomery herself encountered the constraints of publication which insisted on the ethical orientation of children's literature:

> I like doing these [children's stories] but would like it better if I didn't have to lug a moral into most of them. They won't sell without it. The kind of juvenile story I like to write – and, read,

too, for the matter of that – is a rattling good jolly one – "art for art's sake" – or rather "fun for fun's sake" – with no insidious moral hidden away in it like a spoonful of jam. (I, 263)

Forced to comply with this insistence, she subverts it, however, challenging what she saw as merely empty gesturings towards morality. Anne's pragmatic and humanitarian ethics, meaningful because unsullied by the justifications and codification of adult creeds, are not only sympathetically presented in the novel but actually become the means of converting others. Marilla, for instance, contrary to her imbibed conventionalism, finds herself in accord with Anne's criticisms of the local Sunday School:

> . . . some of the things that Anne had said . . . were what she herself had really thought deep down in her heart for years, but had never given expression to. It almost seemed to her that those secret, unuttered, critical thoughts had suddenly taken visible and accusing shape and form in the person of this outspoken and neglected morsel of humanity. (73)

This deconstruction of the typology of the pious child as moral instructor is another aspect of the novel's literary subversiveness. The saintly young heroine (Ellen Montgomery in *The Wide, Wide World*, Gerty in *The Lamplighter*, and Eva in *Uncle Tom's Cabin*) who converts renegade adults is here transformed into the 'freckled witch' (19) who changes attitudes not by her piety and angelic utterances but by overthrowing the dominant social and moral orders; her 'teaching' is effected through her questioning and disregard of the rules by which the surrounding adult world is programmed. Importantly, too, her behaviour is neither God- nor adult-directed; unlike the earlier heroines, she has no mentor or mother to lead her in the right path, since, as has been indicated, Marilla is not the perfect guardian. The narrative thus endorses the autonomous goodness and innate moral clear-sightedness of the child state, and in this it marks a significant development from the earlier texts discussed. Whereas in *The Wide, Wide World*, *The Daisy Chain*, and *Little Women*, the girl is, sooner or later, forced to conform to the pattern of adulthood which surrounds her and shapes her experience, in *Anne of Green Gables* not only does the young heroine redeem her elders but her code of values is prioritized over theirs. The novel thus validates youthful experience more wholeheartedly than its predecessors and denotes a change in the orientation of girls' literature, granting the young reader wish-fulfilment fantasies of power within her own sphere.

Anne is, furthermore, largely untouched by the traditional creeds of sin, atonement and redemption, which even an ostensibly child-centred text such as *What Katy Did* traces as stages of entry to the adult world. Sin and guilt, indeed, play little part in *Anne of Green Gables*. Anne's own despairing abandonment of impossible standards (' "No matter how hard I try to be good I can never make such a success of it as those who are naturally good" ' [152]) foregrounds the novel's rational approach to the nature of virtue. Even when she appears to be enacting conventional moral codes, as at the end of the novel when she gives up her college scholarship in order to stay with Marilla, now threatened with blindness and eviction from the farm, her behaviour is inspired by personal feeling, not by Divine or human command. Anne commits herself to Marilla from love of one who has been a mother to her, refusing to regard her action in terms of heroic self-abnegation:

> "You surely don't think I could leave you alone in your trouble, Marilla, after all you've done for me ... There is no sacrifice. Nothing could be worse than giving up Green Gables – nothing could hurt me more." (249)

Anne's iconoclastic spirit reveals itself not only in the moral sphere but also in the social one. Here particularly the novel's implicit assumptions about female independence and gender orientation are foregrounded. Despite the temporary hiatus in Anne's planned self-improvement (the third novel of the series, *Anne of the Island* [1915], depicts her experience at Redmond, replicating Montgomery's attendance at Dalhousie College, Halifax), the narrative never seriously questions her right to extended education. When Mrs Lynde expresses her complacent satisfaction at the 'womanliness' of her decision – ' "You've got as much education now as a woman can be comfortable with. I don't believe in girls going to college with the men and cramming their heads full of Latin and Greek and all that nonsense" ' (250) – Anne retorts that she is going to study for higher qualifications at home instead. The intelligent girl knows that a life of domesticity will never satisfy her, and even Marilla declares that ' "I believe in a girl being fitted to earn her own living whether she ever has to or not" ' (201). It is never suggested, either, that Anne's fierce competitiveness in battling with Gilbert Blythe for top place in class is unwomanly or morally damaging. Unlike Ethel May, she is allowed to strive alongside her male peers, and her successes are as triumphant as theirs.

This validation of female autonomy is reinforced by the novel's gender emphases. Like many of the other texts discussed, it depicts a world in which women predominate and have control. The few men who figure in Avonlea are either psychologically destructive (Mr Phillips, the schoolmaster who treats Anne so insensitively), ego-threatening (Gilbert Blythe initially), or unable to communicate (Mr Bell, the Sunday School superintendent). The female sphere is foregrounded here; there is much emphasis on food and domestic comfort in the novel, and, as in *The Wide, Wide World*, *Little Women*, and *What Katy Did*, the heroine's introduction to responsibility and decision-making comes through the management of household affairs. Sisterhood is also important, especially in the strong ties between Anne and Diana, different though the two girls are. With the exception of Matthew, all the influential people in Anne's life are women – Marilla, Mrs Allen, the new schoolteacher, Miss Stacy – and it is through their examples that she progresses towards her full potential, intellectually and emotionally.

Anne herself is also empowered through her creative imagination. Central here is her manipulation of language, seen in a propensity for naming which she shares with Katy Carr. Through words, Anne reconstructs and thus reclaims for herself the surrounding environment. She transforms the prosaic into the poetic: Barry's pond becomes the Lake of Shining Waters, the Avenue becomes the White Way of Delight, and the woodland path near Green Gables becomes Lovers' Lane. Anne thus demonstrates her sensitivity to the flexible relationship between words and their signification, and, in creating her own discourse, challenges the privileging of the male Logos. She is also a story-teller: in the tradition of the female mythologist, she captivates her peers with her art of fiction-making, sharing this enabling inventiveness with earlier heroines such as Katy Carr and Jo March, and later Mary Lennox.

In prioritizing female experience and capacities, the novel also deconstructs essentialist notions of gender, and stresses how formulations of sexual identity are cultural, rather than biological. Marilla and Matthew have 'ordered' a 'smart likely boy' (11) from the orphanage, and are horrified when Anne appears instead. But they are rapidly won over by her, and Marilla's initial '"What good would she be to us?"' (30) changes to a recognition of her true value. The girl in fact turns out to offer much more than a boy would have done, and, as the Cuthberts come to realize, the affection and expanded emotional horizons she brings them are far more important than mere (male) provision of labour. Through her, Marilla learns not to distrust her own capacity for love. Similarly, the cranky Miss Josephine Barry, after her initial annoyance when Anne and Diana mistakenly burst into her bedroom at night, is captivated by the girl's freshness and vitality; she becomes aware that '"my imagination is a little rusty – it's so long since I used it"' (134) and realizes that '"If I'd a child like Anne in the house all the time I'd be a better and happier woman"' (196). Anne, then, the substitute boy, disrupts assumptions about gendered behaviour, replacing their binary polarizations with an ideology of individual worth which emanates from a feminized perspective.

Despite its gender deconstructiveness, *Anne of Green Gables* is not a radical text which overtly seeks to overthrow sexual hierarchies. Anne's innocence disorients the orthodoxies on which Avonlea is built, but, unlike Jo March or even Ethel May, she herself never directly rebels against the constraints of femininity; she wants to belong and be accepted, and this desire includes identification with others of her sex. She wants to look like the other girls, and one of her greatest longings is to have a dress with puffed sleeves. Significantly, at the end of the novel the narrative positions her firmly within the domestic sphere. This apparently regressive closure can be partly accounted for by publishing criteria which demanded a conventional conclusion, but it may also reflect Montgomery's own ambivalence about women's roles. She enjoyed being the only woman on the staff of the Halifax *Echo* and *Chronicle*, for which she worked from 1901 to 1902, and questioned biologically separatist notions of function, arguing that 'anyone's sphere – whether man or woman – is where they can be happiest and do the best work.'[16] She also insisted on women's right to speak for themselves:

> I do believe that a woman with property of her own should have a choice in making the laws. Am I not as intelligent and capable of voting for my country's good as the Frenchman who chops wood for me and who may be able to tell his right hand from his left, but cannot read or write?[17]

And though the Boston *Republic* reporter who interviewed her concluded that 'she has no favour for woman suffrage; she believes in the home-loving woman,'[18] her biographer comments that she was actually tougher than this presentation of demureness might suggest. On the other hand, Montgomery was not a thoroughgoing feminist. She considered the roles of wife and mother to be supreme, and in her own married life overtly deferred to ideals of womanly self-abnegation.[19]

If the novel's feminism is only muted, however, the work certainly does not unequivocally valorize the status quo. As recent critics have pointed out, it does not reinforce the doctrines of separate spheres or prioritize essentialist behavioural ideologies.[20] Thus what might be considered gender-specific qualities or roles are not tied to biological sex. As has already been shown, women are textually positioned as figures of strength, in contrast to the men, and their insertion into traditionally masculine arenas of empowerment is indicated by their involvement in the under world beyond the domestic – Marilla's participation in community affairs, Mrs Lynde's interest in politics and support for women's suffrage, and Anne's commitment to education, inspired by Miss Stacy and eventually leading to a career in teaching. In this, they replicate the women of the earlier texts who are active in the public sphere – Mrs March, Meg and Jo in *Little Women* and Mother in *The Railway Children*, for example. Conventionally feminine virtues are not the exclusive attributes of women, either. Gilbert Blythe acts out a self-sacrificial role in giving up his Avonlea teaching post to Anne, so that she need not leave Marilla after Matthew's death and the onset of the elderly woman's blindness. Matthew's womanly characteristics of gentleness and kindness make him naturally more sympathetic than Marilla to Anne's vulnerability; sensitive to the unspoken in her, he is instinctively responsive to her needs and desires, spoiling her with chocolates, obtaining for her the dress with the much-coveted puffed sleeves, and insisting that she be allowed to go to the Debating Club concert. He embodies maternal comfort rather than paternal authority (he is the one who pleads for her to be let off the punishments which Marilla imposes), and it is significant that Anne feels in close harmony with him – '"Matthew and I have such kindred spirits I can read his thoughts without words at all"' (120) – in a female bonding of non-verbal communication. Mocked by the community for his shyness and indecisiveness, he is in fact as much a victim of gender ideology, with its emphasis on male aggressiveness and self-assurance, as are women. Through him and the other main characters in the novel, polarities of masculine and feminine are undermined, being replaced by a more liberal and flexible vision of personal interaction.

It is therefore perhaps more helpful to read *Anne of Green Gables* as a revisionary rather than an ideologically radical or innovative text. This revisionary process is implemented in two main areas – the personal and the literary – which are linked in their purpose of suggesting new and more open attitudes towards girlhood. As indicated at the beginning of this chapter, Montgomery's convincing representation of a girlhood with which her readers could identify is certainly partly dependent on its creator's close personal involvement with the text. Like much of the fiction discussed here, the novel draws heavily on autobiographical experience and many details of Montgomery's own life are incorporated into it, including her school activities, her abandonment of a teaching career in order to look after an elderly relative, and her affection for her schoolmistress.[21] There are, however, significant variations between the 'facts' and the fiction, suggesting that Montgomery is rewriting the past not only in order to come to terms with it but also to place it in a wider perspective of child and gender orientation.

Anne's genuine orphanhood formalizes Montgomery's own abandonment by her father after her mother's death when he left her to the unsympathetic tendance of her grandparents – an act of betrayal which the intense expressions of daughterly devotion in the Journal only foreground more starkly: 'I love him with all my heart – better than anyone else in the whole world – dear, darling father!' (I, 50). A pattern of absent or inadequate fathers has already been noted in many of the texts analysed in this study – a form of covert rebellion against patriarchal dominance, achieved by writing out a potential source of female oppression. In Montgomery's case, the wholesale removal of the father may have had a therapeutic value, proving more psychologically acceptable, as well as more artistically liberating, than the real-life heartlessness. She also recasts her own upbringing by narrow-minded and severe relatives – what she herself describes as an '*emotionally* and *socially* . . . starved and restricted' (I, 377) childhood – into a fictionalized situation which challenges misconceived assumptions about familial affection and the nature of parenting. The care and genuine love which Anne receives from the Cuthberts, then, is not only authorial wish-fulfilment fantasy but a penetrating commentary on the fragile relationship between children and the adults to whom they are entrusted. The narrative is perhaps trying to write out, too, the troubled areas of developing sexuality in Montgomery's own past, particularly her disturbingly passionate (though unconsummated) relationship with Herman Leard, the son of the family with whom she boarded while teaching at Bedeque. Retreating from the psychological and social conflicts which full maturity brings, the novel keeps Anne in a pre-pubescent state, safely within the stasis of childhood. As Montgomery told the *Republic* reporter, ' "I want to leave "Anne" just as she is forever; in her girlhood." '[22] Gilbert never becomes more than a companion to Anne (after she has 'made up' with him), and it is not until *Anne of the Island* that the question of love between them is finally confronted. In her idyllic though not entirely untroubled world, Anne is protected from the lovelessness, isolation, and traumatic sexual awakening experienced by her creator.

Such authorial closeness to the fictional material – avowed by Montgomery herself who said that '*Anne* is as real to me as if I had given her birth – as real and as dear' (I, 332) – has invited criticism of the novel's sentimental celebration of girlhood. Despite her early personal experience of unhappiness, it is true that Montgomery seems to have viewed the child state with a large degree of romanticism. Her Journal entries are suffused with nostalgia for her own passed youth, when, in contrast to her present adult self, she was 'a happy, light-hearted girl with any amount of ideals and illusions' (I, 226) enjoying a Wordsworthian blessedness of being:

> *Then,* everything was invested with a fairy grace emanating from my own imagination . . . all [was] radiant with the "glory and the dream." (I, 121)[23]

The fictional enactment of nostalgic recall does not, however, necessarily mean lack of critical perspective. If Montgomery's heroine is a somewhat idealized replication of herself, she also exhibits more recognizably child-like traits than Warner's or Cummins' girl characters. As Carol Gay has commented, 'Montgomery took the female protagonist and with the realism that Alcott had pioneered, created a worthy successor to Jo March.'[24] More importantly, Montgomery adopts a strategy of self-referential subversion through which the heroine herself undermines the text's potential romanticization of girlhood and female behaviour.

Anne is not only an anti-heroine in the literary sense, she is also a highly self-aware and intelligent young girl who is able to separate herself from and comment on her own conduct. The conscious actor

in her own dramas, she simultaneously fashions roles and demol-
ishes them. In this, she replicates her creator's own highly-developed
sense of self as a fictional construct. Many of Montgomery's Journal
reminiscences read like a novel, with herself as the central character
in the narrative. Rewriting herself in a quasi-imaginary context seems
to have been a kind of therapy for her, a means of formulating an
identity from 'a series of pictures and sensations, at which I could
not choose but look and which I could not choose but feel' (I, 368).
Conscious self-dramatization is also one of Anne's most notable
traits, enabling her both to establish a personal place in an unaccommodating environment and to reveal that environment's shortcomings.

As well as being her own critic, Anne debunks the behavioural
codes of Avonlea society by exploiting them so as to expose their
inadequacies. A close link with the novel's literary subversiveness
can be seen here. As has been shown, many of Anne's attitudes and
actions are directly inspired by the fictional world of melodrama;
enacted in the real world, they reveal not only their own absurdity
but also the absurdities of the social conventions which contextualize
them.

The consciously parodic nature of Anne's self-representation is
evidenced in scenes in which she weeps. Thematically and structurally, mid-nineteenth century women's fiction frequently foregrounds
the tears of young girls, Ellen Montgomery's being probably the
most notorious example. Anne, too, expresses her grief by bursting
into tears. But the tonal shift in the later text can be seen by comparing two passages about weeping from Warner's and Montgomery's novels respectively. A scene from the former describes
Ellen's reaction to her aunt's cavalier authoritarianism in opening
Mrs Montgomery's letter to her daughter:

> Her eyes had been filling and dropping tears for some time, but
> now came the rush of the pent-up storm, and the floods of grief
> were kept back no longer ... Ellen was wrought up to the last
> pitch of grief and passion ... In the extremity of her distress and
> despair ... she sobbed aloud, and even screamed, for almost the
> first time in her life; and these fits of violence were succeeded by
> exhaustion, during which she ceased to shed tears and lay quite
> still, drawing only long sobbing sighs now and then.[25]

In this extract, Ellen is shown as literally possessed by emotion,
beside or rather out of her conscious self. In contrast to this is

Anne's reaction to a similar injustice, when Marilla punishes her for an offence of which she is not guilty:

> Anne realised that Marilla was not to be moved. She clasped her hands together, gave a piercing shriek, and then flung herself face downwards on the bed, crying and writhing in an utter abandonment of disappointment and despair . . . "I don't want any dinner, Marilla," said Anne sobbingly. "I couldn't eat anything, especially boiled pork and greens. Boiled pork and greens are so unromantic when one is in affliction." (86–7)

Anne is genuinely grief-stricken and, at the same time, alert to the histrionic role-playing of her response; she is self-aware in a way that Ellen never is, and can thus parody her own emotional outburst. Montgomery, in recalling the sentimentalism of earlier fiction, ironizes its excesses while simultaneously suggesting that Anne has an inner controlling strength and a healthy capacity for self-ridicule.

This self-awareness, based on the recognition of the ultimate separation between the sphere of imagination and that of reality, surfaces on many occasions in the novel. Anne's adoption of the heroine role, for instance, foregrounds the melodramatic sources from which it draws its inspiration. The highly literary language by which she creates herself as Lady Cordelia Fitzgerald points up the self-posturing of such images:

> "I am tall and regal, clad in a gown of trailing white lace, with a pearl cross on my breast and pearls in my hair. My hair is of midnight darkness, and my skin is a clear ivory pallor." (55)

Anne immediately deconstructs her own fantasy, telling herself, ' "You're only Anne of Green Gables" ' and comfortably sure that ' "it's a million times nicer to be Anne of Green Gables than Anne of nowhere in particular" ' (55). In each instance when she thus 'others' herself, she consciously positions her dream world alongside the everyday, and is always capable of negotiating between the various constructed selves and what she regards as the 'real' Anne.

The same character-centred ironic technique punctures the falsity of Avonlea's moral and social pieties. Again, comparison with *The Wide, Wide World* is illuminating. When Ellen bursts out in a fit of temper at her aunt, the ethical code by which she has been taught to order her behaviour causes her to feel guilt and remorse, not eased until she has acknowledged her sinfulness. When, on the other hand, Anne lets fly at Mrs Lynde for calling her 'terrible skinny and homely' (58), she remains defiant in the face of Marilla's horror, and agrees to apologise only after Matthew's intervention. But the exemplariness of this moral abasement is undermined by the obvious delight which Anne takes in the role of penitent. She exhibits 'an air of subdued exhilaration' as she 'imagines out' what she is going to say (65), and her 'confession' itself is wickedly hyperbolic:

> "I could never express all my sorrow, no, not if I used up a whole dictionary . . . Oh, Mrs Lynde, please, please, forgive me. If you refuse it will be a life-long sorrow to me. You wouldn't like to inflict a lifelong sorrow on a poor little orphan girl, would you, even if she had a dreadful temper?" (65)

A society which can be taken in by such feigned humility should, it is implied, look more carefully at its value systems.

The same kind of moral iconoclasm operates in the incident concerning Marilla's lost brooch. Convinced that Anne is lying to her, Marilla forces a confession from her – a confession which proves to be totally false, as Anne herself readily admits later:

> "Why, you said you'd keep me here until I confessed . . . and so I decided to confess because I was bound to go to the picnic. I thought out a confession last night after I went to bed and made it as interesting as I could." (88)

Not only the deceptiveness of conclusions drawn from appearances, but also the hypocrisies of conventional ethical codes, are exposed here. Anne's honesty triumphs by exploiting and demolishing the narrow-visioned adult morality which seeks to impose on it; like Huck Finn, she acts according to a pragmatism which, without theorizing, radically questions and judges ostensible righteousness.

The subversive power of rational innocence is also shown in another of the novel's parodic replications of sentimental tract literature. During Mrs Barry's temporary absence, Anne saves the life of her three-year old daughter, seriously ill with croup; intensely grateful, Mrs Barry apologises profusely to Anne and reinstates the friendship with Diana, suspended after the disastrous inebriation. Anne herself, however, disrupts the pattern of the generic prototype in which the saintly girl valorizes the Christian/female virtues of nurturance and selflessness and wins the erring adult's eternal respect. She sees the act itself as high adventure rather than as an instance of self-negating charity:

> Anne, though sincerely sorry for Minnie May, was far from being insensible to the romance of the situation and to the sweetness of once more sharing that romance with a kindred spirit. (121)

She also takes a very irreverent attitude to Mrs Barry's admission of injustice, delighting in being in a position of moral superiority and enjoying 'heaping coals of fire on Mrs Barry's head' (124). Once more, the text valorizes the moral insights of disingenuousness, while avoiding a simplistic affirmation of pre-lapsarian wisdom.

Thematically and structurally, then, *Anne of Green Gables* positions itself between two generic literary poles – the Evangelical representation of the sinful child who achieves redemption through self-discipline and obedience to Divine teaching, and the Romantic myth of youthful innocence whose entry into the adult world is a process of corruption and disenchantment. Like many of the other texts discussed here, it offers its own version of *Pilgrim's Progress* (one of Montgomery's favourite books), in this case a more liberal and secularized one. Anne is not fixed in the stasis of the childhood world. She progresses to maturity, learning to control her impulses so as to harmonize more closely with her social environment. She comes to realize the illusoriness of youthful dreams, concluding ruefully that 'the worst of growing up [is that] the things you wanted so much when you were a child don't seem half so wonderful to you when you get them' (195). She also abandons her romance writing, a gesture which seems partly an affirmation of realism ("It was silly to be writing about love and murder and elopements and mysteries' [211]), and partly authorial recognition that in a world dominated by patriarchal and rationalist values the productions of the female literary imagination must be obliterated or suppressed.

And yet the prison bars of adulthood have not yet fully closed on Anne at the end of the novel. She remains in a kind of limbo state, sexually unawakened, and merely looking towards 'the bend in the road' (253) which images her wider future. In common with most of the girl heroines in this genre, she is poised on the edge of maturity. The difference here, however, is that the pattern of her later life seems less determined. Whereas with the earlier works, the narrative conclusion presupposes closure, despite apparent indefiniteness, in this novel the predominant validation of pre-adolescence produces a genuinely ambivalent ending. Anne will of course have to grow up, but the text refuses to formulate the inevitabilities which await her.

Notes

1. Ed. Mary Rubio and Elizabeth Waterston, *The Selected Journals of L.M. Montgomery* (Toronto: Oxford University Press, 1985), I, 331. All subsequent references to this work will be included in the text.
2. Mollie Gillen, *The Wheel of Things: A Biography of L.M. Montgomery, Author of Anne of Green Gables* (London: Harrap, 1976), p.70.
3. Ibid., p.72.
4. Ibid., p.71.
5. Ibid., p.76.
6. Ibid., p.79.
7. Quoted in Gillen, p.72.
8. Ibid., p.162.
9. Ibid., p.166.
10. Ibid., p.78.
11. Ibid., p.81.
12. Ibid., p.165.
13. The autobiographical inspiration is even more prominent in *Emily of New Moon* (1923), in which a substantial amount of material is drawn almost exclusively from Montgomery's own experiences.
14. Lucy Maud Montgomery, *Anne of Green Gables* (London: Puffin Books, 1977), p.17 and passim. All subsequent references are to this edition and are included in the text.
15. In one of the letters which she continues to write to her dead father, Emily describes this attempt:

> Aunt Laura asked me the other day if I would like blue stripes better than red in my next winters stockings and I answered as Anzonetta did when asked a similar question, only different, about a sack,

> Jesus Thy blood and righteousness
> My beauty are, my glorious dress.

> And Aunt Laura said I was crazy and Aunt Elizabeth said I was irreverent. So I know it wouldn't work.

> (*Emily of New Moon* [London: Puffin Books, 1990], pp.113–14).
16. Gillen, p.86.
17. Ibid., p.86.

18. Ibid., pp.85–6.
19. Montgomery married Ewan Macdonald, a Presbyterian minister, in July 1911. Though it was a sensible match, Macdonald was a psychologically unstable man whose inner turmoils imposed a great strain on Montgomery. Moreover, as a loyal wife, she gave up dancing and other more frivolous social activities which she loved, because they would not have been approved of by the local congregation.
20. These points are made in Temma F. Berg, '*Anne of Green Gables*: A Girl's Reading', *Children's Literature Association Quarterly*, vol. 9, no. 4, Winter 1984–5, pp.124–8; and Carol Gay, '"Kindred Spirits" All: Green Gables Revisited', *Children's Literature Association Quarterly*, vol. 11, no. 1, Spring 1986, pp.9–12.
21. The model for Miss Stacy is Hattie Gordon, Montgomery's much-loved teacher at Cavendish, to whom she dedicated *Anne of Avonlea*.
22. Gillen, p.85.
23. Quotations from Wordsworth's 'Immortality' Ode, of which there is an example here, occur throughout Montgomery's Journals.
24. Carol Gay, op.cit. p.10.
25. Elizabeth Wetherell [Susan Warner], *The Wide, Wide World* (New York: The Feminist Press, 1987), p.148.

8

Frances Hodgson Burnett: *The Secret Garden*

Frances Hodgson Burnett's *The Secret Garden* (1911) takes up the subjects of orphanhood, illness and the autonomous world of childhood, which characterize a number of fictions for girls in the late Victorian period. The fantasies of female power which the novel projects so powerfully remain, however, tantalizingly unresolved as the tensions in the text between authority, gender and social class gradually become more pronounced, and the achievements of the heroine correspondingly marginalized. Like *The Wide, Wide World* and *Anne of Green Gables*, *The Secret Garden* focuses on the experience of juvenile isolation and alienation and follows the adaptation of a young girl to a new and initially disturbing environment. Unlike earlier texts, however, the moral emphases are subordinated to a more searching psychological dimension. In its focus on processes of socialization the story of *The Secret Garden* follows a regenerative path, with pervasive images of death and debility transformed to those of life and energy. From the opening chapters when sickly Mary Lennox is found abandoned and forgotten in a desolate house of death, her parents victims of a cholera epidemic, to the final pages which show Colin Craven, bouncing with health, racing headlong into his father's arms, the narrative pattern reinforces this polarization of death and life. In addition, through the dramatic spatial imagery, the dual focus on the enclosed interiors of Misselthwaite Manor and the open natural exteriors of the gardens and the moors beyond, the novel produces a paradigm of psychological growth, a movement from inward-looking self-absorption towards integration and relational activity.

Burnett wrote *The Secret Garden* towards the end of her long and highly successful career as a novelist and dramatist. An Englishwoman who had emigrated with her family to the United States at the age of sixteen, she spent much of her time travelling between Europe and America, and her own experience of cultural tension is realized in the sense of displacement which permeates much of her writing. *The Secret Garden*, written shortly after her naturalization as an American citizen, recreates both the foreignness and the attractions of the English country life which she had enjoyed for almost ten years at Maytham Hall, a large manor house she had rented in Kent and where her own passion for gardening had flourished. After the break-up of her second marriage in 1902 and the death of her first husband in 1906, Burnett had returned to America where she tried to recreate the harmonious idyll of rural England in her new home, Plandome, on Long Island, but the repressed unhappiness of recent experiences continued to surface in her writing. The repeated images of family trauma and boyhood illness in *The Secret Garden*, for instance, recall the death of her adolescent son, Lionel, from tuberculosis. The portrait of Colin Craven, lying pathetically on a sickbed, suggests consumptive symptoms, while his ultimate recovery can be read as a projection of her wish fulfilment, and even as an attempt to assuage her guilt at having spent so much time away from her children during their formative years. Such a reading could also help to explain the shift in interest from Mary to Colin in the final third of the novel, the emphasis on his accomplishments, and the triumphant reconciliation between parent and child in the closing scenes.

Structurally *The Secret Garden* is relatively simple, following the fortunes of the ten-year-old Mary after her parents' death when she is taken from India to live in the Yorkshire mansion of her uncle and guardian, Archibald Craven. From the time Mary arrives in the bleak Yorkshire dwelling which is to be her future home, the story concentrates almost exclusively on this one environment, Misselthwaite Manor and its surroundings. With her uncle absent abroad, mourning the premature death of his young wife ten years earlier, Mary is left alone at the manor without responsible adult guidance, servants her only companions. Her story becomes one of discovery, firstly of a garden, locked for ten years in memory of the dead Mrs Craven, and secondly of her cousin, Colin, a bedridden child, shut away in the house from which he never ventures out. The parallel movements of the restoration of the garden to a flower-filled paradise and the recovery of Colin to full health form the main narrative thrust of the book, informing Mary's process of self-discovery as she becomes the agent of this dual regeneration. She is aided in these acts of transformation by a young local boy, Dickon, whose close affiliation with the countryside helps Mary to understand the processes of the animal world and the 'natural' laws which also govern human behaviour.

This uncomplicated narrative organization belies the text's complex psychological dimension in its analysis of the nature and the requirements of childhood. The treatment of this subject itself reflects the popular contemporary interest in educational theory, heavily influenced by studies in child psychology and in particular by the pioneering work of Froebel, whose *System of Infant Gardens* had been published in England in 1855. Froebel's conviction that education is a 'leading out of nature under the skill of an intelligent gardener' and the view that a correlation between mind and body was necessary for healthy child development clearly inform Burnett's novel.[1] The text further uses the image of the garden to emblematize the idea of a private space as a prerequisite for the development of individual creativity, and identifies this as a crucial factor in the formation of identity. Secrecy, as announced by the novel's title, is also highlighted as fundamental to the concept of personal growth: the knowledge to which children only are privy empowers them to create an enchanted elite circle protected from adult interference. As with Katy's bower and Anne Shirley's imagined world in the forest, Mary's Edenic garden with its associations of enclosure and privacy becomes, albeit temporarily, a domain of female authority. It is, however, important to note how in all three of these works this fantasy retreat becomes integrated into the adult regime, and the girls who have ruled return to a more conventional role. At the end of Burnett's novel when the secrets of the garden and of Colin's renewed vigour are made available to a wider audience and become common currency, the children lose their power and return to a family and community environment which supports the prevailing hegemonic structure.

The appeal of *The Secret Garden* has always been primarily to a female readership. Its emphasis on nurturing, on the importance of a mother figure and on the empowering role of the imagination in personal development repeats a series of narrative norms that have evolved, as this study has shown, as characteristics of literature for girls. The novel directs attention towards personal and family rather than wider community values, and the representation of the male figures, both children and adults, tends to subvert gendered norms; the boys are non-aggressive, non-confrontational and noncompetitive; they are gentle in manner and prepared to absorb themselves in home-loving activities, such as gardening and story-telling.

Similarly Archibald Craven, the absent father/uncle is not the forbidding or authoritative patriarch of much children's fiction, but conforms to the prototype of a sensitive romantic, a recluse who wanders the world heartbroken after his wife's death, a tamed version of Charlotte Brontë's Edward Rochester. And although the book might seem to foreground the attractions of anarchy in its celebration of secrecy and subterfuge, this is only a temporary strategy, and the narrative ultimately retreats into a reassuring conformity.

Furthermore the equality of opportunity which is given to girls and boys in *The Secret Garden* does not initially appear to privilege male experience as do certain other texts of the same period which have a superficially androgynous appeal. In James Barrie's highly successful *Peter Pan and Wendy* (1904), for example, a work whose title immediately announces the equal billing of its hero and heroine, children merely emulate adult behavioural codes. The fantasy of permanent childhood which Barrie's text enacts takes place in a world which recreates the strict gendered division of Edwardian England; the boys go hunting and fight pirates while Wendy becomes a surrogate mother figure who stays at home and cares for her 'children'. *The Secret Garden*'s focus on collective play obviates the need for such a gendered split. It is only in the final chapter of the novel, when the story is nearing completion and the return to a full societal dimension is anticipated that competitive activity is introduced. The race between Mary, Colin and Dickon, when Colin emerges as the clear winner, carries obvious symbolic implications, but the bulk of the novel focuses not on the achievement of external goals, nor on the acquisition of skills, but on personal values of sharing, of selflessness and on the healing properties of love: the same principles which govern earlier sentimental writing for girls such as *Little Women* and *What Katy Did*.

Jacqueline Rose has pointed out how both principles of literary representation and genres in children's writing at the turn of the century were 'busily differentiating themselves from each other' according to a sexual division. As she suggests,

> The distinction between the domestic and fairy story on the one hand and the adventure story on the other, was also a division between literature for girls and literature for boys.[2]

In its mixing of domestic realism and magic fantasy, and in its recapitulation of familiar narrative motifs and patterns of characterization, *The Secret Garden* approximates to the model of a girls' text as described by Rose. Whilst the garden itself creates a magical new world (which liberates children from class and gender restrictions), the fantasy is given validity by the textual reliance on the scrupulously imitative method of classic realist fiction. The details of house and garden, the food that Mary eats, the bulbs that she plants, the visual and tactile recreation of the landscape: all serve to reinforce the solidity of the world that she inhabits. This surface realism (together with the often deliberately deflationary narrative voice which undercuts any sentimentalization of childhood) fails, however, to diminish the power of the fantasy which remains the core of the story. It is the social realism, the legacy of Victorian fiction, that carries the weight of moral conviction of the text, but it is the fairytale plot and romance motifs which establish its mythic dimension and which contribute to its continued popular appeal. Agnieszka Holland's recent film version of *The Secret Garden* (1993), with its move across generic conventions, graphically illustrates the different psychological levels at which the story functions while retaining a superficial rational cohesion. Cinematically, the interior of the house, the servants' quarters and the repressive atmosphere of the sickroom are meticulously rendered: the garden, where animals communicate with humans, summer flowers bloom at an astonishingly rapid rate and evanescent images of a romanticized, ever youthful mother figure melt into the landscape, belongs, however, to a quite different cinematic mode.

Despite its solidity of structure then, and the care with which the domestic and familial setting is assembled, *The Secret Garden* claims its strongest generic affiliations with the fairy-tale and the romance. Feminist critics have argued that the identification of women and romance writing is both powerful and subtle, liberating women writers to act out fantasies of the erotic and the psychic imagination that realistic fiction denies them.[3] The fairy-tale is a narrative with especial relevance for women, focusing as it does upon archetypal female dilemmas and socially acceptable resolutions. As one critic has noted:

> Traditional patterns, no less than fantasy characterization and actions contribute to the fairy tale's potency as a purveyor of romantic archetypes, and, thereby of cultural precepts for young women, . . . By dramatizing adolescence as an enchanted interlude

between childhood and maturity, romantic tales can, however, aggravate the female's psychic helplessness.[4]

In *The Secret Garden*, Mary's imagination is first stimulated by tales of her uncle and his isolated mansion, told her by other children who try to frighten her with a narrative of Gothic intensity in their description of 'a great big desolate old house in the country and no one goes near him . . . He's a hunchback and he's horrid.'[5] To Mary the account sounds 'like something in a book', encouraging her identification with the threatened but resilient heroine of archetypal narrative. The 'house with a hundred rooms, nearly all shut up and with their doors locked – a house on the edge of a moor' reminds her of the Perrault story, 'Ricquet à la Houppe', with 'no knowing what might happen' (16–19). Significantly, as Roderick McGillis has pointed out, that tale which is ostensibly about the transforming power of love is also a story about 'males who dominate females,'[6] and indeed Mary's encounter with a supposed hunchback does ultimately undermine her central narrative position.

The large house, the winding corridors, the locked rooms and the forbidden chambers which comprise Misselthwaite Manor, are also staple features of Gothic fiction, and they endorse the sense of uncertainty and loss of identity that Mary experiences in the early stages of the novel. As a number of critics have noted, several elements in *The Secret Garden* are reminiscent of Bronte's *Jane Eyre*:[7] the desolate location on Yorkshire moorland, the great house from which the master is absent for long periods, the mysterious behaviour of the servants who are guarding a secret which is withheld from the heroine, the strange cry in the night, and the hysterical figure confined to a locked room to which only privileged servants have access. The landscape across which Mary travels on her way to Misselthwaite is dark and menacing, 'the wide, black moor . . . a wide expanse of black ocean through which she was passing on a strip of dry land' (21) and reflects the precariousness of her psychic condition. So too does Jane Eyre initially find the Thornfield surroundings threatening to her own tenuous sense of security.

The hostile settings of Gothic narratives, which also reappear in *Jane Eyre*, carry symbolic resonance, frequently projecting a subliminal landscape of forbidding intensity which echoes the protagonist's alienated condition. Mary, lost and uncertain at the beginning of *The Secret Garden*, finds herself surrounded by mysteries which reflect her personal dilemma, and her search for the origin of the strange cry she hears in the night takes her through winding corridors, past closed doors and portraits of men and women from the past, whose history seems distant from hers and whose significance is withheld. The appearance of Colin as Mary's psychic twin, a personification of her own repressed rage and frustration, is similar to the use of Bertha Mason in *Jane Eyre*, a wild expressive complement to the passionate self that lurks behind Jane's taciturn exterior. And the ultimate return of the manor's master from abroad signals Mary's return to a rightful social position, albeit one of subservience, and as in *Jane Eyre*, is anticipated by an inexplicable telepathic experience.

In *The Secret Garden* then Burnett uses the romance as a main narrative vehicle for exploring hidden areas of the psyche, and the book reinvents fairy-tale and myth in order to apply archetypal plots to Mary's personal experience. The intertextuality which is a self-conscious feature of the novel also places the text firmly within a tradition of female story-telling, with the girl heroine negotiating between the roles of protagonist and narrator. The importance of fiction as a transformational activity is thus endorsed by Mary's role as female author prototype. A story-teller of consummate ability, she can be seen to subsume the role of the woman writer, her creative imagination enabling her to construct a private world that is unconfined by the claustrophobic conditions of the male-dominated Misselthwaite Manor. Narrative in this text is a form of female artistry, demonstrated through Mary's skill at creating enthralling word pictures of India for the Sowerby children, and at visualizing the garden as refuge for Colin, so positive in her effects that Martha can only assume, '"tha must have bewitched him!"' (142). Mary is an enchantress whose control over language captivates her audience and endows her with status. Her articulacy in comparison with Colin's hysterical screams is an empowering device which energizes both self and others, and releases them from a lethargy that is potentially destructive.

Like her literary counterparts, Jo March and Anne Shirley, as well as Burnett's own earlier creation, Sara Crewe of *A Little Princess*, Mary uses fictional paradigms as analogies for her own situation. In *A Little Princess*, a modified version of the Cinderella story, Sara combats the desolation and despair which threaten to engulf her through the transcendent power of narrative. Telling stories to herself and to the poor servant girl, Becky, her faithful companion, she recreates herself as a romantic heroine, taking her inspiration from archetypal heroic models, and overcomes the chilly conditions of her bare attic room by visualizing it as a setting from an adventure story. In *The Secret Garden*, Mary Lennox's fantasies are realized in tangible form: her imaginative revivification of the dead, colourless garden as a living, glowing bower materializes, bringing with it spiritual and psychological fulfilment.

While, however, the central action of the narrative might appear to celebrate female achievement, the novel does contain contradictory messages which warn against too simple a reading. Indeed the equivocal representation of gender in *The Secret Garden* fluctuates between an endorsement of transgressive strategies and a return to conventional norms: like the transference between potentially conflicting narrative genres, this functions as a destabilizing device. The introduction to Mary Lennox as an unfeminine little girl emphasizes the transgressive aspects of her role, and the opening words of the novel – 'When Mary Lennox was sent to Misselthwaite Manor to live with her uncle everybody said she was the most disagreeable-looking child every seen' – are deliberately deflationary, deconstructing past fictional models of idealized childhood and of conventional heroinism. Unlike the pretty, charming and adored Sara Crewe, the little princess of Burnett's earlier novel, Mary is plain, sallow, graceless and badly dressed. Nor does she have the dynamism of the tomboy which so attracts readers' sympathies in *Little Women* and *What Katy Did*. Yet Mary's rejection of the feminine is for the most part unconscious rather than wilful. Marginalized, forgotten, refusing to confirm to the romantic archetypes of either femininity or childishness, she forms a complex study of a problem child. While at one level her moral deficiencies are reminiscent of the naughty children of Victorian tract literature, they are presented here more as a natural consequence of her abandonment and ill-treatment. The victim of systematic neglect by her parents, Mary is depicted as withdrawn, sulky and bad-tempered. She exhibits what have come to be regarded as classic symptoms of abuse which inevitably result in aberrant behaviour, so that at the beginning of the book she is 'as tyrannical and selfish a little pig as ever lived' (2).

This moral encomium is, however, moderated by the psychological realism with which juvenile perceptions are transmitted. The early scenes of the book project a powerful image of disorientation as filtered through Mary's consciousness. Her situation in the plague-ridden house appears as a fragmentary, almost dream-like sequence of isolated images and overheard scraps of conversation, only half-comprehensible to the child's imperfect grasp of events:

> She only knew that people were ill and that she heard mysterious and frightening sounds. Once she crept into the dining room and found it empty, though a partly finished meal was on the table and chairs and plates looked as if they had been hastily pushed back when the diners rose suddenly for some reason . . . she went back to the nursery and shut herself in again, frightened by cries she heard in the huts and by the hurrying sounds of feet. (4–5)

The enclosure of the nursery, both refuge and prison, anticipates the unhealthy interior of Misselthwaite Manor where too illness generates fear and a sense of entrapment.

As mentioned in the Introduction to this study, the imagery of confinement is pervasive in nineteenth and early twentieth century texts by women writers, where in its political and psycho-sexual implications, it carries a particularly feminine resonance. The impact of alienation in the first chapter of *The Secret Garden* is intensified by the unfamiliar oriental setting, the exotic location and the sense of cultural displacement which are used to endorse the experience of non-belonging. As this gives way to a more reassuring, if depressing, English landscape with the description of London, Yorkshire and the rain, the potential for change that becomes the thematic focus of the novel is suggested both in environmental and personality terms. Thrown on her own resources when she arrives in England, Mary's tendency for introspection turns to thoughtful questioning. As the narrator comments, 'Since she had been living in other people's houses and had had no Ayah, she had begun to feel lonely and to think queer thoughts which were new to her' (12), and, her imaginative potential established, the seeds of moral and psychic growth can take root. It could be argued that Mary's socialization is itself reliant on a gendered definition of normality and of Englishness. As she becomes acclimatized to English life, so her process of development is one of increasing feminization: she gains weight, becomes 'almost pretty' and acts as a civilizing influence on her intractable boy cousin.

On the other hand, as Elizabeth Lennox Keyser has argued, it is Mary's aberrance from the conventionally feminine that generates the reader's sympathy.[8] Mary has initiative and qualities of leadership, and it is precisely because of her unorthodox upbringing that she is able to take decisions and follow them through. She seeks and discovers the forbidden garden after her interest has been awakened by stories of its secret location and it is her very 'contrariness' that stimulates her curiosity. 'As she was not at all a timid child and always did what she wanted to do' (35), Mary follows her impulses and is rewarded for her determination. Four years before the publication of *The Secret Garden*, in her novel, *The Shuttle* (1907), Burnett wrote that a girl's duty was to be 'trained to fetch slippers as retrievers to go into the water after sticks,'[9] a training that *The Secret Garden* emphatically refutes. As Peter Keating has observed, during the Edwardian period, 'children were suddenly allowed to be themselves in literature', and Mary in her avoidance of meek obedience follows the evolving trend for the fictional child who was no longer 'pious, industrious and well-mannered: instead the admired child was likely to be seen as imaginative, inventive, self-reliant and constantly in trouble.'[10]

More importantly, the trouble which Mary courts through her disobedience, as she disregards orders to forget the garden and to ignore the source of the mysterious cry in the night, proves to be her salvation and the stimulus for the restoration of order in the disturbed household. The bluntness and obstinacy which make her charmless to the adults who surround her are in fact the real key to Mary's empowerment. Significantly, if the social implications of the text are interpreted as potentially subversive, it is from servants that Mary learns how to exploit her independence to practical effect: Martha teaches her to dress herself on her first morning at Misselthwaite Manor and from this beginning she becomes increasingly adventurous. Her self-reliance leads her to the discovery of the hidden door so that when she eventually steps inside the secret garden, 'she felt as if she had found a world all her own' (79). The garden confers ownership, and the autonomy it grants allows the girl a psychic space in which to realize a personal identity. Her authority and stubbornness also have powerful effects in her relationship with Colin Craven, who responds to her headstrong management tactics when Mrs Medlock's protective coddling has failed.

It is in the representation of the relationship between Mary and Colin that the text engages most interestingly with the debate about gendered ideology and childhood. In drawing attention to the similarities between the two children rather than emphasizing their gendered differences, the novel continues the subversion of gender stereotyping seen in the conceptualization of Mary's character. In its focus on the effects of isolation, the loss of parenting, the emphasis on physiological frailty, and the connection between bodily and psychic health, Colin's plot initially repeats almost precisely the formula of Mary's narrative, that of growth from weakness to strength, from exclusion to acceptance, from egotism to altruism and from ignorance to understanding. Colin acts as Mary's alter ego, enabling her to confront in reality those aspects of the self that she is at first unwilling to acknowledge. On first meeting both children are sickly, spoiled, bad-tempered, and ugly in appearance, disliked by all around them. They are also arrogant and unable to speak politely to the servants who look after them.

In a significant rejection of the policies of colonialist appropriation, the novel challenges the prevailing assumptions about both gender and class in its representation, however temporary, of a new democracy which the children create in their alliance against adults. The social privilege that Colin enjoys as a member of the English squirearchy is made analogous to Mary's position as a child of the ruling class in imperialist India. This privilege is also disabling (literally in Colin's case), and it is a mark of both children's progress that as their relationship flourishes with a concomitant expansion of vision, they reject their establishment positions. This is best illustrated by their attempts to adopt the language of the servant class, the Yorkshire dialect which is, as Mary points out, 'like a native dialect in India', a language that significantly she was never required to learn (197). This division neatly encodes the relegation of servants and women to the realm of the linguistic other, with its own discrete discourse that eludes the rigidities of the symbolic order. When for example Mary hears Martha use the term 'wuthering', her comprehension of it transcends the boundaries of rational explanation:

> Mary did not know what "wutherin" meant until she listened and then she understood. It must mean that hollow shuddering sort of roar which rushed round and round the house as if the giant no one could see were buffeting it and beating at the walls and windows to try to break in. But one knew he could not get in, and somehow it made one feel very safe and warm inside a room with a red coal fire. (49)

The womb-like interior of the nursery, protected from the unseen (male) threat, also anticipates the symbolic cocoon of the walled garden which Mary creates as a female space, away from adult invasion.

Analysis of gender in *The Secret Garden* cannot be isolated from analysis of social class, as the central section of the novel reaffirms the breakdown of established hierarchies in the idealized world of childhood play, an illusion that does not persist into the adult regime. Just as Mary learns to speak politely to Martha and to treat Ben Weatherstaff with respect, so her friendship with Dickon carries no overtones of either sexual or social impropriety but is depicted as a healthy, invigorating relationship between two young people, which thrives on mutual interests and a sense of common purpose. Although the overriding social vision of the text can be interpreted as carrying worrying implications for the feminist critic, with the gradual elimination of both Mary and Dickon from the action and the final reduction of Mary's central role to that of secondary agent, the perspective on childhood as unconditioned by adult social ideologies affirms the tenuous nature of class division as an artificial construct. Similarly the breakdown of gendered distinctiveness as a precondition of pre-adolescent developmental experience is part of the text's iconoclasm which utilises childhood to provide a critique of contemporary ideology.

To complement this the text produces images of gendered displacement which deconstruct conventional models of girlhood and boyhood. The characterization of young boys in *The Secret Garden* if anything conforms more to a stereotypic female than to a male model of development and it could be argued that Dickon and Colin are used to illustrate respectively positive and negative aspects of femininity, which function implicitly as suitable educative models for juvenile readers. Whereas one is a model of how to be, the other represents how not to be. The negative aspects of Colin's imperiousness and fits of temper are moderated by the influence of Dickon and Mary who normalize his behaviour so as to approximate it to a version of the adult male role he will be required to adopt. This reinforces the ambiguity of the text: the atypical boy teaches precisely those masculine codes to which his own feminized value system is antithetical.

Initially Colin's illness, largely imaginary, is reminiscent of classic nineteenth century versions of female frailty which results in a tendency to exploit his debility so as to attract attention to himself and to manipulate the household. As Elaine Showalter has commented:

the portrait of the anorexic painted by Darwinian psychiatry is paradoxically that of the self-sacrificing Victorian heroine. Refusing to eat, she acted out the most extreme manifestation of the feminine role, flaunting her martyrdom, literally turning herself into a "little" woman.[11]

Colin's pallor, his 'sharp, delicate face the colour of ivory' (126), his thin body on which 'every rib could be counted' (181) and his rejection of food are all features which confirm to this type, and in his recourse to tantrums he re-enacts the classic behaviour syndrome of late nineteenth-century theories of the female psyche. No longer, however, is debility seen as a desirable image of the feminine as was the case with Margaret May, Beth March or Cousin Helen. Rather Colin's condition is reminiscent of that of the Victorian woman whose chronic invalidism operated as a form of cultural protest or as a weapon of self-assertion.

Claudia Marquis, in a sustained psychoanalytic reading of *The Secret Garden*, has suggested that the portrait of Colin provides a study of yet another classic female malady, hysteria, and that the text propounds an argument for the necessary reintegration of the hysteric to a full emotional life.[12] At a turning point in the novel, Mary, pushed to the limits of her patience by Colin's frenzied outbursts, shouts at him, ' "Half that ails you is hysterics and temper – just hysterics – hysterics – hysterics!" ' (180). The narrative voice confirms that the boy's condition finds its source in psychological deprivation and enforced introspection:

> If he had ever had any one to talk to about his secret terrors – if he had ever dared to let himself ask questions – if he had had childish companions and had not lain on his back in the huge closed house, breathing an atmosphere heavy with the fears of people who were most of them ignorant and tired of him, he would have found out that most of his fright and illness were created by himself. (181)

As Marquis suggests, 'his is the case history of a hysteric'[13] and as such illustrates the psychic deficiencies of one aspect of a traditional female strategy, the retreat into illness. In this sense *The Secret Garden* forms a significant development from earlier Victorian texts for girls which presented invalidism as an inspirational force for women, with spiritual connotations.

As suggested earlier, Colin also functions as a mirror image of Mary's own disturbance, articulating the anger and frustration that she has internalized. At their first encounter, in the dead of night in Colin's room, each child believes that the other is a ghost or a figure from a dream, and the patterned dialogue and the revelation of their familial ties (' "Mr Craven is my uncle"'. ' "He is my father"' [127]) reinforce their mutual interdependence. As Phyllis Bixler has observed, in this respect *The Secret Garden* is in line with the traditional narrative practices of other nineteenth-century women writers as identified by Sandra Gilbert and Susan Gubar, with the use of 'maddened doubles', 'asocial surrogates' and 'obsessive depiction of diseases like anorexia' as 'symbolic expressions of the disintegration of the psyche, negation of the body, and psychological and physical imprisonment caused by narrow socially approved roles for women.'[14]

Whereas at the time of their first meeting Mary has already begun to act to prevent her own destruction, Colin's behaviour serves as a reminder of the unacceptable face of femininity whose rage and gestures of protest are literally life-threatening. He thus embodies the need for a return to a civilized norm, where extreme feeling must be repressed, so potentially damaging is its expression. Just as Jo March must learn the hard lesson of repression of anger and the need for self-control, so Mary and Colin must acquire socially acceptable attributes of gendered behaviour, resisting the impulse to succumb to the dark rage which is symptomatic of psychic disturbance. Significantly, however, the retreat from a position of rage and self-imposed illness is also a retreat from power.

At the same time the episode of Colin's illness functions as a critique of current medical practice, with its emphasis on medication and rest cures, in favour of alternative holistic approaches. In 1884, Burnett had become interested in the work of Mary Baker Eddy, whose Christian Science principles had helped her to recover from a debilitating attack of nervous exhaustion. Suffering from the effects of strain and overwork, she had responded positively to a course of treatments from a Boston mind-healer, a neighbour of Eddy's and a Christian Science follower.[15] Although Burnett never formally converted to the Christian Science Church, the impact of its teachings remained a powerful influence on her thinking, clearly inspiring *The Secret Garden*'s message of the interdependence of physical and psychic well-being. In the novel, the children's apparent freakishness at the beginning of the story, and their ultimate psychological and cultural destination signal a return to normalcy and a status quo which incorporates a conventional model of male/female relations.

Whilst Colin must be socialized out of his negative femininity, Dickon on the other hand exemplifies a series of positive female traits associated with the strong, but too frequently absent, mother figure. Dickon's personal strength emanates from his own security and bonding with an all-embracing mother in contrast to the troubled children of *The Secret Garden*, Mary and Colin, who can trace the source of many of their anxieties to motherlessness. Their search for an integrated self is closely linked to their growing appreciation of maternal succour in the earth-mother figure of Mrs Sowerby, together with their own developing ability to reproduce nurturing qualities. For, although perhaps insistently motherhood operates as a positive model in this text, primarily through the inspirational spirit of the dead Mrs Craven and the more practical virtues of Susan Sowerby, it is also propounded through male as well as through female characters. Not only does Dickon perpetuate his mother's values in repeating her words of advice and bringing the children food that she has prepared, but he becomes the embodiment of maternal qualities in his protective and stabilizing role. His talent for mothering, for rescuing and sheltering helpless baby creatures and acting as a surrogate parent forms the dominant ethos of his life. The rescue and care of the motherless baby lamb for instance is analogous to his salvation of the two children. Offering the animal a feeding bottle of milk, he addresses it tenderly:

> "Come on, little 'un," and he pushed the rubber tip of the bottle into the nuzzling mouth and the lamb began to suck it with ravenous ecstasy. (205)

In much the same way does he provide both literal and spiritual nourishment for Mary and Colin, bringing them fresh milk and newly baked bread as well as emotional support. Their affirmative response to his influence is a crucial factor in their emotional re-alignment, and the messages of serenity and reliability that Dickon transmits become prerequisites for their acquisition of selfhood.

In these respects, Colin and Dickon together form a recasting of the elements which figure prominently in Burnett's earlier, much maligned but hugely popular child hero, Cedric Erroll in *Little Lord Fauntleroy* (1885). In looks Cedric resembles the healthy Colin, with his long curls, huge eyes and delicate features, while in personality he is reminiscent of Dickon with his universal ability to charm and his penchant for loving. It is significant that in the early twentieth-century stage versions of the novel his role was almost invariably undertaken by a series of child actresses rather than boy actors. Whereas a number of contemporary works for children, whether adventure narratives or family histories, stressed the fact that boys will be boys, in Frances Hodgson Burnett's fictions boys, sensitive, caring and imaginative, are in fact more frequently girls.

The uncertainty which manifests itself in the crossing of gender boundaries in *The Secret Garden* is developed most potently in the ambivalent symbolism of the garden itself. This enclosed, walled space, accessible only through a hidden door, invites entry into a world of licence and release from external constraints: both class and gender hierarchies are abandoned in its revisionary environment. The female value system that operates within the womb-like seclusion of the garden can be seen as analogous to the power of the mother – the spirit of the dead Mrs Craven haunts the place – and which in feminist psychoanalytic theory is all too easily replaced by the law of the father. In Lacanian terms it is the world of the female Imaginary, a world where the symbolic order is temporarily suspended and male authority consequently marginalized. The affiliation of the garden with the romantic figuration of the lost mother (whose portrait insistently recalls girlhood rather than maturity), perpetuates the cultural referents of woman, flowers, nature and paradisal innocence that are traditionally associated with female iconography. As a version of the Edenic world of innocence, the garden is also the site of Mary's transfiguration from moral ugliness to spiritual beauty. Set apart from the power centres of Edwardian patriarchy, it thus has the double function of liberating female potential and reawakening the heroine to new life.

While on one level the garden reformulates Eden, its pre-lapsarian state incorporates a pagan mythology and eulogizes a Nature spirit that responds to mystic rites and incantations. The children believe fervently in the curative powers of Nature and their ritualistic daily invocations result in the 'magic' of Colin's recovery. Dickon's Pan-like status endorses this Pagan element; first observed playing on his 'rough wooden pipe' (97), he is a magnetic centre of attraction for his audience of woodland creatures. The Paganism that Dickon represents forms a complement to Mary's innate 'otherness', visualized through the non-male, non-hierarchical world of Nature which provides a rhythmic process of experience and which counteracts the authoritarian establishment from which she takes her original behavioural impetus. Although Dickon, the main agent of pagan ideology, is a male child, the qualities he embodies are those with strong female connotations: mothering, protective nurturance, tenderness and nature. Blending in to the landscape of the garden he inspires the spirit of motherhood with which the garden is endowed to work its 'magic' so that its identification with the lost mother figure of the beautiful, girlish Mrs Craven becomes complete. Mary's immediate empathy with Dickon, even before the two have met, activates her latent femininity, which merely requires an appropriate channel for expression. Dickon, the substitute mother, thus acts as the agent of Mary's feminization just as she in turn functions as the civilizing force for Colin's return to the norm. In its defence of paganism as a healing force effectively replacing conventional Christian theology, and by associating the pagan with Nature and by extension with the female principle, the text constructs a significant opposition between the male establishment and the ability of women to deconstruct that order and to invest it with new meaning.

The garden, however remains a highly ambivalent image. Significantly, the swing, which in Susan Coolidge's version of the Fall served a didactic purpose, here functions as a reminder of the vulnerability of woman even within the charmed sanctuary of the garden. The young, beautiful Mrs Craven dies when the swing on which she is seated collapses and forces her into premature labour, giving birth to Colin. The episode is significant in terms of the double-edged meaning attributable to the symbolism of the garden. For at the same time as it provides opportunities for its heroine to establish her authority and dictate her own terms of reference, the secret garden also represents a world characterized by transience, as the effects of seasonal change demonstrate. The associative imagery of flowers and the 'magic' ascribed to the garden where animals appear to talk and Dickon is 'a sort of wood fairy' emphasize the provisional nature of its enchantment. In accordance with the conventions of the pastoral romance, democratic allegiances which flourish in the protected enclosure also dissolve when confronted with the return of the master of Misselthwaite to the reins of control, and the garden itself becomes marginalized as a temporary place of shelter.

So although the secret garden is the site of Mary's growth to self-assurance and provides her with the opportunity to exercise initiative and application, it simultaneously becomes the locus of her cultural imprisonment. Even within the safety of the garden differences between male and female begin to emerge as Colin's return to normal health results in renewed interests. His passion for science and for isometric exercises is balanced against Mary's more sedate love of story-telling and her patient absorption in watching plants bloom, the essentialist division between male rationalism and female imagination becoming apparent as the novel approaches closure. Having then created the conditions for the exercise of female power in Mary's autonomy over the garden, Burnett causes her heroine to relinquish that power by exposing its limits: Colin, in the final episode of the novel, leaves the garden behind and returns to the real power centre, the house, which he is to inherit as master. Mary, the prime mover of his recovery, is significantly absent from the closing tableau where Colin and Archibald Craven, heads held high, stride across the lawn in a demonstration of male bonding that excludes female participation. The preservation of this patriarchal order reinforces the division between male and female spheres of experience which the bulk of the novel has up to this point effectively blurred.

The Secret Garden thus stands in the direct line of literature for girls that offers its readers provocative possibilities of excitement and adventure, only to withdraw the promise in the terms of their ultimate resolution. Like Alcott's *Little Women*, which relies on Jo March's resistance to convention for its narrative dynamic merely to have her sink into being a 'little woman' for the approving gaze of her father, *The Secret Garden* concludes by foregrounding the conservatism which has also been implicit in its portrayal of class relations. Just as Mary is removed from the focus of attention at the end of the novel, so Dickon, the working-class child who has been central in the regenerative process, is completely forgotten in the finale's emphasis on reconciliation between father and son. The novel's main narrative experience of childhood freedom is thus framed by the removal and the return of parents. Similarly the social hierarchy of prevailing English class and gender divisions is perpetuated by the unashamed return to the status quo and the exclusion of Mary and Dickon from the centre of love as well as from power.

In its realization of dual, often conflicting modes of gendered behaviour and their determining contexts, the novel exhibits tensions such as are common to other fictions in this study without being necessarily feminist in its orientation. The eventual narrative progression of *The Secret Garden* reverts to the conventional model of the feminine, offering a model of woman as an apotheosis of motherhood, and showing girls as feminizing and civilizing influences on a sterile male culture. Yet the main action of the novel gains its magnetism from a diametrically opposed position as it glorifies female intransigence and freedom and establishes a psychic personal space for the talented, creative girl who is its heroine. This textual instability thus provides scope for readings of the novel's covert 'message', contained in its very incoherence.

Anthea Trodd has argued that the confines of the genre of children's literature allowed women writers during this period to explore their situation without drawing hostile attention to themselves, and that despite the conservatism of its conclusion, the appeal of *The Secret Garden* 'lies in its exploration of the heroine's discovery of a space of her own.'[16] Commentators are generally agreed that the image of the garden and the potency it confers on those who succumb to its magic generates the narrative dynamic of the text, even if, like Humphrey Carpenter, they assume that Burnett did not fully understand the significance of what she was about.[17] The preceding discussion shows how confusions regarding gender and models of female behaviour which had affected women writers of earlier periods remained problematic for twentieth-century authors for children, despite a shift in emphasis from a moral to a psychological agenda. In its explicit alignment of gender with power relations, *The Secret Garden*, a text by a hybrid English/American woman writer, forms a fascinating coda to the tradition of evangelical and sentimental literature for girls which has provided a benchmark in this study's analysis of fictional ideologies of girlhood.

Notes

1.   Froebel, *System of Infant Gardens* (1855), quoted in Juliet Dusinberre, *Alice to the Lighthouse: Children's Books and Radical Experiments in Art* (London: Macmillan, 1987).

2.   Jacqueline Rose, *The Case of Peter Pan or The Impossibility of Children's Literature* (London: Macmillan, 1984), p.84.

3.   See, for example, Laurie Langbauer, *Women and Romance: the Consolations of Gender in the English Novel* (Ithaca and London: Cornell University Press, 1990); Rosalind Miles, *The Female Form: Women Writers and the Conquest of the Novel* (London and New York: Routledge

& Kegan Paul, 1987); Jean Radford, *The Progress of Romance: The Politics of Popular Fiction* (London: Routledge, 1986).

4. Karen E. Rowe, 'Feminism and Fairy Tales', *Women's Studies*, 1979, vol. 6, p.248.

5. Frances Hodgson Burnett, *The Secret Garden* (Oxford and New York: Oxford University Press, 1987), p.10. All subsequent references are to this edition and are included in the text.

6. Roderick McGillis, ' "Secrets" and "Sequence" in Children's Stories" ', *Studies in the Literary Imagination*, 1985, Fall, vol. 18 (2) p.37.

7. See particularly Fred Inglis, *The Promise of Happiness: Value and Meaning in Children's Fiction* (Cambridge: Cambridge University Press, 1981); Ann Thwaite, *Waiting for the Party: The Life of Frances Hodgson Burnett 1849–1924* (London: Secker & Warburg, 1974).

8. Elizabeth Lennox Keyser, 'Quite Contrary: Frances Hodgson Burnett's *The Secret Garden*', *Children's Literature: An International Journal*, The Modern Language Association Division of Children's Literature, 1983, vol. 11, pp.1–13.

9. Quoted in Thwaite, op.cit. p.52.

10. Peter Keating, *The Haunted Study: A Social History of the English Novel 1875–1914* (London: Secker & Warburg, 1987), p.220.

11. Elaine Showalter, *The Female Malady: Women, Madness and English Culture 1830–1980* (London: Virago Press, 1987), p.128.

12. Claudia Marquis, 'The Power of Speech: Life in *The Secret Garden*', *Journal of the Australasian Universities Language and Literature Association*, 1987, Nov., vol. 68, pp.163–187.

13. Marquis, p.166.

14. Phyllis Bixler Koppes, *Frances Hodgson Burnett* (Boston: Twayne, 1984), p.100.

15. For a fuller description of Mary Baker Eddy's philosophy and influence on Burnett see Thwaite, op.cit., pp.88–9.

16. Anthea Trodd: *A Reader's Guide to Edwardian Literature* (Hemel Hempstead: Harvester Wheatsheaf, 1991), p.72.

17. Humphrey Carpenter, *Secret Gardens: The Golden Age of Children's Literature* (London: George Allen & Unwin, 1985), p.189.

9
Angela Brazil:
The Madcap of the School

Angela Brazil's *The Madcap of the School* (1917) is included in this study of classic works for girls, not for the enduring qualities of the individual text, but because it functions as an exemplar of the school story genre that Brazil pioneered and that was to have such a profound impact on girls' reading experience during the twentieth century. Unlike earlier works considered in this study, such as *Little Women* or *The Secret Garden*, *The Madcap of the School* is no longer enjoyed by a modern audience, nor is it even easily available in print. Yet, together with forty-eight other full-length novels by Brazil, and approximately seventy short stories of boarding-school life that she produced for magazines, it played a significant part in the creation of a new and highly influential literary genre, a genre that addressed a specifically female juvenile readership in a direct challenge to the sentimental tradition of much previous fiction for girls.

As the subject of the final chapter of this work, *The Madcap of the School* is particularly important for the way in which it signals a crucial change of direction in girls' reading and reflects the contemporary shift in ideologies of girlhood from the Victorian to the modern period. Published during the First World War, the novel also dramatizes something of the uncertainties relating to female education and women's social roles that the war experience itself threw into sharp relief. In its incorporation of certain fundamental generic features of earlier school tales and its negotiation between variant models of the feminine, *The Madcap of the School* stands at a literary cross-roads. It demonstrates a debt to past traditions of literature for girls while clearly indicating future directions that were to break with those traditions in establishing alternative imaginative possibilities for a young female readership.

Born in 1869, Angela Brazil had written several whimsical and fantasy tales for children before she published her first school story, *The Fortunes of Philippa*, in 1906. Its success was immediate and commissions for further similar stories followed, until Brazil was producing on average two full-length novels and five short stories of boarding-school life annually. The popularity of the format she initiated was such that other writers quickly followed suit and as early as the 1920s, books appeared in sub-Brazil mode, which make explicit reference to the schoolgirl culture as embodied in her work and to the precise nature of its imaginative attraction for young readers. In Elinor Brent Dyer's *The Princess of the Chalet School* (1927), for instance, the motherless Princess Elisaveta of Belsornia, living in a royal household with only a governess for company, indulges in a fantasy that she should be allowed to attend a boarding school,

> where there were lots of nice girls who were all anxious to be friendly and work and play with her, as she had read of girls doing in the school-stories which her father had given her.[1]

Elisaveta's fantasy reflects in miniature the shift in middle-class education for girls that was taking place during this period, in its move from private tuition to collective schooling. In common with those of real and less privileged children of the period, the princess's imagination is fired by a literary vision of a community of equals, where her unnatural isolation will be alleviated by a network of female friends, and where work and play are indivisible. This vision of a female community, self-sufficient and mutually supportive, is a central element in Brazil's version of school as it appears in *The Madcap of the School*. In this novel, Marlowe Grange School comprises twenty-six pupils whose sense of solidarity invests them with a corporate strength that extends into the society at large. As the head girl announces, in a thrilling exhortatory speech to her fellows:

> "If a whole school makes up its mind to a thing, it ought to have some effect, and it would be splendid to feel that our school had been an inspiration, and helped to build up a new and better nation after the war. There are only twenty-six of us here at present, but suppose when we leave we each influence ten people, that makes two hundred and sixty, and if they each influence ten people more, it makes two thousand six hundred, so the thing grows like circles in a pond."[2]

It is this ideal of a defined communal ethic with its associated vision of pupil power that the school story as developed by Brazil

foregrounded, and that was to exercise such an influence over subsequent writers who reproduced its formula and its ethos. Within
it girls were realized as individuals, not types (although they later
became so); individuals, moreover, who, through their distinctive
status as schoolgirls, re-invented the boundaries of the feminine in
their extension of what was possible for young women to achieve.
As Gill Frith has observed,

> If we see ideologies of femininity in terms of a unitary, if
> overdetermined, progression towards passivity, domesticity and
> a reproductive role, then the representation of femininity within
> the school story clearly stands as an expression of resistance and
> subversion.[3]

In the late twentieth century, the girls' school story itself has
become something of a cliché. Its standard characters (the madcap;
the plucky new girl; the sporty games captain; the fair but firm
headmistress) and stock situations (the schoolgirl prank; the midnight feast; the end of term concert; the heroic rescue) have become
so familiar to generations of readers that a whole parodic cult has
evolved with its own sophisticated intertextual allusions that draw
heavily on a self-referential linguistic code. As Jan Montefiore has
pointed out, 'the parody of the girls' school story has entered popular culture', inspiring films, cartoons, drama and allusions in reviews, skits and poems such as 'John Betjeman's erotic celebrations
of Myfanwy, "ringleader, tomboy and chum to the weak."'[4] It is,
however, easy for contemporary readers to forget Brazil's pioneering role in the definitive establishment of a genre which has now
gained such mythic status that it forms a ready cultural target for
subversion. Jeffrey Richards has argued a similar point with reference
to the development of the boy characters in Frank Richards' *Greyfriars*
series:

> the idea that they are stereotypes, which some later commenta-
> tors have advanced, is quite untenable. They are instead arche-
> types, something quite different. A stereotype is a carbon copy
> of a well-established model; an archetype is the creation of a
> definitive idealization.[5]

Brazil's schoolgirls, conceptually innovative, do not reproduce existing patterns of behaviour but initiate new approaches to girlhood

which in the hands of some later authors were to become over-determined and simplistic. Yet the archetypal characters and narrative situations which *The Madcap of the School* establishes produce models of female behaviour and potential that result in a literary image of the girls' school as a positive source of female power. It is this construction of an inviolable power base, corresponding to a precise social phenomenon (i.e. the growth in girls' formal schooling and the changing views about female education), that is perhaps responsible for the particular contemporary appeal of Brazil's work. As Rosemary Auchmuty has observed in her sustained analysis of several post-Brazil school-story series, the link between narrative action and the realization of fictive identity is strong, and:

what seems conventional – even reactionary – now, was radical then in contrast to the Victorian girl's almost complete lack of physical freedom and her attenuated sense of self-worth.[6]

Within the enclosed territory of Marlowe Grange, the setting for *The Madcap of the School*, girls and women are able to adopt positions of authority that were relatively inaccessible to them in the outside world. Through the focus on sport and the existence of extra-mural school activities (both denied Brazil in her own schooldays), they can realize qualities of leadership and initiative that allow them to engage in heroic action and that inspire the admiration of their peer group. The new educational opportunities themselves are thus seen as directly responsible for encouraging a perception of self that revises conventional female models. Moreover, in Brazil's recognition of adolescence as a formative stage of development, girl characters can experiment with female identities in an environment of licence that was frequently withheld from them in real life.

Before analysing the generic and specific textual motifs of *The Madcap of the School*, Brazil's seventeenth novel of boarding school life, it is important to place its distinctive elements in their literary and contemporary social context. Although she transformed it, Brazil did not invent the boarding-school story *per se*, and her work needs to be seen as part of the well-established tradition of juvenile fiction which deals with the place of school experience in the process of female maturation, and which so far this study has not addressed.

Sarah Fielding's *The Governess or, Little Female Academy*, published in 1749, is generally credited with being the first boarding-school story. With its declared moral bias and inclusion of didactic digressive tales, it concentrates on abstract behavioural principles, made accessible through personalized narratives, as each of the nine girls at Mrs Teachum's establishment tells her own history. At the same time the novel does contain certain embryonic features of the later school story that Brazil was to establish as fundamental to the genre as it subsequently developed. Mrs Teachum's school in *The Governess* is, like Brazil's schools, a self-contained community, whose pupils rarely if ever venture into the outside world. The nine girls who are the subject of the narrative are invited to adopt a communal as opposed to individualistic identity and one of the major lessons they learn is how to live harmoniously together. Within the discrete social unit of the school they thus develop a sense of social responsibility, and Mrs Teachum delegates authority to the eldest pupil, aged fourteen, who, like Brazil's monitresses, is given the opportunity to demonstrate her skill at sensitive leadership. In addition, *The Governess* stresses the impact of moral lessons on the emotional life of the young. Miss Sukey Jennett, for instance, is so overcome with anxiety about her relationships with other girls:

> that she could not utter one Word more; but sat herself down, reclining her Head upon her Hand, in the most melancholy Posture that could be: Nor could she close her Eyes all Night; but lay tossing and raving with the Thought how she should act, and what she should say to Miss Jenny the next Day.[7]

The sleepless night, a standard element in the fictional schoolgirl experience, creates the world of school as one of emotional crises, where friendships, jealousies and tensions are played out within the structure of an educational establishment. Sukey's despair is certainly comparable to that of Brazil's Raymonde Armitage, the protagonist of *The Madcap of the School* when:

> the whole of her gay, careless world seemed to have crumbled to ashes. She wondered what her chums were thinking of her. Did they, like Veronica, mistrust her conduct? A sense of utter desolation swept over her, and, pushing aside the tea things, she leaned her arms on the table, with her hot face pressed against them. (280)

The inspirational quality of Fielding's work, and in particular her original conception of the girls' school as an appropriate narrative vehicle for young readers, can be seen both in the number of her contemporary imitators and in the way in which variations on *The Governess* formula persisted well into the nineteenth century.[8] Both Susan Coolidge and Frances Hodgson Burnett, authors whose work has already been discussed in another context, make use of the setting of a girls' school in respectively *What Katy Did at School* (1873) and *Sara Crewe: or What Happened at Miss Minchin's* (1887), later to reappear as *A Little Princess* (1905). In an early Brazil text, *The Third Class at Miss Kaye's* (1908), these two works are quoted as providing archaic portraits of the Victorian girls seminary. Sylvia, the heroine in this novel, finds the modern boarding-school very different from her expectations, which are based on readings of Coolidge and Burnett. Perhaps the greater influence on Brazil among nineteenth-century writers for girls was, however, L.T. Meade, whose *A World of Girls* (1886) anticipates *The Madcap of the School* in a number of significant ways without the radical implications of the later novel. Meade herself was probably the most widely read of Brazil's immediate predecessors, being voted the most popular author of 1898 in a poll organized by *Girls' Realm*,[9] and *A World of Girls* contains many of the salient features that have come to be associated with schoolgirl fiction. The correspondences between her work and Brazil's subsequent transformation of it are substantial and worth exploring in more detail.

Like Marlowe Grange, Lavender House, the school that provides the setting for *A World of Girls*, is envisaged as an enclosed but not isolated community, where girls are removed from home and family but where they are still able to relate socially to the village life which surrounds them. Hester Thornton, who enters Lavender House at the age of twelve, is, like Burnett's Sara Crewe, sent to boarding-school following the death of her mother and, after her father's decision to live abroad, her stay there is unrelieved by visits home. Burnett in *Sara Crewe* uses the framework of the school as a background against which her heroine can re-enact a version of the Cinderella myth, triumphing over two ugly sisters in her progress from rags to riches. Meade exploits the school setting more purposefully and, despite the inclusion of stock sentimental episodes, with a greater degree of realism. In the world of Lavender House, girls from the ages of five (even younger once Hester's baby sister comes to the school) to sixteen are made forcefully aware of its communal ethic, with divisions between the classes and choices of room-mates reinforcing the relational ethos of the text. In common with Brazil's later schoolgirls, Meade's pupils can win privileges within a clearly established internal hierarchy and they look on the headmistress's approval as the ultimate accolade to be fought for. The narrative focus of the book, as with *The Madcap of the School*, concerns personal allegiances and tensions, the development of friendships, exclusive alliances between groups or pairs of girls, jealousies and experiences of exclusion and alienation. And, as in Brazil's text, Lavender House girls enjoy midnight feasts and prize-giving ceremonies and prepare end of term entertainments.

Much more central for Meade than for Brazil, however, is the emphasis on conventional ethical instruction, the moral and emotional crises of the novel being presented within a traditional understanding of Christian conduct. Brazil's secularization of school society in *The Madcap of the School* and in her other school stories realigns the moral dimension of the text with a personal code of behaviour that establishes internal parameters rather than relying on external religious agencies. *A World of Girls* introduces a clergyman as the ultimate representative of authority who is brought in to minister to and discipline the girls when internal measures have failed. In contrast to the gravity with which the authority of the church is invoked by Meade, *The Madcap of the School* satirizes the visiting clergyman, the Rev. T. Beasley, who comes as a representative of the outside world to examine the pupils and whose inflexible standards of judgement are shown to be inadequate in dealing with the subtle dilemmas that girls encounter. It is the headmistress's authority which is finally validated in *The Madcap of the School*, and her judgement proved to be sound, while the arrogant and patronizing figure of the clergyman (who is also the headmistress's brother), is removed from the action at the end of the novel, much to the girls' relief. The final vision of *The Madcap of the School* is thus an endorsement of female culture, and the school, retained as a unit which can operate effectively without male interference, consequently functions implicitly as a critique of masculine hegemony.

Brazil's depiction of a female community managed solely by women continues a debate about the propriety of such communities that had become prominent in the late nineteenth century. As Pauline Nestor points out in her study of women's friendship in Victorian fiction, contemporary discussions on the subject shared

a common conviction that the feminine temperament was particularly vulnerable, and that women's grasp on rationality and control was dependent on proper occupation and supervision. There was then an inherent danger in any community which might paradoxically leave its female members too completely to themselves, and the constitutional vulnerability of women could, it seemed, be exacerbated by the potential for "contagion" within a community.[10]

It is this conviction that underlies Burnett's scepticism about Miss Minchin's establishment in *Sara Crewe* where petty abuses of power are rife, that informs the presentation of Coolidge's parochial Hillsover 'nunnery', in *What Katy Did at School*, and that requires the intervention of the Reverend Mr Everard in Meade's Lavender House. The female community that Brazil depicts, however, emphatically refutes this perception, its inversion of gendered hierarchies establishing feminized principles of government as being both sensitive and progressive in the handling of disciplinary issues.

More significantly, in its realization of alternative possibilities for girls, *The Madcap of the School* develops and revises the figure of the schoolgirl so as to create her anew as a distinctive breed. The very title of the novel draws attention to the centrality of the 'madcap'. Any analysis of Brazil's treatment of Raymonde Armitage needs to recognize its radical revision of Victorian principles of gendered behaviour, and in particular the unbending attitude to female insubordination as depicted in Meade's *A World of Girls*, which also takes an embryonic tomboy as a central character. This study has already drawn attention to the way in which the figure of the tomboy makes a regular appearance as a dynamic focus of attention in nineteenth-century juvenile American texts while noticeably absent from English fiction of the same period. As Gillian Avery has remarked, as shown in American novels tomboys 'are appealing; on English soil they would seem dangerously bold.'[11] Susan Coolidge's mischievous schoolgirl, Rose Red, in *What Katy Did at School*, is admired by Katy Carr for her irrepressible sense of fun, but the scrapes she gets into are never serious and display nothing more than light-hearted high spirits. *The Madcap of the School* clearly draws some inspiration from contemporary American texts for girls. Gene Stratton Porter's *Freckles* (1904) and *The Girl of the Limberlost* (1909) are both referred to within Brazil's novel as promoting exciting models of girlhood freedom such as have been denied to their English counterparts. Meade's *A World of Girls*, in contrast, finds the whole issue of the tomboy more problematic:

Without any doubt, wild, naughty, impulsive Annie Forest was
the most popular girl in the school. She was always in scrapes –
she was scarcely ever out of hot water – her promises of amendment were truly like the proverbial pie-crust; but she was so
lovable, so kind-hearted, so saucy and piquante and pretty, that
very few could resist the nameless charm which she possessed. . . .
her courage was of just the sort to captivate school-girls, and her
moral weakness was not observed by these inexperienced young
eyes.[12]

Although Meade asserts the fact of Annie's appeal, she fails to engage
the reader's sympathy with the character, and in keeping with the
moral direction of a Victorian educative text, Annie's charm is
represented as insidiously dangerous. Popularity and moral righteousness are incompatible here, and the book suggests that the
judgement of young people is fallible and requires continual guidance. Attractive but posing a threat to fixed principles of gendered
behaviour, Annie is consequently made into the protagonist of a
melodramatic narrative so that her high spirits, her love of daring
and her winning ways become only salutary illustrations of the
'moral weakness' she embodies. Attempting to rescue a child who
has been kidnapped by gypsies, the kidnap itself an indirect result
of Annie's carelessness, she falls dangerously ill, recovering consciousness just at the moment when her long-lost father, whom she
thought had abandoned her, appears to reclaim his daughter. Because her irresponsibility stems from thoughtlessness rather than
criminality, Annie is allowed to survive as a reformed character,
having been shown the error of her madcap ways.

While elements of this character and her situation resurface in
Brazil's work – *The Madcap of the School* contains both gypsies who
are potentially menacing and a heroic rescue carried out in dangerous circumstances – the tomboy figure herself carries no suggestion of impropriety nor of moral fallibility. Rather, Raymonde
Armitage carries the undivided imaginative sympathy of the novel,
and her introduction in the first chapter of the book establishes her
disruptive potential as a major ingredient in her appeal:

Raymonde Armitage would certainly not have won a medal for
exemplary behaviour, had any such prize been offered at the
school. There was no harm in her, but her irrepressible spirits
were continually at effervescing point, and in fizzing over were

liable to burst into outbreaks of a nature highly scandalizing to the authorities. (12)

Unlike Annie Forest, Raymonde poses no threat to her companions. Her vivacity and her anarchic high spirits, while scandalous to those in authority (and it is noteworthy that those who are 'scandalized' are those whose notions of girlhood are seen as antediluvian), contribute to her qualities of leadership. Her scepticism of and impatience with discipline are valued as evidence of her independent mind, and when one of the more strait-laced members of staff describes Raymonde as 'the naughtiest girl in the school', she is immediately reproved by the headmistress:

> "Pardon me!" corrected Miss Beasley. "The most mischievous, perhaps, and the most troublesome; full of bubbling spirits and misplaced energy, but straightforward and truthful. There is something very lovable about Raymonde." (37)

As J.S. Bratton has commented with relation to early twentieth-century juvenile fictions of imperialism:

> In practical terms, new narratives and character models, which would maintain the old values but offer a more modern standard of activity for girls, were not easy to set up. A century of writing for girls had established the norm of the domestic tale, in which the trials of the heroine were involved with the learning of discipline, the internalization of the feminine values of self-abnegation, obedience and subordination.[13]

Brazil's Raymonde Armitage effectively subverts the conventions of the feminine which earlier stories for girls, even those which utilized the school for the narrative framework, implicitly relied upon. Raymonde and her fellows reject discipline, welcome insubordination and find in the hierarchy of school life an alternative to the domestic as offering scope for female accomplishment to flourish. Moreover, Raymonde's success as a leader is paradoxically dependent upon her disruption of order. Rules are there to be broken, the teachers (apart from the ultimate arbiter, the headmistress) are the acknowledged enemy, and part of Raymonde's remit is to establish an oppositional regime of schoolgirl power. As she stresses to her companions:

"I've told you already, it's my mission to enliven the school, and if you don't have a jinky term I'll consider myself a failure." . . . The six kindred spirits who revolved in Raymonde's orbit turned to her with a gush of admiration. (17)

The Madcap of the School has no clearly articulated narrative structure. Its form is episodic, following the adventures of a group of girls through the events of a single term, with Raymonde as the focus and instigator of action. 'The Mystic Seven', the charmed circle of friends who are at the heart of the story, become the determinants of the value system that the novel implicitly upholds. The text's strength thus rests on its projection of a distinctive culture and its creation of highly individualized girl characters, who contribute to and support that culture and its ideals. To some extent of course, Brazil was drawing upon the model of the boys' English public school story, which had acquired popularity during the late nineteenth century, for the exploits and characteristics she ascribed to girls. The Marlowe Grange girls have adventures that replicate those of boyhood play, including going camping, birds'-nesting, exploring secret passages and capturing German spies – this *is* 1917. And there are overtones of Jo March in Raymonde's awareness that it is her gender that has been a crucial obstacle in her frustrated path to action: '"If only I'd been a boy, I'd have run away to the front long ago"', she announces melodramatically *pace* Alcott.

But Brazil's radicalism goes much further than this. In depicting girls within a totally female environment, *The Madcap of the School* liberates its characters from the prescriptive conditions that determine gendered division in the heterosexual community. As Gill Frith has commented:

In a world of girls, to be female is *normal*, and not a *problem*. To be assertive, physically active, daring, ambitious, is not a source of tension. In the absence of boys, girls break bounds, have adventures, transgress rules, catch spies. There is no taboo on public speech.[14]

Brazil's reinvention of the school story needs then to be seen both against previous models of narratives of school life and as a positive endorsement of new ideologies of girlhood that isolate a female culture. *The Madcap of the School* thus rewrites earlier narratives for girls so as to produce a revised concept of female identity which appears, on the surface at least, to be unproblematic.

The book opens at the start of the summer term and with the girls' arrival at a new school building, Marlowe Grange. This Tudor mansion has a history of female independence and bravery. It was once used as a temporary convent when taken over as a refuge by nuns fleeing from the French Revolution. It was also the scene of a dramatic story of female courage when a teenage girl escaped from the besieged garrison to help relieve the household during the Civil War. Its present thus provides a continuum with its past, as an enclosed female sanctum which also offers its inmates opportunities to demonstrate heroic potential. *The Madcap of the School* makes continual explicit and implicit reference to other texts and earlier narratives so as to show women reworking traditional fictive subject positions. The moated grange itself which 'might have come straight, slap-bang out of a novel!' (10) introduces the self-reflexive tone of the text which contextualizes its own narrative devices by means of literary complements. Set in a walled garden, where spring flowers bloom and bees buzz for nectar, the school's very location which 'seemed to hold all the promise of the coming summer' (14) appears to symbolize the condition of the adolescent girls within it, ripening for adulthood. Moated and undisturbed for centuries, with a wood beyond the garden, the Grange recalls a sleeping beauty's palace and carries something of its suggestive sexual connotations. Like the garden of Burnett's *The Secret Garden*, the school, carefully placed in natural surroundings, becomes a female sanctuary, enclosed and tranquil.

Beyond it, however, lie exciting possibilities for discovery and in her desire to explore beyond the confines of the garden, Raymonde Armitage indicates the tension that is partly realized in this book between the secure self-government of the women's world and the attractive but fraught external environment. Just as the tomboy figure herself has her literary origins in North American literature, so Raymonde models herself on the fictive version of girlhood that she finds in Gene Stratton Porter's writing. It is the vision of the American Limberlost, the wilderness that liberates female potential and that contains a threatening undercurrent of swamp and untamed nature, which inspires her thoughts of escape from the constrictions of the school grounds. With her closest friend, Fauvette Robinson, Raymonde sets out on an illicit adventure to invade this forbidden territory with its subliminally subversive appeal. When the girls reach the wood, it fulfils their fantasies, being 'a little terrestrial paradise' (44) where nature is riotous, thick, and gloriously uncultivated. It is, also, as in *What Katy Did*, a paradise where they fall. Discovered by their teacher, they are punished by being made to copy out Milton's *Paradise Lost*, a particularly appropriate text with its subject of female transgression, both sexual and political.

The literary evocation of North American culture continues to stimulate thoughts of freedom. Raymonde's imagination is subsequently captured by stories of Canadian pioneer women, active, strong, and enterprising, with a landscape that provides scope for their capabilities, and she attempts to emulate their achievements by building a log cabin on the island in the river beyond the school. Again, at the end of the novel, the girls mount a Coon Concert as part of their fund-raising contribution for the War effort. However politically suspect their venture might seem to the modern reader, it needs to be set within its period when the imaginative appeal of the pre-Jazz Age music is offered as a refreshing antidote to the Victorian songs thought suitable for young ladies. The concert, held in a barn, with songs 'sufficiently spicy to entertain the girl portion of the audience' (233) confusedly recalls a conglomeration of American myths, including that of the Wild West as well as the plantation. Yet while *The Madcap of the School* reveals its debt to American cultural myths, it transforms these so as to communicate a specifically English bias. Boarding-school fiction has evolved very much as an English literary genre and, as has been argued, Brazil's work shows clear evidence of its British antecedents, such as the work of L.T. Meade. The boarding-school itself, as an English cultural construct, remains the central vehicle for Brazil's exploration of girlhood strength. In its assessment of female possibility in a changing culture, the school setting also provides a rich field for psychoanalytic interpretation. As Angela McRobbie points out, the boarding school in fiction for girls:

> legitimates the reader's desire to imagine a hypothetical space where the dilemmas and difficulties of everyday life are magically resolved through the working-out in fantasy of precisely that which cannot be admitted – that is, their ambivalent and changing relations with their parents, their rivalries and resentments against their brothers and sisters, their desire to move towards the outside world which because it is too threatening is itself contained in the narrative in the form of a school.[15]

Whereas in *Little Women* sisterhood was a familial construct, in *The Madcap of the School* the family is replaced by the metaphor of school. Girls, removed from the security of their families, recreate an alternative source of bonding which allows them to discover an independent identity within a mutual support system that is distinctively female. And in Raymonde and her friends who form the nucleus of narrative attention, Brazil also provides revolutionary models of girlhood to set against received versions of the feminine. In contrast to the ambivalence with which Burnett's or Nesbit's girl characters are depicted, Brazil's adolescents are unequivocally celebrated for being disorderly, active, articulate, and intent on breaking down repressive conventions of behaviour and language. The opening sentences of the novel establish the linguistic code of the schoolgirl, with the slang expressions – 'jubiliate', 'how ripping!' 'jinky', 'what a chubby place!' (9–11) – that construct their private, gendered and youth culture. Brazil has been criticized for her invention of a schoolgirl slang as 'silly' and for her lack of irony in its use as 'limiting and wrong and absurd.'[16] What such a criticism fails to take into account is the creation of social exclusivity that this unique communication system effects. Brazil's slang, considered sufficiently outrageous by contemporary readers for her books to be banned from some schools, effectively creates its own antiauthoritarian code that is distinctively juvenile *and* female.

In *The Nicest Girl in the School* (1909), one of Brazil's earlier experiments in the genre, her heroine receives a copy of Ruskin's *Sesame and Lilies* as a school prize. Such an award would be greeted with contempt by the unruly group at the centre of *The Madcap of the School*, a text which self consciously dismantles the Victorian image of the 'angel in the house' with its imposed behavioural and linguistic standards. As one pupil grumbles:

"This isn't a school for saints."
"If we followed all Gibbie's pet precepts we should have halos round our heads."
"And be sprouting wings!" added Raymonde. 'A very uncomfortable process too. I expect it would hurt like cutting teeth, and it would spoil the fit of one's blouses. I don't want to be an angel! I'm quite content with this world at present." (59)

This deliberate recall of the angelic ideal only to undermine it is integral to the text's general resistance to preconceived notions of femininity. It is explored most extensively in the portrait of Fauvette Robinson, Raymonde's close friend, who, in her parody of the traditional iconography of womanhood, serves merely to subvert it.

Fauvette is 'a little, blue-eyed, fluffy-haired, clinging, cuddly, ultra-feminine specimen', whose stereotypic features are deployed in a highly self-conscious fashion. Her exploitation of the convention-ally feminine is mocked in the text as an outdated throwback to the nineteenth-century romantic heroine. She is sentimental, infantile and with 'just a sufficient talent for acting to make her absolutely invaluable in scenes from Dickens and Jane Austen, where a heroine of the innocent, pleading, pathetic, babyish, Early Victorian type was required' (18). She is incapable of fending for herself, incom-petent – she can't even keep her locker-drawers tidy without help – and sees herself in relation to a romantic configuration of literary femininity that the other girls are intent on discarding. At the same time her friends are aware of the manipulative value of this pose of helplessness, and use Fauvette to plead on their behalf for a favour from the Principal, knowing that her 'big, pathetic, innocent blue eyes' (178) will work to their advantage. Traditional femininity then is explicitly acknowledged as a political strategy, its fictive quality recognized at the very moment of its tactical exploitation.

Fauvette's ambition to construct herself according to a literary ideal is pursued in her obsession with appearance and dress. Her self-image has value for her only as it is appreciated by others, and she is constantly constructing herself imaginatively as the object of another's gaze, whether it be as a version of Gene Stratton Porter's Swamp Angel, 'photographing rare birds and shooting villains with revolvers, and looking her best through it all' (41), or playing the part of a girl in a punt with a white boating costume, leaning back 'against blue cushions while HE rows' (179).

Brazil's deconstruction of traditional models of the feminine utilises Fauvette and Raymonde as classic polarities in theories of gender relations, only slightly complicated by the fact that both characters are female. As Laura Mulvey has suggested in her sem-inal article, 'Visual Pleasure and Narrative Cinema':

> The determining male gaze projects its fantasy onto the female figure, which is styled accordingly. In their traditional exhibition-ist role women are simultaneously looked at and displayed, with their appearance coded for strong visual and erotic impact so that they can be said to connote *to-be-looked-at-ness*.[17]

According to Mulvey's analysis, the gender of the spectator is ir-relevant in the determination of the feminine object. In this context it could be argued that in *The Madcap of The School* Fauvette and Raymonde embody models of scopophiliac self-projection, with Fauvette as the object of Raymonde's displaced voyeurism. As Fauvette projects herself into a variety of fictive scenarios 'with all the authority of an experienced reader of magazine stories', so her fantasy of self captures Raymonde's vicarious imagination. While firmly rejecting a personal romantic future, Raymonde:

> felt that she should look forward to her chum's inevitable engagement almost as much as Fauvette herself. It would be as good as a Shakespeare play, or one of the best pieces on the kinema [*sic*]. (180)

Indeed Raymonde's encouragement of Fauvette's role-playing forms an intrinsic element in her own self-realization. Raymonde helps the other girl to dress in the mornings, does her hair, trims her underwear with ribbon, all stages in the process of domination which keeps Fauvette's infantilism intact so that ultimately Raymonde

> formed her opinions, and generally dominated her school career. Fauvette was one of those girls who all their lives lean upon somebody, and at present she had twined herself, an ornamental piece of honeysuckle, round the stout oak prop of Raymonde's stronger personality. (18)

The latent sexual imagery of this passage could suggest a subliminal lesbian dependency in this relationship, with Raymonde adopting the traditional masculine role of protector and leader, a role which historically acquires its superior status only through the perpetuation of its antithesis as inferior.

The narrative situations of the text, however, and the variety of female roles both encoded within it and overtly addressed, make this too simple a reading. While friendship between girls is accepted as enduring, the novel has a vigorous anti-romantic impetus that mitigates against emotionalism or even affection. In a passage fraught with teasing psychoanalytic implications, Brazil describes the ethos of school itself as being in direct opposition to the conventional positioning of woman as sentimental object:

> Sentiment was not encouraged at the Grange. Miss Beasley very rightly thought that girls should keep their childhood as long as

possible, and that premature love affairs wiped the bloom off genuine love experiences. The school in general assumed the attitude of scoffing at romance, except in the pages of the library books. It was not considered good form to allude to it. Tennis or hockey was a more popular topic. (166)

In *The Madcap of the School*, adolescence remains determinedly asexual, despite the fact that the girls who are its subjects are typically aged between thirteen and sixteen. School, the territory of childhood, takes over the parental role as the guardian of female innocence, a view in accordance with contemporary theories of adolescence which advised, 'Keep the girl a child in the physical sense as long as possible.'[18] In keeping with the popular opinion that 'the principle should be to broaden by retarding,'[19] physical exercise has replaced erotic encounter as suitable conversational material at Marlowe Grange, presumably as a subject that will engage the girls' bodies as well as their attention. While sub-lesbian attachments, such as that between Raymonde and Fauvette, might flourish unacknowledged, heterosexual romance exists as a literary construct only. The moral encomiums attached to displays of affection emphatically ignore the transitional aspect of adolescence as a state of increasing sexual awareness, but indicate too the altered attitudes towards concepts of female nature, no longer deemed to be instinctively sentimental.

As part of the demythologizing of romance in *The Madcap of the School*, The Mystic Seven make it their mission to expose amatory sentiment as an illusion. Cynthia Greene, a girl who is foolish enough to indulge in fantasizing about an admirer, is quickly made the object of general derision. Thinking that she is in love clearly has a disastrous effect on Cynthia, who becomes so self-absorbed that she loses concentration on more important tasks, and misses two catches when fielding at cricket. Her clothes become a parody of the romantic poseur and her sighing, gazing into the distance and propensity for tears are dismissed by Raymonde as 'sickly sort of stuff' (171). Cynthia's dreams of romantic love are indeed shown to be without foundation, having been artificially fed by Raymonde who, disguised as a love-lorn admirer, has been sending Cynthia secret notes and arranging assignations before finally unmasking her grand passion as nothing more than the result of a schoolgirl prank.

The anti-romantic dimension of Brazil's schoolgirl culture is not, however, replaced by any complementary adoption of explicit

feminist principles. Quite the reverse. Although Marlowe Grange is
a school devoted to expanding opportunities for girls in the new
educational climate of the early twentieth century, the pupils
themselves resist any attempt to pre-programme their behaviour
according to any imposed theory. The main target for Brazil's satire
of the New Woman is Miss Gibbs, a teacher whose high ideals of
girlhood are shown to be as unrealizable as were the nineteenth-
century attitudes of angelic iconization:

> She was determined to work on the most modern methods, and
> to turn her pupils out into the world, a little band of ardent
> thinkers, keen-witted, self-sacrificing, logical, anxious for the
> development of their sex, yearning for careers, in fact the vanguard
> of a new womanhood. Unfortunately her material was not alto-
> gether promising. . . . They listened to her impassioned address
> on women's suffrage without a spark of admiration, and sat
> stolidly while she descanted upon the bad conditions of labour
> among munitions girls, and the need for lady welfare workers.
> The fact was that her pupils did not care an atom about the
> position of their sex, a half-holiday was far more important to
> them than the vote, and their own grievances loomed larger than
> those of factory hands. (60)

Living according to the precepts she has imbibed from her recent
attendance at an educational congress, Miss Gibbs fails to instil a
similar enthusiasm for such precepts in her pupils. Much of the
novel's action concerns an ongoing battle between Miss Gibbs in
her strenuous efforts to modernize the girls' education, both in the
syllabus and in extra-curricular activities, and the Mystic Seven's
equally strenuous resistance to being made the subject of a socio-
logical experiment. This rejection of theory is central to Brazil's
vision of the schoolgirl as requiring freedom to develop naturally,
both in mind and body. Miss Gibbs' indifference to games is a sign
of her insensitivity to girls' need for physical action. Her emphasis
on their intellectual development, providing for them such treats as
lectures on geology or archaeological expeditions, is represented as
being out of touch with the interests of the young. Indeed over-
emphasis on formal education is generally seen as being unhealthy.
One of the Mystic Seven's early exploits concerns Maudie Heywood
who by working too hard is setting a bad example to the school.
Her intellectual ambitions are seen as 'swanky' and by completing

extra assignments she is represented as setting a precedent that might result in extra prep for the other girls. When Raymonde glues down Maudie's desk to prevent her from doing her exercises, the headmistress treats the act with tolerance. Maudie's complaints are dismissed and she is advised to mix more with the other girls and not to over-value the importance of study. ' "Part of the training of school life is to learn to accommodate yourself to a community" ', Miss Beasley tells her, and to Miss Gibbs she comments that ' "Maudie . . . must be able to take her share of teasing. Humour is her one deficiency" ' (37).

In its mistrust of female intellectualism at the same time that it promotes new opportunities for girls, the book precisely reflects its historical moment. Gillian Avery, in her history of girls' public schools, has described how:

> The public schools evolved in reaction to the strained, bespectacled and anaemic bluestockings that the high schools were felt to be turning out. There was far more to education than cultivating brains; it should prepare pupils to make the most of their talents, to work and play hard, and to take a responsible place in the community.[20]

The Madcap of the School locates its girl characters in a world of changing gender relations and revised concepts of female identity, contextualized by the impact of the First World War. The school itself functions as an effective system for educating girls to an awareness of community values and for allowing their freedom to explore and develop identities. It is, however, a world where this licence is bound by inevitable limits. As in Nesbit's *The Railway Children*, there is an understanding that the holiday atmosphere, like childhood itself, cannot continue eternally. Although Marlowe Grange offers a model of good educational practice, Brazil intimates that there are disadvantages to all closed communities and that:

> when there is no home-going until the end of the term, little trifles are sometimes unduly magnified, and a narrow element – the bane of all communities – begins to creep in. (204)

Towards the end of the novel – and in this sense *The Madcap of the School* involves a significant shift in narrative emphasis – the girls are encouraged to expand their perception of self in order to accommodate their newly acquired personalities to the post-war society they will enter. As Miss Beasley, the authoritative voice of reason and vision, declares:

> "I believe this war will have broken down many foolish old traditions and customs, and that people will be ready afterwards to live more simple, natural lives than they did before. The schoolgirls of today are the women of to-morrow, and it is on you that the nation will rely in years to come." (239)

The contemporary unease about gender and girlhood is transmitted in the dialogue between divergent models of femininity that is represented in this novel. The challenge to 'old traditions and customs' that the figure of the schoolgirl encodes is very real, particularly in her rejection of conventional notions of decorative female passivity and repression. Conversely, however, the modern is problematized in Brazil's often traditional use of female imagery, such as the convergence of nature and the feminine, and the anxiety about feminist ideologies that the mockery of Miss Gibbs subsumes. What does remain indisputable is the recoding of the female world as positive and empowering. The banishment of Rev. T. Beasley at the end of the novel, an episode referred to earlier, inverts the traditional hierarchy of brother/sister, male/female relations and leaves the final image of the girls' school as one that is self-sufficient and progressive. The boarding-school as Angela Brazil communicates it in *The Madcap of the School* offers a new and positive vision of developing girlhood whose appropriation by later twentieth-century readers was enduring.

Notes

1. Elinor Brent-Dyer, *The Princess at the Chalet School* (London: Armada Books, 1927), p.8.
2. Angela Brazil, *The Madcap of the School* (London: Blackie, 1917), p.240. All subsequent references are to this edition and will be included in the text.
3. Gill Frith, 'The Time of Your Life: The Meaning of the School Story', in eds Carolyn Steedman, Cathy Urwin, Valerie Walkerdine, *Gender, Language and Childhood* (London: Routledge & Kegan Paul, 1985), p.123.

4. Jan Montefiore, 'The fourth form girls go camping: sexual ambivalence and identity in girls' school stories', in eds Michael Worton and Judith Still, Textuality and Sexuality: Reading Theories and Practices (Manchester and New York: Manchester University Press, 1993), p.174.

5. Jeffrey Richards, 'The School Story', in ed. Dennis Butts *Stories and Society: Children's Literature in its Social Context* (London: Macmillan, 1992), p.10.

6. Rosemary Auchmuty, *A World of Girls* (London: The Women's Press, 1992), p.64.

7. Sarah Fielding, *The Governess or, Little Female Academy* (Oxford: Oxford University Press, 1968), p.115.

8. See Jill E. Grey's introduction to *The Governess*, op.cit., for the details of the publishing history of the text, and an account of imitators of Fielding's narrative.

9. Mary Cadogan and Patricia Craig, *You're a Brick, Angela: A New Look at Girls' Fiction 1839–1975* (London: Victor Gollancz, 1976).

10. Pauline Nestor, *Female Friendships and Communities* (Oxford: Clarendon Press, 1985), p.20.

11. Gillian Avery, 'Home and Family: English and American Ideals in the Nineteenth Century', in ed. Butts, op.cit., p.38.

12. L.T. Meade, *A World of Girls: A Story of a School* (London: Cassell, 1908), p.59.

13. J.S. Bratton, 'Girls' Fiction 1900–1930', in ed. Jeffrey Richards, *Imperialism and Juvenile Literature* (Manchester and New York: Manchester University Press, 1989), p.197.

14. Gill Frith, op.cit., p.121.

15. Angela McRobbie, *Feminism and Youth Culture: From 'Jackie' to 'Just Seventeen'* (London: Macmillan, 1991), p.207.

16. Isobel Quigly, *The Heirs of Tom Brown: The English School Story* (London: Chatto & Windus, 1982), p.218.

17. Laura Mulvey, 'Visual Pleasure and Narrative Cinema', *Screen* 16(3), Autumn 1975, reprinted in eds Robyn R. Warhol and Diane Price Herndl, *Feminisms: An Anthology of Literary Theory and Criticism* (New Brunswick, NJ: Rutgers University Press, 1991), p.436.

18. Gillian Avery, *The Best Type of Girl: A History of Girls' Independent Schools* (London: André Deutsch, 1991), p.316.

19. Ibid., p.317.

20. Ibid., p.86.

Bibliography

PRIMARY TEXTS

Alcott, Louisa May, *Little Women* (London: Puffin Books, 1953)

Brazil, Angela, *The Madcap of the School* (London: Blackie n.d. 1917)

Burnett, Frances Hodgson, *The Secret Garden* (Oxford: World's Classics, 1987)

Coolidge, Susan (Sarah Chauncey Woolsey), *What Katy Kid* (London and Melbourne: Ward, Lock, n.d.)

Montgomery, Lucy Maud, *Anne of Green Gables* (London: Puffin Books, 1977)

Nesbit, Edith, *The Railway Children* (London: Puffin Books, 1960)

Wetherell, Elizabeth (Susan B. Warner), *The Wide, Wide World* (New York: The Feminist Press, 1987)

Yonge, Charlotte Mary, *The Daisy Chain: or, Aspirations* (London: Macmillan, 1870)

SECONDARY TEXTS

Altick, Richard, *The English Common Reader: A Social History of the Magazine Reading Public, 1800–1900* (Chicago: University of Chicago Press, 1957)

Auchmuty, Rosemary, *A World of Girls* (London: The Women's Press, 1992)

Auerbach, Nina, *Communities of Women: an Idea in Fiction* (Cambridge, Mass.: Harvard University Press, 1978)

Avery, Gillian, *The Best Type of Girl: A History of Girl's Independent Schools* (London: André Deutsch, 1991)

——, *Childhood's Pattern: a Study of the Heroes and Heroines of Children's Fiction 1770–1950* (London: Hodder & Stoughton, 1975)

——, *Nineteenth Century Children: Heroes and Heroines in English Children's Stories 1780–1900* (London: Hodder & Stoughton, 1965)

—— and Julia Briggs (eds), *Children and Their Books* (Oxford: Oxford University Press, 1990)

Battiscombe, Georgina, *Charlotte Mary Yonge: The Story of an Uneventful Life* (London: Constable, 1943)

—— and Marghanita Laski (eds), *A Chaplet for Charlotte Yonge* (London: The Cresset Press, 1965)

Baym, Nina, 'Portrayal of Women in American Literature, 1790–1870', ed. Marlene Springer, *What Manner of Woman: Essays on English and American Life and Literature* (Oxford: Basil Blackwell, 1977), pp.211–34

——, 'Rewriting the Scribbling Women', *Legacy: A Journal of Nineteenth Century American Women Writers*, vol. 2, no. 2 (Fall 1985), pp.3–12

——, *Women's Fiction: A guide to novels by and about women in America 1820–1870* (Ithaca: Cornell University Press, 1980)

Berg, Temma F., '*Anne of Green Gables:* A Girl's Reading', *Children's Literature Association Quarterly*, vol. 9, no. 4 (Winter 1984–5), pp.124–8

Bratton, J.S., *The Impact of Victorian Children's Fiction* (London: Croom Helm, 1981)

Brent Dyer, Elinor M., *The Princess of the Chalet School* (London: Harper-Collins, 1992)

Briggs, Julia, *A Woman of Passion: The Life of E. Nesbit* (London: Penguin Books, 1987)

Bronfen, Elisabeth, *Over Her Dead Body: Death, Femininity and the Aesthetic* (Manchester and New York, Manchester University Press, 1992)

Burnett, Constance Buel, *Happily Ever After: A Portrait of Frances Hodgson Burnett* (New York: Vanguard Press, 1969)

Butler, Francelia, Margaret Higonnet and Barbara Rosen, (eds), *Children's Literature* 17 (New Haven, Conn.: Yale University Press, 1989)

——, and Richard Rotart, (eds), *Triumphs of the Spirit in Children's Literature* (Hamden, Conn.: Library Professional Publications, 1986)

Butts, Dennis (ed.), *Stories and Society: Children's Literature in its Social Context* (London: Macmillan, 1992)

Cadogan, Mary and Patricia Craig, *You're a Brick, Angela: A New Look at Girls' Fiction 1839–1975* (London: Victor Gollancz, 1976)

Carpenter, Humphrey, *Secret Gardens: A Study of the Golden Age of Children's Literature* (London: Allen & Unwin, 1985)

Cheyney, Ednah D. (ed.), *Louisa May Alcott, her Life, Letters and Journals* (London: Sampson, Low, Marston; Searle & Rivington, 1889)

Chodorow, Nancy, *The Reproduction of Mothering: Psychoanalysis and the Sociology of Gender* (Berkeley and Los Angeles: University of California Press, 1978)

Coleridge, Christabel, *Charlotte Mary Yonge: her Life and Letters* (London: Macmillan, 1903)

Cott, Nancy F., *The Bonds of Womanhood: 'Women's Sphere' in New England 1780–1835* (New Haven: Yale University Press, 1977)

Crouch, Marcus, *The Nesbit Tradition: The Children's Novel 1945–1970* (London: Ernest Benn, 1972)

Cruse, Amy, *The Victorians and Their Books* (London: George Allen & Unwin, 1935)

Darling, Frances C., 'Susan Coolidge 1835–1905', *Horn Book Magazine*, June 1959, pp.232–45

de Chaignon la Rose, Pierre, *Notes and Reviews by Henry James* (Freeport, NY: Dunster House, 1921)

Dennis, Barbara, *Charlotte Yonge (1823–1901): Novelist of the Oxford Movement* (Lewiston/Queenston/Lampeter: The Edwin Mellen Press, 1992)

Dobson, Joanne, 'The Hidden Hand: Subversion of cultural ideology in three mid-nineteenth century American women's novels', *American Quarterly*, vol. 38, no. 2 (Summer 1986), pp.223–43

Douglas, Ann, *The Feminization of American Culture* (New York: Alfred A. Knopf, 1977)

Drain, Susan, 'Community and the Individual in *Anne of Green Gables*: the meaning of belonging', *Children's Literature Association Quarterly*, vol. 11, no. 1 (Spring 1986), pp.15–19

Dusinberre, Juliet, *Alice to the Lighthouse: Children's Books and Radical Experiments in Art* (New York: St. Martin's Press, 1987)

Dyhouse, Carol, *Girls Growing up in late Victorian and Edwardian England* (London: Routledge & Kegan Paul, 1981)

Edgeworth, Maria, *Moral Tales* (London: George Routledge, 1893)

Elbert, Sarah, *A Hunger for Home: Louisa May Alcott's Place in American Culture* (New Brunswick, NJ: Rutgers University Press, 1987)

Estes, Angela and Kathleen Laut, 'Dismembering the Text: the Horror of Louisa May Alcott's *Little Women*', *Children's Literature* 17 (1989), pp.98–123

Fielding, Sarah, *The Governess or Little Female Academy* (Oxford: Oxford University Press, 1968)

Freeman, Gillian, *The Schoolgirl Ethic: The Life and Work of Angela Brazil* (London: Allen Lane, 1976)

Gay, Carol, 'Kindred Spirits All: Green Gables Revisited', *Children's Literature Association Quarterly* vol. 11, no. 1 (Spring 1986), pp.9–12

Gilbert, Sandra and Susan Gubar, *The Madwoman in the Attic: The Woman Writer and the Nineteenth Century Literary Imagination* (New Haven, Conn.: Yale University Press, 1979)

Gillen, Mollie, *The Wheel of Things: A Biography of L.M. Montgomery, Author of Anne of Green Gables* (London: Harrap, 1976)

Gorham, Deborah, *The Victorian Girl and the Feminine Ideal* (London: Croom Helm, 1982)

Green, Roger Lancelyn, 'The Golden Age of Children's Books', *Essays and Studies XV* (1962), pp.59–73

Harris, Susan K., *19th Century American Women's Novels: Interpretive Strategies* (Cambridge: Cambridge University Press, 1990)

Heilbrun, Carolyn G., *Hamlet's Mother and Other Women* (London: The Women's Press, 1991)

Heininger, Mary Lynn Stevens, et al., *A Century of Childhood 1820–1920* (Rochester, NY: Margaret Woodbury Strong Museum, 1984)

Hiatt, Mary, 'Susan Warner's subtext: the other side of piety', *Journal of Evolutionary Psychology*, vol. 8, parts 3–4 (1987), pp.250–61

Hughes, Felicity A., 'Children's Literature: Theory and Practice', *English Literary History* 45 (1978) pp.542–56

Hunt, Peter, *Children's Literature: the Development of Criticism* (London: Routledge, 1990)

——, *Criticism, Theory and Children's Literature* (Oxford: Basil Blackwell, 1991)

Inglis, Fred, *The Promise of Happiness: Value and Meaning in Children's Fiction* (Cambridge: Cambridge University Press, 1981)

Jacobus, Mary, *Women Writing and Writing About Women* (London: Croom Helm, 1979)

Keating, Peter, *The Haunted Study: A Social History of the English Novel 1875–1914* (London: Fontana, 1991)

Kelley, Mary, *Public Woman, Private Stage: Literary Domesticity in Nineteenth Century America* (New York and Oxford: Oxford University Press, 1984)

Kirkland, C., 'Novels and Novelists: Queechy and The Wide, Wide World', *North American Review*, vol. 76 (January 1853), pp.104–23

Knoepflmacher, U.C., 'Of Babylands and Babylons: E. Nesbit and the

Reclamation of the Fairy Tale', *Tulsa Studies in Women's Literature*, 6 (2) (1987), pp.299–325

Koppes, Phyllis Bixler, *Frances Hodgson Burnett* (Boston: Twayne, 1984)

——, 'Tradition and the Individual Talent of Frances Hodgson Burnett', *Children's Literature*, vol. 7 (1978), pp.191–207

Kornfield, Eve and Susan Jackson, 'The Female Bildungsroman in Nineteenth Century America: Parameters of a Vision', *Journal of American Culture*, vol. 10, Part 4 (1987), pp.69–75

Lesbian History Group (ed.), *Not a Passing Phase: Reclaiming Lesbians in History* (London: The Women's Press, 1989)

Lurie, Alison, *Not in Front of the Grown-Ups* (Reading: Cardinal Books, 1990)

MacDonald, Ruth K., *Louisa May Alcott* (Boston: Twayne, 1983)

McGillis, Roderick, 'Secrets and Sequence in Children's Stories', *Studies in the Literary Imagination*, vol. 18, no. 2 (1985), pp.35–46

McRobbie, Angela, *Feminism and Youth Culture: From 'Jackie' to 'Just Seventeen'* (London: Macmillan, 1991)

Mare, Margaret and Alicia C. Percival, *Victorian Best Seller: the World of Charlotte M. Yonge* (London: George G. Harrap, 1948)

Marquis, Claudia, 'The Power of Speech: Life in *The Secret Garden*', *Journal of the Australasian Universities Language and Literature Association*, 68 (1987), pp.163–87

Mills, Sara, Lynne Pearce, Sue Spaull, Elaine Millard (eds), *Feminist Readings/Feminists Reading* (Hemel Hempstead: Harvester Press, 1989)

Moi, Toril (ed.), *The Kristeva Reader* (Oxford: Basil Blackwell, 1986)

Mordell, Albert (ed.), *Literary Reviews and Essays by Henry James* (New York: Grove Press, 1957)

Morey, Ann-Janine, *Religion and Sexuality in American Literature* (Cambridge: Cambridge University Press, 1992)

Murphy, Ann B., 'The Borders of Ethical, Erotic and Artistic Possibilities in *Little Women*', *Signs: Journal of Women in Culture and Society*, vol. 15, no. 3 (Spring 1990), pp.562–85

Myers, D.G., 'The Canonization of Susan Warner', *New Criterion*, vol. 7, no. 4 (December 1988), pp.73–8

Nestor, Pauline, *Female Friendships and Communities* (Oxford: Clarendon Press, 1985)

Payne, Alma J., 'Louisa May Alcott', *American Literary Realism*, vol. 6, no. 1 (Winter 1973), pp.27–43

Papashilvy, Helen Waite, *All the Happy Endings: A study of the domestic novel in America, the women who wrote it, the women who read it, in the nineteenth century* (New York: Harper, 1956)

Prickett, Stephen, *Victorian Fantasy* (Brighton: Harvester Wheatsheaf, 1979)

Quigly, Isabel, *The Heirs of Tom Brown: The English School Story* (London: Chatto & Windus, 1982)

Reynolds, Kimberley, *Girls Only? Gender and Popular Children's Fiction in Britain, 1880–1910* (Hemel Hempstead: Harvester Press, 1989)

Richards, Jeffrey (ed.), *Imperialism and Juvenile Literature* (Manchester and New York: Manchester University Press, 1989)

Romanes, Ethel, *Charlotte Mary Yonge: An Appreciation* (London: A.R. Mowbray, 1908)

Rose, Jacqueline, *The Case of Peter Pan or the Impossibility of Children's Fiction* (London: Macmillan, 1984)

Rousseau, Jean-Jacques, *Emile* (London: J.M. Dent, 1974)

Rowbotham, Judith, *Good Girls Make Good Wives: Guidance for Girls in Victorian Fiction* (Oxford: Basil Blackwell, 1989)

Rowe, Karen E., 'Feminism and Fairy Tales', *Women's Studies* 6 (1979), pp.237–57

Rubio, Mary and Elizabeth Waterston, *The Selected Journals of L.M. Montgomery* (Toronto: Oxford University Press, 1985)

Salmon, Edward J., 'What Girls Read', *Nineteenth Century*, vol. 20, no. 116 (1886), pp.516–27

Schnog, Nancy, 'Inside the Sentimental: The Psychological Work of *The Wide, Wide World*', *Genders*, no. 4 (Spring 1989), pp.11–25

Sewell, Eleanor L. (ed.), *The Autobiography of Elizabeth M. Sewell* (London: Longmans, Green, 1907)

Sewell, Elizabeth Missing, *Principles of Education* (London: Longman, 1865)

Sherwood, Martha Mary, *The History of the Fairchild Family*, 17th edn (London: J. Hatchard, 1848)

Showalter, Elaine, *A Literature of Their Own: British Women Novelists from Brontë to Lessing* (London: Virago Press, 1978)

——, *Sister's Choice: Tradition and Change in American Women's Writing* (Oxford: Oxford University Press, 1991)

——, (ed.), *The New Feminist Criticism* (London: Virago Press, 1986)

Spacks, Patricia Meyer, *The Female Imagination* (New York: Alfred Knopf, 1972)

Steedman, Carolyn, Cathy Urwin, Valerie Walkerdine (eds), *Language, Gender and Childhood* (London: Routledge & Kegan Paul, 1985)

Stern, Madeline B. (ed.), *Critical Essays on Louisa May Alcott* (Boston: GK Hall, 1984)

——, *Louisa May Alcott* (Norman: University of Oklahoma Press, rev. edn. 1971)

Stimpson, Catherine R., 'Reading For Love: Canons, Paracanons and Whistling Jo March', *New Literary History* 21 (1990), pp.957–76

Streatfeild, Noel, *Magic and the Magician: E. Nesbit and her Children's Books* (London: Ernest Benn, 1958)

Thwaite, Ann, *Waiting for the Party: A Life of Frances Hodgson Burnett* (London: Secker & Warburg, 1974)

Tillotson, Kathleen, *Novels of the Eighteen Forties* (Oxford: Oxford University Press, 1954)

Tompkins, Jane, *Sensational Designs: The Cultural Work of American Fiction 1790–1860* (New York: Oxford University Press, 1985)

Trodd, Anthea, *A Reader's Guide to Edwardian Literature* (Hemel Hempstead: Harvester Wheatsheaf, 1991)

Tuchman, Gaye, *Edging Women Out: Victorian Novelists and Social Change* (London: Routledge, 1989)

Vicinus, Martha, *Independent Women* (Chicago: Chicago University Press, 1985)

Warhol, Robyn D. and Diane Price Herndl (eds), *Feminisms: an Anthology of*

Literary Theory and Criticism (New Brunswick, NJ: Rutgers University Press, 1991)

Warner, Anna B., *Susan Warner ('Elizabeth Wetherell')* (New York: G.P. Putnam's Sons, 1909)

Weedon, Chris, *Feminist Practice and Post-Structuralist Theory* (Oxford: Basil Blackwell, 1987)

Weiss-Town, Janet, 'Sexism Down on the Farm? *Anne of Green Gables', Children's Literature Association Quarterly*, vol. 11, no. 1 (Spring 1986), pp.12–15

Williams, Susan B., 'Widening the World: Susan Warner, her readers, and the assumption of authorship', *American Quarterly*, vol. 42, no. 4 (December 1990), pp.565–86

Worton, Michael and Judith Still (eds) *Textuality and Sexuality: Reading Theories and Practices* (Manchester and New York: Manchester University Press, 1993)

Yonge, Charlotte, 'Children's Literature of the Last Century', *Macmillan's Magazine*, vol. 20, nos 117–19 (1869), pp.229–37, 302–10, 448–56

Index

Alcott, Anna 95
Alcott, Bronson 95, 97
Alcott, Louisa May 3, 61, 63, 85–106, 107, 110, 127, 128, 138, 157, 165, 202; *Good Wives* 90, 96, 105n, 106n; *Hospital Sketches* 89; *Life, Letters and Journals* 20, 34n, 92, 95, 97, 105n; *Little Women* ix, xiii, 5, 9, 10, 13, 14–18 *passim*, 20, 27, 29, 30, 31, 34n, 47, 52, 67, 68, 85–106, 107, 108, 114, 119, 121, 122, 125, 129, 132, 141–4, 145, 154, 155, 156, 157, 159, 161, 163, 175, 178, 179, 184, 189, 192, 204
Alder, Mrs G.R. 154
Altick, Richard D. 33n, 59n
America, culture and society 14–18, 26, 46, 52–3, 99, 203–4; cf British, 16–17, 53, 94–5; fiction, 4, 5, 13–19, 109, 132; cf British, 17, 19, 66–7, 134, 199
Ardener, Shirley and Edwin 29
Auchnuty, Rosemary, 195, 212n
Auerbach, Nina 25, 47, 60n, 100, 106n, 114, 125n
autobiography and fiction 26–8, 64, 95, 96–7, 109, 111, 120–1, 164–5, 173
Austen, Jane 206
Avery, Gillian vii, xi, xiiin, 2, 13, 17, 32n, 33n, 34n, 66, 83n, 147n, 199, 210, 212n

Baldwin, Stanley 151
Barrie, Sir James; *Peter Pan and Wendy* 175
Battiscombe, Georgina 83n
Baym, Nina 24, 32n, 34n, 37, 59n, 108, 125n
Beauvoir, Simone de 85
Beer, Gillian xii, xiiin
Berg, Temma F. 171n
Betjeman, John 194
Bildungsroman 51–2, 108
Bland, Hubert 129
Blau du Plessis, Rachel 126n
boys' literature 2, 3, 21, 146–7
Boys' Own Paper 21
Bratton, J.S. 32n, 201, 212n
Brazil, Angela xi, 18, 24, 73, 138, 192–212; *The Fortunes of Philippa* 192;

The Madcap of the School xiii, 15, 16, 29, 30, 192–212; *The Nicest Girl in the School* 205; *The Third Class at Miss Kaye's* 197
Briggs, Julia vii, 2, 20, 32n, 34n, 129, 132, 138, 147n, 148n
Bronfen, Elisabeth 137, 148n
Bronte, Charlotte; *Jane Eyre* 113, 175, 177–8
Brontes, the 86
Browning, Elizabeth Barrett 39
Bunyan, John; *The Pilgrim's Progress* 52, 67, 89, 90–1, 108, 169
Burne-Jones, Edward 3
Burnett, Frances Hodgson 7, 15, 76, 172–91, 205; *Little Lord Fauntleroy* 15, 186–87; *A Little Princess* 15, 178–79, 197; *Sarah Crewe, or What Happened at Miss Minchin's* 197, 199; *The Secret Garden* ix, 11, 12, 15, 16, 27, 30, 31, 33n, 113, 123, 145, 154, 158, 161, 172–91, 192, 203; *The Shuttle* 181
Butts, Dennis vii, 33n, 83n

Cadogan, Mary 212n
Cameron, Lucy Lyttleton 5, 63
Carpenter, Humphrey 131, 132, 133, 147n, 148, 190, 191n
Carroll, Lewis 3, 9
Charlesworth, Maria Louisa; *Ministering Children* 22
Cheyney, Ednah D. 34n, 105n
Chodorow, Nancy 28, 35n, 143, 148n
Chopin, Kate; *The Awakening*, 118
Christian Science 185
Cixous, Helene 28, 118
Coleridge, Christabel 9, 33n, 62, 65, 67, 83n
Conrad, Joseph 86
Coolidge, Susan (Sarah Chauncey Woolsey) 8, 13, 16, 53, 63, 78, 107–26, 157, 197; *The Autobiography and Correspondences of Mrs Delany* 110; *The Diary and Letters of Frances Burney, Madame D'Arblay* 110; *The Letters of Jane Austen* 110; *The New Year's Bargain* 110; *Nine Little Goslings* 33n; *An Old Convent School*

219